Founding Fictions

AMY BOESKY

Founding Fictions

UTOPIAS IN EARLY MODERN ENGLAND

The University of Georgia Press ATHENS & LONDON

Designed by Kathi Dailey Morgan
Set in Janson Text by Books International, Inc.
Printed and bound by Braun-Brumfield, Inc.
The paper in this book meets the guidelines for
permanence and durability of the Committee on
Production Guidelines for Book Longevity of the
Council on Library Resources.

Printed in the United States of America

00 99 98 97 96 c 5 4 3 2 1

Library of Congress Cataloging in Publication Data

Boesky, Amy.
    Founding Fictions : Utopias in early modern England /
Amy Boesky.
        p.   cm.
    Includes bibliographical references and index.
    ISBN 0-8203-1832-9 (alk. paper)
        1. English prose literature—Early modern, 1500–1700—
History and criticism. 2. Utopias in literature. I. Title.
PR756.U86B64   1996
820.9'372—dc20   95-52473

British Library Cataloging in Publication Data available

Frontispiece: Ambrosius Holbein, "Map of Utopia." By
permission of the Houghton Library, Harvard University.

To the memory of my mother,

Elaine Berlow Boesky

CONTENTS

ACKNOWLEDGMENTS

Like many projects long in the writing, this book has gathered debts as it developed. My first thanks are to the teachers who helped me to care about early modern literature and culture. Both have generously and thoughtfully guided this project—John Carey, in its nascent stages as a topic for an examination paper at Oxford; and Barbara Lewalski, in its development as a doctoral dissertation and in its subsequent and manifold revisions. For their mentorship and supervision I am very grateful. I would also like to thank members of the Renaissance Colloquium at Harvard between 1987 and 1989, the Draft Group at Georgetown University between 1990 and 1992, and former and current colleagues and students at Boston College. I have benefited as well from a wide community of teachers, students, and friends, especially Katy Aisenberg, Nancy Bentley, Mary Crane, Gail Finney, Anne Fleche, Melanie Forman, Roland Greene, Alan Heimert, Marybeth Martin, John Norman, Jason

Rosenblatt, and Lucienne Thys-Senoçak. Students in my courses on utopian literature at Georgetown University and Boston College have helped me with their curiosity and insights, and I have also benefited from the questions and suggestions posed by colleagues in the Society for Utopian Studies and in the Renaissance Society.

Support for this project has come from the Whiting Foundation, Georgetown University, the NEH, and Boston College. The official readers for the University of Georgia Press have been extremely helpful, as have librarians in numerous places, especially at Widener Library, at the Houghton Library, and at the Folger Library. Thanks are also due to the University of Texas Press for permission to reprint chapter 5, which appeared first in *TSLL*. An earlier version of chapter 2, "A Land of Experimental Knowledge: Francis Bacon's *New Atlantis*," is forthcoming in a collection of essays to be published by Cambridge University Press, *The Project of Prose in the Early Modern West*.

Finally, there is the support I have received from my family, and it is to them that I owe the deepest thanks: to my father, Dale; to my late mother, Elaine; to my sisters, Sara and Julie; to my daughters, Sacha and Elisabeth; and most of all, for all things, to Jacques.

Founding Fictions

INTRODUCTION

In Francis Bacon's *New Atlantis* (1627), a band of Portuguese mariners (lost at sea on their way back from seeking gold in Peru) wash up on a technologically "perfect" island ruled by a band of scientific priests. After a period of quarantine and decontamination, the mariners are told a story about the island's birth as a nation. The culture of Bensalem was not always homogeneous or Christian. Some eighteen hundred years earlier, after a great insurrection had devastated the surrounding populations, an ark was found floating in a band of light in Bensalem's waters. From this ark Bensalem's disparate inhabitants—some Indian, some European, some Asian—removed a book and a letter. The book was the Bible, in both testaments, and the letter was a document identifying its recipients as a community and mandating their blessed future. They were to become Christians, scientists, and patriarchs, their culture dedicated to the study of God's perfection as it manifested itself in the perfection of nature. Bensalem's letter in the ark was less a prognostication than a charter. It was a founding fiction, a chronicle to which the people could repeatedly return to recall their most prized values: their insularity, their empiricism, and their strict internal hierarchies. In the unfolding of this narrative of communal election, Bensalem enacts what Regis Debray has claimed are the nation's dual responses to the "twin threats of death and disorder":

> These are, first of all, a delimitation in time, or the assignation of origins, in the sense of an *Ark*. This means that society does not derive from an infinite regression of cause and effect. A point of origin is fixed, the mythic birth of the *Polis*, the birth of Civilization or of the Christian era, the Muslim Hegira, and so on. This zero point or starting point is what allows ritual repetition, the ritualization of memory, celebration, commemoration—in short, all those forms of magical behaviour signifying defeat of the irreversibility of time. . . . The second founding gesture of any human society is its delimitation within an enclosed space.[1]

The letter in Bensalem's ark epitomizes the foundational role of the utopian narrative. The "found" nature of the utopia is one of its most prized fictions, as the ideal commonwealth claims to have been discovered (often by chance) rather than built or conquered. This fortunate accident underscores the utopia's belief in its own election. Rather than finding a wilderness or arcadia, the traveler to utopia finds a complex culture, urban, developed, politically or technologically advanced. Moreover, as the ideal commonwealth is found rather than made, the text of the utopia is discovered rather than written. Either somebody else dictates the narrative and the author has only to serve as scribe (as in the utopias of More, Bacon, and Cavendish) or the utopia's history has already been written down and needs merely to be exported (as in Neville's *Isle of Pines*). In each instance the violent and competitive procedures of invention are concealed, and the myths of divine election and benediction are foregrounded. While the utopia depends on and promotes nationalism's sense of "imagined community," the narration of the utopia is always disjunctive, disrupting what Homi Bhabha has called "the homogenizing myth of cultural anonymity."[2]

This book is a study of English utopias written between 1516 and 1688. I argue that utopian discourse rose alongside the emergent institutions of the early modern state: the new schools, laboratories, workhouses, theaters, and colonial plantations that became crucial centers of authority as power shifted in England from the court and church to a widening aristocracy and growing bourgeoisie. In confining myself to works by English writers (and, after Ralph Robinson's translation of *Utopia* in 1551, to works written in the English language), I necessarily leave aside important connections between English utopias and Continental texts and traditions—works by such writers as Erasmus, Eberlein, Rabelais, Campenello, Brahe, Comenius, de Bergerac, and Fontanelle. While fruitful work has been done on the interconnections between early modern utopias in France, Germany, the Netherlands, and Switzerland, I will argue that national demarcations (however blurry) not only are crucial to the strategies of utopian fictions but are actually part of their subject.[3]

Much about the utopia as a genre is paradoxical, not least that the form, which I will argue was instrumental in the formation of emergent "Englishness," should have begun with a text written in Latin, published in Louvain, and adumbrated by Dutch, French, and German humanists. Thomas More's rather academic detachment from English customs and institutions helped to establish the peculiarly disjunctive quality of utopian discourse. In *Utopia* More writes as an exile, displaced at home as abroad, finding English customs and problems everywhere and their solution nowhere. In its curious alternation between idealization and irony, *Utopia* is both the progenitor of a new genre and a new articulation of national consciousness.

This book began for me with two questions: what kind of a fiction is a utopia, and why did it emerge when and where it did? Despite manifold imitations of *Utopia* on the Continent, the genre was especially (and explosively) popular in seventeenth-century England. Both the long lapse between More's text and later English utopias and the form's consequent popularity can be attributed to the unique relationship between the English Reformation and Civil War. In England, emergent nationalism facilitated by the break from Rome was rapidly succeeded by its own revolutionary self-assessment. The seventeenth century in England, like the eighteenth century in France, witnessed the transfer of power from a tiny elite to the great new organs of statecraft—the legal and educational systems, the army, the new workhouses, and early factories. Many of the changes associated with the Continental Enlightenment were already established in England by the time of the Restoration. It is not that English nationalism was precocious but rather that in England national consciousness was from its beginnings deeply implicated in literacy and in authorship. As Liah Greenfield has argued, the most important source of nationalism in early modern England was the Bible, that sacred book discovered in the ark by Bacon's Bensalemites. The Reformation stimulated literacy, and emphasis on the interpretation of the "word" nurtured "a novel sense of human—individual—dignity." During the Marian reign the martyring of English Protestants enforced a new association between Protestant and national causes. Greenfield observes that while no exact equivalent of the word *nation* appears in the Hebrew or Greek Bibles, "all the English Bibles use the word"; the Authorized Version uses *nation* 454 times. Reformation Englishness becomes explicitly visible in the Elizabethan period, with the founding of the Society of Antiquaries, the writing of histories and history plays, and the celebrations of England evident in chorographies, maps, epics, and even playing cards.[4]

The mere identification of "Englishness" was by no means simple or uniform in this period, as Richard Helgerson demonstrates in his study of Elizabethan nationalism. "Was the nation—itself a problematic though widely used term—to be identified with the king, with the people (or some subdivision of the people), or with the cultural system as figured in language, law, religion, history, economy, and social order? Which of these or what combination of them was to define and control the state?"[5] Given the vast differences among the utopists I study in this book, it would be a gross simplification to assume each defined national interests in the same way. The authors I cover include a future Catholic saint

(Thomas More), a rusticated natural philosopher (Francis Bacon), an artisan who starved to death (Gabriel Plattes), a communist agrarian (Gerrard Winstanley), a misogynist Republican (Henry Neville), and two Royalist women, one a duchess, one a professional writer and sometime spy (Margaret Cavendish and Aphra Behn). Some of these writers traveled or lived extensively abroad; others never left English soil. Yet surprisingly, for all their differences these authors share in their utopias a number of ideas and assumptions about cultural and national formations. Most important, English utopists in this period shared a representation of the ideal commonwealth as shaped by institutions rather than by individuals, monarchs or otherwise. In each of the utopias I study here, Englishness is formed and reformed through the mechanisms of a new institution. For More, it is the new public school that functions as a simulacrum for reform, a model offered to him by St. Paul's, founded by his friend Dean Colet in 1509. For Bacon, it is the emergent laboratory, modeled on those established by John Dee, Cornelis Drebbel, and Salomon de Caus, which offered the best homology of the state in the 1620s. For Gabriel Plattes, Samuel Gott, and Gerrard Winstanley in the 1640s and 1650s, the public workhouse provided the best model for industry and employment during the Civil War. Margaret Cavendish, whose utopia was published just after the ravages of the Great Fire in 1666, found in the Restoration theater a model for the rehearsal and containment of spectacle. Finally, for Henry Neville and Aphra Behn in the late 1660s and 1680s, respectively, the colonial plantation provided the delimited space in which English mastery could best be performed and perfected. In each instance the utopist praises the institution for its capacity to produce citizens trained and trainable, citizens who possess the prominent values of the modern state: obedience, discipline, and order. Paradoxically, as Ernest Gellner observes, nationalism does not advertise "the establishment of an anonymous, impersonal society, with mutually substitutable atomized individuals"—even if this is what the state most requires. Instead, nationalism celebrates the "folk," the distinctiveness of certain customs or costumes, vernacular languages, literature, and architectures.[6] In the same way utopias, like the "histories of the individual" so

Io.Clemens.   **Hythlodæus.**

Hans Holbein, "Conversation in the Garden." From Thomas More's *Utopia* (1518). By permission of the Houghton Library, Harvard University.

ho. Morus.   Pet. Aegid.

prominent in the seventeenth century, promulgate a sense of specialness, of election. The very anonymity of the utopian commonwealth emphasizes the individualism of that crucial character in the utopian dialogue: the reader. As Peter Ruppert has demonstrated, the reader, like the traveler, is an exile in utopia, and this position allows him or her to accept utopia's "lessons" without sacrificing a belief in individual agency.[7]

Utopias rely on both an elevated sense of human ability (for instance, the belief in the ability to make an ideal commonwealth and to abide in it) and a far less benign view of citizenry, a suspicion that, unbridled, the self is always untrustworthy. Robert Burton remarks in his brief utopia embedded in *The Anatomy of Melancholy* that he wanted his citizens to dance together once a week—"(but not all at once)."[8] Early modern utopias are partly colonialist fables, and the discovery of the ideal commonwealth bolsters imperialist self-confidence and self-importance. But the profound distrust of all human endeavor written into these narratives cannot be overestimated. If the utopia promotes the bourgeois, the adventurer, and the empiricist, as I will argue in subsequent chapters, it also censures the very idea of the self, depersonalizing citizenry and granting only the exile or malcontent a "name." In the same way utopias unsettle as they promote the idea of nationhood, revealing both the nation's power to organize and to aggrandize itself as well as the limits and consequences of such endeavors. In most early modern utopias the nation functions as a machine for the production of "perfected" citizens, but it is not always clear whether the author is praising or bemoaning the nation's burgeoning power.

Utopias often strike modern readers as restrictive or totalitarian. It is hard to see retrospectively the incendiary power of such texts, which are now often dismissed as inefficacious, closer to political cartoons than to radical slogans. In fact, debates about the political function of utopian literature actually began alongside the new genre in the Renaissance: whereas Philip Sidney praised More in 1595 for creating in *Utopia* a "speaking picture" and remarked, "That way of patterning a Commonwealth, was most absolute though hee perchaunce hath not so absolutely performed it," Milton in the 1640s was already distinguishing real activism from the dreamy commonwealths of *Utopia* and *New Atlantis*, warning his compatriots against "sequestering out of the world" into "Utopian polities."[9]

One of the fiercest debates about utopian writing in the critical literature has centered on its ability to effect change rather than to represent it. Some readers maintain that the utopian text opens up a horizon of possibility for the society that conceives it. In the 1920s Karl Mannheim argued that while utopias are not ideologies, they are politically transcendent; after him Marcuse, Ruyer, Mucchielli, and Bloch all worked to further the idea that utopias work primarily by countering extant (flawed) governments. Widely divergent critics have supported this view, from the structuralist Northrop Frye, who has claimed that the utopia as speculative myth is essentially comic, to the Marxist Raymond Williams, who has argued that the form offers "a strength of vision against the prevailing grain." Opposing this view are the critics who foreground the ironic or darker aspects of utopian commonwealths, emphasizing the utopia's limitations, its inability to escape the problems it censures. Like the neo-Marxists Louis Marin and Fredric Jameson, such critics have tended to see the utopia as a "rearticulation" of the "real" or, as Darko Suvin puts it, an "estrangement" of the society it claims to counter.[10]

This book is an effort toward a third position. Utopian fiction advocates a reorganization of human activity that initially seems liberal or progressive but is always set forth in self-critical or qualitative ways. Utopias are not blueprints for reform so much as representations of the contradictory status of "improvement." The utopia is thus neither a heuristic model nor a historical mirror but a representation of the tensions and ambiguities surrounding the very ideas of nationalism and reform.

Ursula LeGuin has remarked that the future, in fiction, is a metaphor.[11] While postindustrial utopists often employ a temporal shift through the device of time travel, in the early modern period utopia is more often discovered through spatial relocation. As Bhabha writes in another context, "the difference of space returns as the sameness of time, turning Territory into Tradition, turning the People into One."[12] Like postindustrial utopists, writers like

More, Bacon, Plattes, Gott, Winstanley, Cavendish, and Neville were chiefly interested in the particularity of their own here and now. Distance is thus as much a mirror as a metaphor, for the procedures of dislocation make more sharply visible the outlines of one's own domain. The early modern period did not locate the best society in the secular future. Christian teleology (fall-salvation-millennium) was interwoven in this period with reminders of mortality, degeneracy, guilt, and deterioration, and the idea of the golden age, borrowed from Hesiod's *Works and Days*, was set not in the future but in the distant past. When More wrote a series of epigrams celebrating the succession of Henry VIII in 1509, he suggested, with politic flattery, that the new king would restore the golden age to England: "The golden age came first, then the silver, after that the bronze, and recently the iron age. In your reign, Sire, the golden age has returned." But despite its extravagant praise, this epigram hints at contemporary degeneration; even a golden age, as More of all people would come to learn, was not necessarily stable. Though all eras can be claimed as tumultuous, the rapid changes in England between 1516 and 1688 must have made the static world of utopia seem particularly appealing.[13]

Two separate dates mark the beginning of English utopian literature. One is 1516, the year More published his Latin "libellum" or handbook in Louvain. The second is 1551, the year Ralph Robinson translated *Utopia* into English, resituating Utopia in what has been called the "language-of-power" of the vernacular.[14] Though Robinson's translation might appear to reclaim More's text for English (and Protestant) audiences, one has only to open the first book of More's *Utopia* to be reminded, Latin or no Latin, of its self-conscious nationalism. More's text begins with a drumroll of syllables introducing England's king—"The most invincible King of England, Henry the Eighth of that name, a prince adorned with royal virtues beyond any other"—and the further More moves away from England as his conscious subject, the further his text is authorized by English customs and manners. England becomes the text's absent presence. The famous "Debate of Counsel" which dominates book 1 is staged (through flashback) at an English dinner party, and for Morus and Giles, the text's fictitious audience,

England is the political backdrop against which the drama of Utopia unfolds.

This self-conscious nationalism is one of the most strikingly novel features of More's "libellum." While a host of models and sources for the utopia can be traced from Plato, Plutarch, and Lucian of Samosota through the *Civitas Dei* of Augustine and the travelogues of Prester John and Mandeville, More's *De Optimo Reipublicae Statu* signals its departure from such texts, insisting on and advertising its own novelty.[15] In subsequent decades, *Utopia* was so widely reprinted, analyzed, and interpreted that by the end of the sixteenth century the terms *utopia* and *utopian* were fully incorporated into the English vocabulary, appearing in works by Sidney, Donne, Lyly, and Shakespeare and ironized in Joseph Hall's *Mundus Alter et Idem* (1600).[16] But with the exception of two dialogues on the imaginary land of Mauqsun (Nusquam) written by Thomas Lupton in the 1580s, *Utopia* was not imitated in England until Francis Bacon wrote *New Atlantis* in the 1620s. It was in the first decades of the seventeenth century that the English utopia was transformed into what Fredric Jameson has called the "social contact" of genre.[17] After Bacon, dozens of utopias were written and published in England. Robert Burton embedded a utopia in *The Anatomy of Melancholy* (1627–1639). Others include Gabriel Plattes's *A Description of the Famous Kingdome of Macaria* (1641), Samuel Gott's *Nova Solyma* (1648), Thomas Hobbes's *Leviathan* (1651), Gerrard Winstanley's *The Law of Freedom* (1652), James Harrington's *Oceana* (1656), the anonymous R.H.'s continuation of *New Atlantis* (1660), Margaret Cavendish's *The description of a new world, call'd The Blazing-world* (1666), Henry Neville's *The Isle of Pines* (1668), and the anonymous *Antiquity Reviv'd* (1693).[18] Historically, then, the so-called classical utopia in England belongs more to the seventeenth century than to the sixteenth. As English self-consciousness intensified prior to and during the Civil War, the utopia as a discursive form offered a particularly potent space for representing historical rupture.[19]

It is difficult to account for the lapse in English utopian fiction between More and Bacon, a lapse that has largely gone unremarked. It is possible that Elizabethan satire, drama, and romance were accessible and popular enough in the 1580s and 1590s to afford the kind of social interrogation that would later be taken up by utopists, rendering utopian fiction either unfeasible or unnecessary between More and Bacon. Another possibility is that the flood of travel narratives written and published in the later decades of the sixteenth century promulgated renewed English interest in travelers' tales as a narrative form as well as in the remote and exotic destinations they represented. It could also be that before Bacon risked imitating More in *New Atlantis*, the idea of such imitation seemed untenable or unappealing, whereas after Bacon it felt acceptable, "done." Most important, ideas about England (and Englishness) were fundamentally altered in the Stuart period, allowing for the development of a new sociology of nationhood.[20] Partly this alteration had to do with English ventures away from England. The kind of colonialist expansion described by More (and in part endorsed by him) only really began to be institutionalized in the beginning of the seventeenth century. Numerous English voyages to Virginia, Newfoundland, and Guiana took place during Elizabeth's reign, recorded in Richard Hakluyt's *Principal Navigations* (1598). But as Jeffrey Knapp has argued, Elizabethan efforts to colonize the New World were generally failures, so imaginative literature in the sixteenth century valorized an enterprise that could happen only in the realm of Nowhere.[21]

By the early Stuart period a new seriousness began to color English imperialism. In 1607 the English established the first successful settlement in Virginia, almost a hundred years after More's brother-in-law set off for that purpose from Bristol, and in the seventeenth century the English organized colonial enterprises by forming most of the great joint-stock and trading companies: the East India Company in 1600, the Virginia Companies in 1607, the Dorchester Company (1624), the Newfoundland Company (1610), the Massachusetts Bay Colony (1629), and the Royal African Company (1660).[22] As Kenneth R. Andrews notes, "It was the reign of James that saw the effective beginnings of the British Empire: the establishment of colonies in North America, the development of direct trade with the East, and even the first annexation of territory in a recognized Spanish sphere of influence—the West Indies."[23]

From Stuart endorsement of the joint-stock companies and colonial settlements to Oliver Cromwell's nationalist "Western Design," the seventeenth century saw occasional encounters with the New World becoming organized on a large scale. The planting of settlements in North America and the West Indies precipitated renewed interest in organizing populations, at home as well as in the colonies. One consequence of English colonial activity in the New World was that the English crusade to reform laborers at home was intensified by its experiments with new populations overseas. Less sensational than colonialist atrocities, these species of domestic reforms were predicated on similar ideas, for the idle poor, like rebellious slaves in the West Indies, became a cipher for the unmanageable during the early phases of the Civil War. Their control could thus be trumpeted as a triumph of national reform, a reminder of the insufficiency of rebellion in the face of state control.

Settlements beyond English borders in the seventeenth century raised questions about national identity, whether it could be maintained elsewhere, and what it would take for England to be expanded and reformed as a nation. At the same time, England's rapid consolidation of colonial activity in the West Indies coincided with domestic identity crises brought about by the Civil War, the Interregnum, and the Restoration. Concerns about what it meant to be English outside of England—in Virginia, Bermuda, Barbados, Jamaica, St. Christopher, and Guiana—took shape during the period in which England was turning itself from a monarchy to a commonwealth and back again, and the identity of the nation had to be redefined—not once, as it happened, but twice.

For twenty years in the middle of the century, it was unclear what kind of government England would have or how it would reshape its foreign and domestic policies. Domestically as well as imperially, ideas of English nation and nationhood were dramatically reshaped during this period. One consequence of sectarianism and dissent during the Civil War and Interregnum was an enormous outpouring of political tracts in which debates about national identity intensified. Paradoxically, such debates worked in part to solidify social and national classifications after the Civil War. As texts by Margaret Cavendish, Henry Neville, and Robert Filmer make clear, the Restoration enabled the turbulent previous decades to speak more forcibly for the powers of containment than for resistance.

James Holstun has suggested in his analysis of Puritan utopias that it was a new sense of demographics—a need to organize a population displaced by economic changes in the early modern period—that was the chief contributor to the rise of utopian literature in the seventeenth century.[24] I approach demography rather differently, as I argue that English utopias recorded a novel set of responses to such changes by establishing institutions as new organs for organizing people and ideas. After the break from Rome in 1534, England began a steady and gradual reorganization of power that by the early seventeenth century was in evidence in a rash of new charters, societies, houses, companies, and exchanges. The century began with the opening in 1602 of the Bodleian Library in Oxford. Successive decades saw the establishment of the Royal Society and the Royal Observatory, the London Stock Exchange and the Bank of England, the first official English museum (the Ashmolean), the first public workhouses, England's first organized national militia (the New Model Army), and even the first public fire departments. A desire to make things official evolved parallel to utopian fiction in England, a desire to acquire charters and public funding, to house institutions in buildings rather than to meet casually or sporadically—in short, to authorize practices through the procedures of institutionalization, procedures, as the anthropologist Mary Douglas has pointed out, which work principally by their capacity to "confer sameness."[25]

MOST STUDIES OF utopias begin with a system for separating this kind of literature from its generic neighbors.[26] While the category of the utopia is itself rather narrow, the category of the utopian is broad, including travelogue, bucolic or pastoral, romance, as well as embedded bowers or ideal places, such as Kalendar's House in Sidney's *Arcadia*, the Bower of Bliss in Spenser's *Faerie Queene*, or any of Shakespeare's transformative woods or isles. Similarly, the political and didactic treatises on the "good commonwealth" or literature advising the king or his advisors—works like Sir Thomas Elyot's *The Boke named the Governour* or Baldassare Castiglione's

The Courtier—might be "utopian" without being utopias. I am less concerned with such distinctions for their own sake than with utopias' self-reflexive anxiety about them. In the early modern period the utopia incorporates a sense of generic relatedness into its form; it is keenly aware of neighbors, of proximity, and for this reason often defends itself through isolation and through boundaries, walls, moats, or difficult access. At the same time, the utopia insists on and advertises its own distinctiveness.

I define utopia as a "speaking-picture" of an ideal commonwealth. I see the utopia as both a fiction and a sociology of statehood, centrally concerned with organization, with new institutions, and with institutionalism. The utopia is primarily urban, though its representation of urbanness varies; it is a self-conscious and necessarily intertextual form, signposting itself as a utopia through strict adherence to previous formal conventions, through puns or allusions, or through prefatory labels. In most cases the utopia is a dialogue based on the traveler's tale. Its plot is spare: someone (usually a man) has been to the utopia, distant in place and/or time, and returns to report on its practices. Often the utopian community is discovered by accident after a storm, shipwreck, or confusion at sea. The traveler learns about the culture he or she visits through a lengthy central dialogue with a host or hosts; he is instructed in the habits and rituals of the utopia and perhaps permitted to take part in some phases of its life or to ask questions of its citizens. If the utopia is complete, the visitor returns to his native country, taking back the valuable impression of the ideal commonwealth and making it known. While the utopia develops its plot from travel narrative, its purposes and methodologies are indebted to a wide range of classical and contemporary dialogues, from Plato and Lucian to Castiglione, Machiavelli, Elyot, and Starkey. The twin organizing features of the utopia, then, are the travel romance and the wisdom dialogue or Socratic exchange, and while the wisdom dialogue may appear to interrupt the travel narrative, the purposes of the two interrogations are similar: something is searched for, and something of value is brought back home.[27]

Most utopias in this period are masculinist, visited by, ruled by, and explained by men. Most are situated in ideal places (temperate, beautiful, mild), which are eventually revealed to have been formed by colonial conquest or some other violent disaster. In its form the utopia is characterized by an ironic, dialectical quality related to adjacent kinds such as satire, paradox, and riddles. Critics have used various terms for discussing the distinguishing complexity of the utopian narrative. Louis Marin has seen the utopian form as "neutralizing" historical anxieties. Darko Suvin claims the utopia "estranges" the real; for Stephen Greenblatt, it is "anamorphic art."[28] These multiple terms attest to the power of the splitting and doubleness that informs the utopia at every level: as dialogue, as place, and as representation.

Like the evolving institutions in this period, utopias distinguish themselves from adjacent literary kinds by putting a new emphasis on *system* as the best means for reorganizing populations and ensuring their improvement. Utopias set forth a belief in reform through routine, through a bureaucratization of the ideal. No other world is ordered as scrupulously as the world of the utopia. Like the "total institutions" studied by the sociologist Erving Goffman in the 1950s and 1960s (penal colonies, convents, asylums), the utopia reifies its barrier to the outside world with such boundaries as "locked doors, high walls, barbed wire, cliffs, water, forests, or moats."[29] The utopia, itself a new institution, contains within it a nest of nodal institutions: the school, the market, the army, the family. English utopists from More to Neville represent these institutions in complex and contradictory ways. Initially the utopia seems to serve as a model for the one nodal institution that stands at its center. But subtly, through metaphor, through digression, through rupture, regendering, or aporia, this nodal institution is challenged even as it is praised. Utopian fictions are thus "complete and perfect works," in the words of Pierre Macherey, anticipating not only the social changes they advocate but also the consequences—good and bad—that such changes might incur.[30] This may be why definitions of utopia that do not include "dystopia" or "anti-utopia" within them feel so unsatisfactory. Utopian fiction powerfully anticipates our desire to separate the utopian from the dystopian, but it prevents our ability to do so. The utopia derives its force less from a series of meanings, in other words, than from a series of contradictions. In early modern England, those contradictions were primarily organized around the belief in the modern state as an organ for reform and the discordant sense that its institutions would prove, as Nietzsche and Foucault were later to argue, the enemies to freedom.[31]

Utopia's Two Voices

In one of the fragmentary Hellenistic novels of the fourth century, Diodorus Siculus recorded the travels of a man named Iamboulous, an adventure that was anthologized in collections of travel writing well into the sixteenth century and was, like Mandeville's travels, believed by many early explorers to have been true.[32] In Iamboulous's account, the narrator was blown off course near the equator; his ship found its way to a cluster of seven paradisical islands reminiscent of the Hesperidean islands of the West. Iamboulous found in these islands a peaceful race of people who were described as having no hair on their bodies and possessing flexible, almost rubbery bones. They were abstemious and long-lived. When they reached one hundred and fifty years of age they practiced a kind of self-induced euthanasia, putting themselves to sleep by eating medicinal plants. What Iamboulous found most striking about these unusual people, however, was that they were double-tongued:

> And they have a peculiarity in regard to the tongue, partly the work of nature and congenital with them and partly intentionally brought about by artifice; among them, namely, the tongue is double for a certain distance, but they divide the inner portions still further, with the result that it becomes a double tongue as far as its base. Consequently they are very versatile as to the sounds they can utter, since they imitate not only every articulate language used by man but also the varied chatterings of the birds, and in general, they can reproduce any peculiarity of sound. And the most remarkable thing of all is that at one and the same time they can converse perfectly with two persons who fall in with them, both answering ques-

tions and discoursing pertinently on the circumstances of the moment; for with one division of the tongue they can converse with the one person, and likewise with the other talk with the second.[33]

Iamboulous's praise for these islanders' double tongues is itself complexly reported. On the one hand, he commended the islanders' ability to record ("since they imitate not only every articulate language used by man but also the varied chatterings of the birds"), a demonstration of their endless capacity to give back, absorb, and give back again. His initial praise makes the islanders seem a composite Echo to the explorer's Narcissus: whatever he says they give back to him; they record his language, rather than their own. In this sense, Iamboulous's praise for the islanders points ahead to the impressions of New World populations recorded by Europeans in the early modern period—to Columbus, for example, who recorded in his logbook that the Indians on the island of Dominica were excellent mimics and thus "should be good and intelligent servants for I see that they say very quickly everything that is said to them."[34] The islanders confirm and validate Iamboulous's presence; their voices matter only insofar as they reproduce the language of the people who have found them.

Iamboulous's praise for the islander's divided tongues begins with efficiency: the islanders can carry on two conversations at the same time, not having to wait to finish one speech to take up another. But Iamboulous also recognizes that they can carry on two kinds of discourse at once: they can answer questions and simultaneously discourse "pertinently on the circumstances of the moment." They can respond while they converse; they can speak with two different people at the same time. Iamboulous's utopians emblematize utopian discourse: they speak with two tongues at once.[35]

The marvelousness of Iamboulous's islanders resides in their capacity for a certain kind of discourse. Their speech is not really dialogue, a word whose derivation (from the Greek) means to speak through or across, to speak *alternately*, first one voice, then another, then the first again.[36] Rather, these islanders speak with two voices concurrently, dialectically rather than dialogically.[37] In the early modern period the utopia takes the "dialogic" quality of dialogue as part of its subject. The utopia organizes itself around not one but several dialogues, each occupying different positions on the continuum between the monologic and the dialogic: the traveler's initial dialogue with his hosts; the traveler's report, often delivered in a dialogue with his peers; the author's (presumed) dialogue with his or her readers; and the utopia's implied (ideological) dialogues between citizen and culture, New World and Old World, individual and institution, freedom and repression. The centrality of the dialogue as a form is signposted in utopian fiction by acute self-consciousness about the ways in which dialogues are conducted and recorded. In Bacon's *New Atlantis*, for example, each carefully orchestrated dialogue between the visiting mariners and their hosts is abruptly interrupted, making dialogue itself less a form of alternation than of disruption or aporia. In both Margaret Cavendish's *The Blazing-world* and Henry Neville's *The Isle of Pines* dialogue within the utopia is compared negatively with the written chronicle or cabbala, superior importance being attached to what the utopian culture has written down about itself rather than to what it says. But within the utopia's flattened-out dialogues can be found submerged and important debates about the nature of reform and about the value of central institutions, such as colonialism, capitalism, science, monarchy, and slavery. Through these debates the utopia records the culture's difference from itself, its ambivalence about expansion, improvement, and reform. These debates erupt not through the pat yes and no of the utopia's formal exchange but through moments of rupture or aporia in the utopia's self-representation. Like Iamboulous's islanders, the utopia speaks with two tongues at once, offering praise as well as censure, advertising what it disqualifies, speaking a language that endorses what is new while hinting at its failure.

The Place of Utopia

More's *Utopia* distinguishes itself from Plato's *Republic*, a dialogue on the nature of the just state, by giving the ideal commonwealth a place. Utopia is an island shaped like a new or rising moon. As its capital city, Amaurotum, is bordered by a river, the island itself is defended by a deceptive harbor, its water covering treacherous rocks, at once inviting and impeding entry.

Utopia, More's narrator Hythlodaeus explains, was not always an island. At one time it was a peninsular country called Abraxa, inhabited by a "rude and rustic people" unconverted to wisdom, philosophy, or culture. It was Utopus who discovered and conquered Abraxa, cutting the peninsula from the mainland by ordering "the excavation of fifteen miles on the side where the land was connected with the continent" so that water could flow all around it, and giving this reshaped land mass his own name. In Hythlodaeus's account, Utopus's conversion of Abraxa is described as pacific, benign; like Hythlodaeus, who also discovers Utopia on a colonialist mission, Utopus is said to have been welcomed by the "rude and rustic people" he put to work building his capital city. But this seamlessness is a partial concealment, for Utopia has its geographic and cultural origin in Abraxa's ruin, in its territorial "cutting," in its dominion, and in the forced labor of its inhabitants, commanded to build a new culture on the site of their own.

Seventeenth-century utopists inherit from Utopia/Abraxa the location of utopia in a conquered or contested site. Bacon's *New Atlantis* is built by its founding ruler, Altabin, to replace the great nation of Atlantis, destroyed in a violent "inundation" or deluge that broke down an interconnected ancient world order. Gott's New Jerusalem is a millennial reconstruction of the fractious city of Zion; Winstanley's *Law of Freedom* is a manifesto defending the Diggers' colony in Surrey, destroyed by hostile neighbors in 1649–1650. Margaret Cavendish's *Blazing-world* is an imperial utopia built on the devastation of London's Great Fire and the English Civil War. Neville's *Isle of Pines* locates itself on an island disrupted by slave rebellions, anarchy, and cyclical executions, and Behn's *Oroonoko* revisits Guiana, a site legendary both for its promise and loss of El Dorado. In each case the utopia as an ideal place establishes itself over and against the subtext of national devastation. The ideal commonwealth is represented for the early modern utopist as a symbolic reconstruction, a new site with an ancient history, a place whose ideal terrain is shadowed by previous ruin. The construction of utopia entails both a geographical displacement and a partial repetition of its violent past.

Despite the utopia's professed statelessness, the utopian institution is a political organ that reveals itself working closely with the state to manufacture the values it prizes most highly. Those values—good citizenship, empiricism, industry, filial obedience—are not extrinsic to society but constructed within it. The state's institutions—its schools, research centers, workhouses, and families—not only restructure and reorganize its populations but actually confer on that population a series of identities. These identities in turn shape the utopia's collective memory, its rituals, its self-representations in poetry, architecture, or dialogue. Working against the utopias' manifest claims to alterity (their distant settings, their ethnographies of customs and rituals) I suggest that these narratives are less explications of the "other" than they are sociologies of emergent institutions.

Utopias are bounded sites—walled, moated, found only by accident or shipwreck, difficult to relocate or reenter. One of the most subtle but important of these boundaries is the utopia's insistence on its own transparency as a kind of discourse. Readers are barred from "reading in," as Ruppert has pointed out, from interpreting, from dislocating the narrative's claims to "truth." In this regard, a surprising number of readers take utopias at their word. Readers often overlook the complexities of utopian fiction, marginalizing if not ignoring its strategies of self-representation. Thus, critics have tended to resort to aesthetic or evaluative criteria when faced with the utopias' didacticism, rather than questioning that didacticism or historicizing its agenda. Miriam Eliav-Feldon's sociological study of European utopias in the early modern period begins by claiming that "utopias as a rule have little literary value despite their fictional frameworks," an assessment that recurs in criticism of later utopias as well.[38] James Redmond, an editor of William Morris's *News from Nowhere*, claims in his preface that he believes (and is certain Morris would have agreed) that the "literary" qualities of *News from Nowhere* are beside the point, for it "speaks plainly and directly," freeing itself from the need for "literary criticism."[39] Utopias are thus seen to occupy a special place as discourse, free from what More in his letter to Giles calls "fancy terms."[40] This insistence on utopian obviousness is in fact a mystification, an acceptance of the utopia's "truth claim," which is always a self-conscious and highly crafted literary device.

Utopias are about the fictional nature of nonfiction. They work by demonstrating that all texts—statutes, sermons, declarations of war—are representations, that states are not discovered but made, and that values are not innate but artfully (and artificially) constructed. Given the web of connections between early modern utopias and contiguous cultural practices—exploration and the planting of colonies, the establishment of city schools and research institutes, the reordering of government, theories of political and domestic organization—I think it is imperative to read these texts in the contexts that they themselves take seriously. Readers of utopias are particularly susceptible to privileging meanings over methods and hence to re-estranging the genre, for example, reading Bacon's *New Atlantis* (a prose fiction) "like a play," or trying to measure the "literariness" of one utopian text over another.[41] Utopias may encourage such responses because these works are so self-consciously hybrid, positioning themselves between genres and overtly advertising their strategies of rhetorical adaptation, translation, and transmutation. Nevertheless, it is important to resist (or at least to make conscious) the ways in which these texts keep us outside of them as readers, to keep asking how the utopia gets told as well as to analyze what it claims to be saying. To read utopias in this way we must continually be on the watch for what is not described as well as what is. For even to admit a problem exists, as Marx put it, is to assume that there is a possibility it can be solved. Silences or gaps in these utopias may testify less to indifference than to a kind of unarticulated despair.

No man is born to himself, no man is born to idleness. Your children are not begotten to yourself
alone, but to your country; not to your country alone,
but to God.—Erasmus, *Upon the Right Method of
Instruction*

There is a close historical correlation between the
national formation and the development of schools
as "popular" institutions, not limited to specialized
training or to elite culture, but serving to underpin
the whole process of the socialization of individuals
. . . . The state, economic exchange and family life are
also schools in a sense, organs of the ideal nation
recognizable by a common language which belongs
to them "as their own."—Etienne Balibar, "The
Nation Form"

1. Founding the "Best State of the Commonwealth"

THE SCHOOL OF THOMAS MORE

In 1509, six years before the publication of More's
Utopia, John Colet established a school in the churchyard of St.
Paul's Cathedral. One hundred and fifty-three students (the num-
ber of the miraculous draught of fishes recorded in John 21.2)
were to be admitted "free" to St. Paul's, provided that they knew
English and some Latin.[1] Colet's invitation to "my countreymen
Londoners specially" to attend the "scole-house of stone" he built
in the "est ende of the church-yerde of Paulis" heralded a new con-

junction between education and Englishness. St. Paul's was a striking departure from the ecclesiastical schools of the fourteenth and fifteenth centuries, instituted to educate sons of the citizens of London rather than those of the nobility. Everything from the curriculum to the spatial design of St. Paul's was designed to train up a new class of citizens. While recognizing the extant models of Winchester and Eton, St. Paul's emphasized a new separation of schoolboys into distinct groups (based on age and ability) called "forms." The boys sat on fixed benches, one behind the other, in ascending rows. Erasmus, who visited the school in its early years, described it as a single round room divided into four parts by curtains. These quadrants systematically divided the boys into separate classes, each governed by a pupil chosen to serve as head or captain:

> He [Colet] divided the school into four apartments. The first,
> viz., the porch and entrance is for catechumens, or the chil-
> dren to be instructed in the principles of religion; where no
> child is to be admitted, but what can read and write. The
> second apartment is for the lower boys, to be taught by the
> second master or usher; the third, for the upper forms, under
> the headmaster: which two parts of the school are divided
> by a curtain to be drawn at pleasure. . . . The boys have their
> distinct forms, or benches, one above another. Every form
> holds sixteen; and he that is head or captain of each form
> has a little kind of desk by way of pre-eminence.[2]

The school's design emphasized hierarchy and place, the students' "eminence" or subjection, and the consummate control of the headmaster. Within forms, the elevation of the captain's desk reminded the boys that hierarchy existed even among so-called equals. Colet dedicated the school to the boy Jesus, whose portrait was hung at the front of the school in a position of spiritual vigilance. If one kind of supervision slipped at St. Paul's, another would supersede it.

St. Paul's was a city school, placed in the trust of the Mercer's Company and identified not with noblemen but with merchants of the middle classes. Its headmasters were to be chosen from among the laity rather than the priests, and its students were trained to be-

Hanc *Scholæ Paulinæ* faciem poſt Incendium renovatam denuo æri incidi ſuis ſumptibus fecit *Joh. Bridges* Armig. Hoſpitij Lincolnienſis Socius ejuſdem Scholæ quondam Alumnus.

St. Paul's School, 1516. From Samuel Knight, *The Life of Dr. John Colet in the Reigns of Kings Henry VII and Henry VIII* (London, 1724). By permission of the Houghton Library, Harvard University.

come not clergymen but well-behaved, Christian-minded citizens. They were, in Colet's terms, "little Londoners," and it was as such that their discipline was to be organized. With the help of Erasmus and Lily, Colet set up a strict curriculum concerned not only with what the boys would learn but also with the methods by which they were to learn it: "The children shall come unto school in the morning at 7 of the clock, both winter and summer, and tarry there until 11, and return again at one of the clock, and depart at 5, and thrice in the day prostrate they shall say the prayers with due tact and pausing, as they be contained in a table in the school, that is to say, in the morning and at noon and at evening."[3]

"Contained in a table"—the taxonomy both for the grid of behaviors and their codification in writing—describes the form of Colet's statutes as well as their prescription. The rigidity of the timetable, of rank, and of function in the enclosed world of St. Paul's was detailed by Colet down to the elimination of waste: "To their urine they shall go thereby to a place appointed, and a poor child of the school shall see it conveyed away from time to time, and have the avail of the urine. For other causes if need be they shall go to the water-side."[4]

Every minute of every day in the schoolboy's life was to be strictly supervised. Penry Williams has reckoned that the average English schoolboy in the Tudor period spent 1,826 hours of each year in school. Colet strictly forbade "remedies," or days allotted off in addition to holy days: "I will also they shall have no remedies. If the Master granteth any remedies, he shall forefeit 40.s. tociens quociens, except the King or an archbishop, or a bishop present in his own person in the school, desire it."[5] This rigor seems to have been intended to toughen boys for the exigencies of city life and its demands—to prepare them to become hardworking and diligent citizens. In the reformist literature a new emphasis is discernible on civic obligation and service allied with education and training. "Instead of the display of innate superiority at such courtly pastimes as hunting, singing, dancing and romantic interchange, English humanists sought to establish a serious demeanor, aphoristic style, and constructive use of time as the signs of a powerful subject," Mary Crane remarks.[6] This change in style led to new emphasis on obedience. William Lily, the first high master of St. Paul's, detailed in his *Carmen de Moribus* the proper sign of respect from his students: "When thou shalt see me thy master, salute me, and all thy school-fellows in order." John Strype, a student at St. Paul's before the original structure was destroyed in the Great Fire, remarked on Colet's delight in "Inscriptions and Mottoes," which he "appointed to be set up in several Parts and Places of the School, as short and pithy Intimations of his Mind and Intentions." Each window was inscribed on the inside with the phrases "AUT DOCE, AUT DISCE, AUT DISCEDE, which I remember the upper Master, in my Time, used often to inculcate upon such Scholars, as were idle and negligent: Either Learn or be gone."[7] Evidence for corporal punishment in Tudor schools can be found almost everywhere, from school seals that advertised whippings to eyewitness accounts. Crane points out that John Stanbridge's phrasebook, widely used in Tudor schools, offered English schoolboys a veritable conjugation of beatings: "I was beten this mornynge," "The master hath bete me," "I shall be bete."[8] In fact, corporal punishment was so notorious a feature of the English public school—and has so long remained so—that it has become part of the popular myth about England in novels and films, suggestively linked to English manners and mores. While English schools would not become explicitly nationalist in their curricula until the late Elizabethan or early Jacobean era (James I required a text entitled *God and the King* in Scottish schools), the religious and moral aspirations of the Tudor grammar schools were, as Foster Watson observes, implicitly nationalistic.[9] The schoolboy's obedience was ultimately to the state, not just to the headmaster; discipline was a matter of patriotism as well as piety.

During the late fifteenth and early sixteenth centuries schools' ties to the church were loosened, and one paradigm of service was replaced with another. Liah Greenfield claims that nationalism emerged in England as a new (Henrician) aristocracy formed itself as an official elite, an aristocracy "open to talent" marked by "remarkable abilities and education."[10] Unquestionably the rapid changes in Tudor grammar schools, both before and after the Reformation, reflected this burgeoning nationalism. Between 1480 and 1660 fifteen grammar schools were founded in London and many more in rural or outlying areas. To varying degrees, these schools reflected reformists' concern with a new kind of training. Their timetables differed from the agenda of medieval religious orders— also exacting—by the new relations they drew between schedules and utility. In the monastery or religious school, "hours" had been structured along ecclesiastical lines; often a rigid timetable was followed to demonstrate mastery over the body or the will or as an enactment of one's duty to God. In the secular English grammar schools established in the late fifteenth and early sixteenth centuries, timetables increasingly were enforced to ensure productivity. Discipline was no longer seen as the final product of labor, maintained for its own sake, but rather for the sake of service, self-improvement, and duty to the state. Use and profit became the new measures of productivity, and increasingly it was the nation to whom such service was to be devoted and who was to benefit from its labors: "Whereas the thirteenth century friar says that 'all the studies of learners ought to be for theology, that is, to tend to the knowledge of God,' his sixteenth century followers aimed at molding 'the nature of man as a citizen, an active member of the state.'"[11]

As Joan Simon has observed, St. Paul's exemplified these changes, founded as it was on "a new model and with a radically new curriculum." "Here was a public school of the kind that all humanist writers advocated: a school open to all comers, placed in the city and not shut away in a monastic precinct, held in a building of its own and under the control of a public authority."[12] Colet's chief concern at St. Paul's was for the inculcation of "good Christian life and manners in the children." For this reason the method of the boys' instruction—close supervision, rigid timetables, and a hierarchical system even among the students themselves—was as important to the molding of character as the Greek or Latin authors taken up for study. The mastertext for schoolboys in this period was the grammar, which broke meaning down into coherent parts, provided rules for place and use, and codified the importance of order. The *Sulpicius*, a set of Latin elegiacs learned by rote at Eton and elsewhere, transformed these principles into a grammar of conduct and etiquette: "Spread the tables neatly, see that the trenchers . . . are clean. Don't champ your jaws when eating, sit upright, don't put your elbows on the table, take your food only with three fingers and in small mouthfuls. . . . Use your napkin often . . . don't bite your food but cut it, nor gnaw your bones. Only lift the cup with one hand . . . don't look over it while you are drinking, don't swallow it too fast or drain the pot, or whistle when you drink. Wipe your hand after it, and wash your hands and mouth when you leave the table. Bend your knee, join your hands, and say 'Prosit' for grace."[13]

The school in the early modern period dismantled barriers between public and private behavior, teaching schoolboys that no area in their lives was beyond its disciplinary control. In the terms of the sociologist Erving Goffman, the public school thus became a "total institution," marked by the following features: "First, all aspects of life are conducted in the same place and under the same single authority. Second, each phase of the member's daily activity is carried on in the immediate company of a large batch of others, all of whom are treated alike and required to do the same thing together. Third, all phases of the day's activities are tightly scheduled, with one activity leading at a prearranged time into the next, the whole sequence of activities being imposed from above by a system of explicit formal rulings and a body of officials. Finally, the various enforced activities are brought together into a single rational plan purportedly designed to fulfill the official aims of the institution."[14]

The following excerpts from the statutes of the Westminster School (1560) make clear the extent to which the Tudor schools corresponded to Goffman's definition:

> There shall be two Masters, one of whom shall be called Head Master. . . . All the scholars shall be under their government, both of them shall be religious, learned, honourable and painstaking, so that they may make their pupils pious, learned, gentlemanly, and industrious. . . . Their duty shall be not only to teach Latin, Greek, and Hebrew Grammar, and the humanities, poets, and orators, and diligently to examine in them, but also to build up and correct the boys' conduct, to see that they behave themselves properly in church, school, hall, and chamber, as well as in all walks and games, that their faces and hands are washed, their heads combed, their hair and nails cut, their clothes both linen and woollen, gowns, stockings, and shoes kept clean, neat, and like a gentleman's . . . and that they never go out of the college precincts without leave.[15]

One of the most striking characteristics of the "total institution" is its division of populations into two basic groups—a "large managed group" and a "small supervisory staff." The imbalance between these two populations puts special emphasis on the need for surveillance—"a seeing to it that everyone does what he has been clearly told is required of him, under conditions where one person's infraction is likely to stand out in relief against the visible, constantly examined compliance of the others."[16] As if anticipating Goffman's description, the Westminster statutes conclude the list of masters' duties with the appointment of surrogate inspectors, or monitors: "They shall further appoint various monitors from the gravest scholars to oversee and note the behavior of the rest everywhere and prevent anything improper or dirty being done. If any monitor commits an offence or neglects to perform his duty he shall be severely flogged as an example to others."[17]

The culture of vigilance born from the appointment of internal monitors worked against the unifying tendencies of these emergent schools. If the schools helped to consolidate groups of children into classes based on age, uniting them and calling attention to their needs as distinct from those of adults, the election of peer-police also divided these classes, setting schoolboy against schoolboy, turning peers into spies or malefactors. This culture of vigilance seems to have been shared by most if not all English schools in the early sixteenth century. Given the size of their classes, masters depended on pupil-informants to help supervise their charges, and by the early sixteenth century, the process of selecting such informants was becoming official practice. The monitor might be called the "excitator," the "custos," the "asini," or the "prepostor," but whatever his title, his duty was to police his peers. At Eton, prepostors were obliged to report delinquencies to their masters, be they "fyting, rent clothes, blew eyes or sich like" or "yll kept hedys, unwassh'd faces, folwe clothis and sich other." Eton required two prepostors for each form: "Two in the body, i.e., nave of the church; two in the choir. In every house a monitor. They go home two and two in order and have a monitor to see that they do till they come their 'hostise' or Dame's door. Privay monitors—to spy on the others—'how many the master will.'"[18] At the Westminster School (fl. 1560), monitors were in charge of getting the other boys out of bed ("At 5 o'clock that one of the Monitors of the Chamber . . . shall intone 'Get up'") as well as with supervising cleanliness and ensuring that no blot be visible, either in character or in domestic order: "Prayers finished they shall make their beds. Then each shall take any dust or dirt there may be under his bed into the middle of the chamber, which, after being placed in various parts of the chamber, shall then be swept up into a heap by four boys, appointed by the Monitor, and carried out."[19]

At St. Paul's, Colet officialized the role of monitor and gave it prominence by selecting one "principal child" from every form to be "placed in the chair, president of that form." The social and civic aims of the humanist school made this internal authority especially important in the first decades of the sixteenth century. The appointment of monitors, prepostors, or prefects meant that the possibility of being spied on infiltrated the school at every level, and the use of peers to police behavior came to be seen as part of the educational system, construed as a practical means of preparing "little Londoners" for future life. The effect of this internal vigilance may have been even greater than its masters had anticipated, for the election of internal monitors splintered horizontal ties, maintaining authority at the top in part by disseminating suspicion, uneasiness, and paranoia below. As one's loyalty could not safely be given to peers, it could be preserved intact for the larger institution of the school or for that nascent abstraction the school was devised to serve, the state itself. That structures of authority were changing in this period—and that the shift made itself strongly felt in schools—is tellingly demonstrated by the fate of Colet's portrait of the boy Jesus hung at St. Paul's. When it was removed by reformers during the seventeenth century, it was replaced by a bust of Colet himself, his stony gaze secularizing the role of monitor and making its office finally—and unmistakably— English.[20]

LITTLE HAS BEEN written about More's own schooling (he attended St. Anthony's School in Threadneedle Street, a "free school" attached to St. Anthony's Hospital). As far as any influence on *Utopia* is concerned, greater weight has been ascribed to the years More spent as a member of the Charterhouse community, where he lived, according to his son-in-law, Will Roper, "without vow about four years."[21] But the Tudor school, with its internal mechanisms for surveillance and control, can be seen as an important paradigm or "pattern" for the commonwealth More fashioned in 1515–1516. More had known Colet from childhood; though More was twelve years younger, the two had been students together at Oxford and had studied together under Grocyn and Linacre. More was greatly interested in Colet's efforts at St. Paul's, and he supported many of Colet's efforts to reform education.[22] More's own household was famously modeled as a kind of school. His inclination to solitary study led him to construct a separate building on his estate "a good distance from his mansion" housing a library, chapel, and gallery "in which as his use

Bust of John Colet. From Samuel Knight, *The Life of Dr. John Colet in the Reigns of Kings Henry VII and Henry VIII* (London, 1724). By permission of the Houghton Library, Harvard University.

was upon other days to occupy himself in prayer and study to-gether." Roper recounts More's insistence that his wife and children join him in such contemplative pursuits. "Thus delighted he evermore not only in virtuous exercises to be occupied by himself, but also to exhort his wife, and children, and household to embrace the same". Roper, who spent sixteen years in this household, adds that More would often urge his children "to take virtue and learning for their meat, and play but for their sauce."[23] This prescription is borne out by a letter from More to his children in which he boasts that even while riding on horseback through driving rain he was able to compose Latin verses to them—an example he urged them all to take to heart. In a letter to his daughter, Margaret, More demanded enthusiasm for study and the avoidance of idleness: "Later letters will be even more delightful if they have told me of the studies you and your brother are engaged in, of your daily reading, your pleasant discussions, your essays, of the swift passage of the days made joyous by literary pursuits . . . for I assure you that, rather than allow my children to be idle and slothful, I would make a sacrifice of wealth, and bid adieu to other cares and business, to attend to my children and my family." In March 1521, More sent a letter to his children with the following address: "Thomas More to his whole school, greeting."[24]

In Utopia the domestic and pedagogic are similarly conjoined: dinners, for example, become occasions for testing the wits of young men, for hearing edifying readings, and for absorbing the protocol of place, order, and subservience. Household and school are conflated in *Utopia*, with its appointed hours for waking and sleeping, working and eating, even for periods of relaxation or play; both house and school are supervised and controlled by the state. The Utopian state controls the smallest details of its citizens' daily timetable. As Hythlodaeus reports: "The Utopians . . . divide the day and night into twenty-four equal hours and assign only six to work. There are three before noon, after which they go to dinner. After dinner, when they have rested for two hours in the afternoon, they again give three to work and finish up with supper. Counting one o'clock as beginning at midday, they go to bed about eight o'clock, and sleep claims eight hours."[25]

FAMILIA THOMÆ MO

Thomas Morus A. 50. Alicia Thomæ Mori uxor A. 57. Iohannes Morus pater A. 76. Iohannes Morus Tho
Elisabeta Damea Thomæ Mori filia A. 21. Cæcilia Heroina Thomæ Mori filia A. 20. Margareta Giga Clem

Hans Holbein the Younger, "The Family of Thomas More."
Oeffentliche Kuntstsammlung Basel, Kupferstichkabinett.

iohannis
.... Thom
.. anno 19

hēricus patenson9
Thomæ mori moro
anno XL

oliem fil9

alitia thomæ mor
uxor anno 51

margreta roper
thomæ mori filia
anno 22

cicilia herona thomæ mori filia anno 20

NGL : CANCELL :

..19. Anna Grisacria Iohannis Mori Sponsa Aᵒ 15. Margareta Ropera Thomæ Mori filia Aᵒ 22.
..Mori filialis Condiscipula et cognata Aᵒ 22. Henricus Patensonus Thomæ Mori morio Aᵒ 40.

Hythlodaeus's precision here is intended to demonstrate that Utopian efficiency guarantees plenty of time for learning, but it is the micromanagement of the calendar that is most instructive in Utopia, more than the popular predawn lectures or the exemplary games in which the virtues take on the vices. The rigidity of the Utopian routine is enforced less to encourage a certain kind of behavior ("the intervals between the hours of work, sleep and food are left to every man's discretion") than to maximize utility and to discourage loafing ("not to waste [time] in revelry or idleness"). Waste in every sense of the word is abhorrent in Utopia; every minute of every day must be accounted for, justifying the need for government certificates and permission to travel. As Hythlodaeus approves, "Nowhere is there any license to waste time." He also remarks that "the chief and almost the only function of the sypho-grants [utopian officers] is to manage and provide that no one sit idle" (127, 147). What Foucault has identified as the tripartite method of the timetable—the establishment of rhythms, the impositions of particular occupations, and the regulation of cycles of repetition—is deeply embedded in Utopia.[26] Like Cardinal Morton's table, which stands at the center of *Utopia*'s first book, the timetable becomes the site at which public and private intersect, the grid which assures that order will not be disrupted and that every citizen will be apportioned voice, place, and function. The timetable, like the hierarchical design of Colet's classroom, imposes its own logic and direction. What it teaches above all else is obedience to the state.

In Utopia, as in the early Tudor schools, the culture of vigilance not only encourages virtuous behavior but makes virtue possible. "Being under the eyes of all, people are bound either to be performing the usual labor or to be enjoying their leisure in a fashion not without decency," Hythlodaeus explains (147). This principle of visibility (which brings the Utopians to use gold and silver for chamberpots, deflating the values of precious metals by exposing them and making them ordinary) works as a code of ethics, as if what is seen can never be dangerous. The greatest shame in Utopia is for private malefaction to be used as a public example. Slaves are circulated as visible signs of disgrace, marked with gold to signify their crimes. The Anemolian ambassadors provoke similar snickers and derision from the Utopian onlookers, as their ceremonious attire renders them ridiculous rather than important. Conversely, being singled out for public esteem is a great pleasure in Utopia. The panoptic possibility that someone is watching (always associated with the dread of shame) forms the very basis of Utopian ethics. In battle, for example, courage is produced not from any innate quality in a soldier but rather from the dread of being seen as cowardly: "Shame at being seen to flinch by their own side, the close quarters with the enemy, and the withdrawal of hope of escape combine to overpower their timidity, and often they make a virtue of extreme necessity" (209).

As the living bear witness in Utopia the dead also "travel freely where they please," moving about the living as "witnesses of their words and actions." These spirits form a supernatural police force, for "the belief, moreover, in the personal presence of their forefathers keeps men from any secret dishonourable deed" (225). Presumably these invisible monitors ensure that even the rare moments of solitude in Utopia can never be entirely private. Like the gaze behind "the curtain to be drawne at pleasure" at St. Paul's, the dead in Utopia keep a perpetual and invisible watch over the performance of citizenship.

Should anything secret or dishonorable occur in Utopia, it must be immediately exposed, like the dust and dirt beneath the beds of the boys at the Westminster School. Grave offenses are handled by senators, who generally dispense a sentence of slavery "since this prospect, they think, is no less formidable to the criminal and more advantageous to the state than if they make haste to put offenders to death and get them out of the way at once" (191). At the domestic level confession is regulated by the head of household, always male: "On the Final-Feasts, before they go to the temple, wives fall down at the feet of their husbands, children at the feet of their parents. They confess that they have erred, either by committing some fault or by performing some duty carelessly, and beg pardon for their offense" (233). Once again the household is patterned here on an institutional model, and even the most intimate of speech acts—the domestic confession—is ritualized, given a place in the schedule, and made a part of state routine. Presumably this ritu-alized confession and absolution is meant to reinforce patriarchal authority as well as filial devotion. Discipline in Utopia, as in the humanist schools, is enforced at the microlevel; there is no escape from actual surveillance or its possibility, and citizens are trained not only to obey laws but to enforce them.

More subtle than Utopia's penal system and more suggestive is the commonwealth's tacit code of decency through which certain kinds of behavior are encouraged and others prohibited. While it is not required that citizens take their meals in the public halls, for example, it is considered bad form to reject the halls for the privacy of one's own home. Privacy is seen both as inefficient and as a dem-onstration of bad taste. Everything in the Utopians' training works against solitary pursuits, for they are trained to rely both on par-ticipation and on witnesses. Utopians believe values are the fruits of careful training. Valor on the battlefield, as Hythlodaeus de-scribes it, comes from "good and sound opinions, in which they have been trained from childhood both by teaching and by the good institutions of their country" rather than from native courage (211). Values are publicly held, and a watchful audience is necessary to ensure that they are appreciated and reinforced.

If Hythlodaeus does not bother to describe in detail the proce-dures for training the tiny "class of learning" in the common-wealth, it may well be because all of Utopia, at every level, operates like a great school. Like St. Paul's, the commonwealth of Utopia is divided into four quadrants, each identical in shape and design; as at St. Paul's, citizens are divided into classes or households, each with its "head" to maintain order. As the entire commonwealth functions like a school, descriptions of schools within the com-monwealth are redundant. Most Utopians do not, in fact, attend schools. They learn through apprenticeship agriculture and crafts, generally those learned by their fathers before them. Before and after the hours devoted to labor, however, Utopian citizens not destined for the "class of learning" enjoy a busy curriculum of military training, edifying games, or gardening (a stock metaphor in humanist educational tracts for the tending and improving of the human character). Extra hours at one's craft or in attendance at predawn lectures are held in high public esteem, as is participation in one of several species of war games, in which "one number plunders another" or "the vices fight a pitched battle with the virtues" (129). While Utopia has been variously accused of being a static society, much of its pressure actually comes from the possibility of promotion: "Not seldom does it happen that a craftsman so industriously employs his spare hours on learning and makes such progress by his diligence that he is relieved of his manual labor and advanced into the class of men of learning" (133). Demotion, conversely, is also possible: a scholar who "falsifies the hopes entertained of him" may be "reduced to the rank of workingman" (131–33). The citizen's position is not fixed; he or she has always to be on guard to ensure that status will stay high or improve if it is low. In Foucault's terms, this system of rewards and punishments hierarchizes "good" and "bad" subjects, placing them in relation to each other and making all subordinate to the disciplinary mechanisms by which their positions are fixed.[27]

One value especially prized in Utopia is the ability to reproduce patterns or to imitate forms of production. This is most strikingly revealed when Hythlodaeus tries to explain to Morus and Giles what it was like teaching the Utopians to read Greek. At first, he admits, the Portuguese only bothered to teach the Utopians to seem like good sports ("more at first that we should not seem to refuse the trouble than that we expected any success"), but the Utopians, "not only fired by their own free will but acting under orders of the senate," proved to be both tractable and enthusiastic. In fact, if the disruptive and mocking guests at Cardinal Morton's table in book 1 epitomize the worst sort of students, the Utopians in their zeal for the classics epitomize the best: "They began so easily to imitate the shapes of the letters, so readily to pronounce the words, so quickly to learn by heart, and so faithfully to reproduce what they learned that it was a perfect wonder to us"(181). Hythlodaeus commends the Utopians here for their productivity: their easy imitation, ready pronunciation, and quick memorization are all skills allowing them rapidly to reproduce letters, just as the Portuguese methods of printing enable them to increase "their stock [of books] by many thousands of copies" (185). Such imitation exemplifies a highly specialized form of labor, and in fact the Utopians may well be model students because they have been trained as model workers, zealous in a pursuit that is, in Hythlodaeus's terms, just another form of reproduction.

Nor are imitation and "faithful reproduction" the only characteristics that link learning in Utopia to capitalist performance. Education in Utopia relies at almost every level either on testing or "besting"; prizes are given for the most beautiful gardens, promotions are given for the keenest moral and intellectual excellence, and even the relaxed atmosphere of the dinner table is used to refine through dialectic. The terms used in Utopia to suggest progress—*industry, employment, diligence, advancement*—are more commonly associated with economics than with pedagogy. Whereas at St. Paul's, each of the four quadrants of the circular schoolroom was controlled by a "master" or "head," in Utopia the four quadrants of the commonwealth are centrally governed by the institutional hub of the marketplace. These markets function as schoolrooms for the exposure and containment of desire, teaching Utopia's citizens the value of "plenty" and its intrinsic ties to state control.

Regulating Want

In book 1 of *Utopia*, Hythlodaeus, a stranger to Utopia and England alike, provides a brief ethnography of English culture. England, like Utopia, is a "nursery . . . of institutions," but England's institutions are corrupt, bankrupt, dominated by the inescapable and grim exigencies of the marketplace. Masterless men are hanged for stealing food they need to survive. Nobody listens to anybody. Courts are ruled by avarice. Morus hears all of this while in Flanders as the king's spokesman, disputing Dutch import duties on English cloth. In this world, all business is at once political and economic, governed by the demands of unequal goods and uneven forms of exchange.

If England is characterized by the binary poles of excess and want, Utopia, according to Hythlodaeus, is characterized by balance and moderation. Exchange is used at every level to offer the "desirable society," as Northrop Frye puts it, rather than the writer's own world.[28] Citizens are rotated out of cities for periodic stints as farmers, and goods are exported from cities to keep excesses down. There must never be too much, too many, too few, or not enough. Populations are carefully regulated so that no household grows beyond sixteen inhabitants or drops to fewer than ten. Six thousand households are the limit for each city, a limit "easily observed by transferring those who exceed the number in larger families into those that are under the proscribed number. Whenever all the families of a city reach their full quota, the adults in excess of that number help to make up the deficient population of other cities"(137).

Should the population of the entire island "happen to swell above the fixed quotas," colonies are established on the adjacent mainland: "They enroll citizens out of every city and, on the mainland nearest them, wherever the natives have much unoccupied and uncultivated land, they found a colony under their own laws. They join with themselves the natives if they are willing to dwell with them. When such a union takes place, the two parties gradually and easily merge and together absorb the same way of life and the same customs, much to the great advantage of both peoples"(137).

Hythlodaeus's account here occludes the procedures of colonial interaction. He describes it as a "union," as gradual and easy "merging" that enables both parties "together to absorb the same way of life and the same customs." But as each of these Utopian colonies is established under Utopian laws, we must presume that what Hythlodaeus means by "the same way of life and the same customs" is not a blending of two cultures but an enforced submission on the part of the colonized to Utopian polity. In a subsequent passage, Hythlodaeus is more explicit about the potential consequences of such gradual and easy merging: "The inhabitants who refuse to live according to their laws, they drive away from the territory which they carve out for themselves. If they resist, they wage war against them. They consider it a most just cause for war when a people which does not use its soil but keeps it idle and waste nevertheless forbids the use and possession of it to others who by the rule of nature ought to be maintained by it" (137).

Regulating the Utopian population, in other words, begins with carefully calculated exchange (so many per household, so many per city, so many per nation) and ends, at least potentially, in colonial conquest and warfare. What justifies this outcome is the doctrine of fair use: wasted land is a greater crime to the Utopians than conquering natives, and "the rule of nature" entitles the stronger of two countries to "the use and possession" of land. A similar rhetorical slippage can be seen in the operation of the Utopian marketplace. The alleged function of the markets, according to Hythlodaeus, is to abolish "the fear of want." Through regulation and exchange, the market disqualifies the possibility of shortage or excess. This institution strikes us as all the more powerful, given our indoctrination in book 1 into what could be described, according to Pierre Macherey, as the ideological motif of shortage.[29] Nowhere in the prefatory letters or the first book of *Utopia* is there enough. Just as our initial account from Morus begins with lack— no time to write, not enough information about the location of the island, nostalgia for family, home, and country—Hythlodaeus picks up and elaborates this theme, lamenting his own lack of appropriate position, England's lack of arable land and food, monarchy's lack of wisdom in curtailing dominion rather than aggrandizing it, and his own lack of suitable audience (39, 43, 49). In each of the three micro-utopias Hythlodaeus narrates in book 1, shortage and absence are foregrounded, and someone is described either as stealing or being stolen from. Nowhere in this world is there enough—nowhere but Nowhere, in Utopia, where want is eradicated, where commodities are regulated so that all are equivalent, treasure and not-treasure, citizen, slave, and king.

Given the centrality of the marketplace to the Utopian economy, it is surprising that Hythlodaeus should qualify his praise for it with a string of imaginary objections. Richard Halpern has suggested that the Utopian marketplace is the "point at which . . . competing logics are both condensed and globalized," claiming, I think quite rightly, that the marketplace is "the most volatile site in all *Utopia*."[30] My own sense is that the marketplace in *Utopia* is what Macherey calls a "perfect and complete institution," in that it has subsumed within it the whole range of its own potential limits and qualifications.[31] In this sense the market, like the school, is the epitome of the utopian institution. Not only can the marketplace be described only in terms of the very things it is said to nullify—*greed, want, superfluous display*—but the procedures for describing the marketplace partially curtail its potency. Here is Hythlodaeus's description:

> Every city is divided into four equal districts. In the middle of each quarter is a market of all kinds of commodities. To designated market buildings the products of each family are conveyed. Each kind of goods is arranged separately in store-houses. From the latter any head of a household seeks what he and his require and, without money or any kind of compensation, carries off what he seeks. Why should anything be refused? First, there is a plentiful supply of all things and, secondly, there is no underlying fear that anyone will demand more than he needs. Why should there be any suspicion that someone may demand an excessive amount when he is certain of never being in want? No doubt about it, avarice and greed are aroused in every kind of living creature by the fear of want, but only in man are they motivated by pride alone— pride which counts it a personal glory to excel others by superfluous display of possessions. The latter vice can have no place at all in the Utopian scheme of things. (137–39)

Hythlodaeus describes the market as a kind of machine: products are conveyed there, goods are arranged separately in storehouses, but no personnel are affiliated with the distribution of such goods. In fact, the only real action Hythlodaeus describes here is *seeking*, as the head of household comes for what he and his household require and carries off what is desired without payment. What in Europe would be considered theft (and punished by hanging) is in Utopia a mechanistic procedure, anticipated and controlled by the state. But Hythlodaeus's description of the market and its functions is shadowed by the urgent rhetorical questions appended to his précis. Why should anything be refused? Why should there be any suspicion? The initial image of "plentiful supply" is quickly succeeded by anxious, if not urgent, descriptions of shortage: "no underlying fear," "suspicion," "avarice and greed," "the fear of want." Hythlodaeus begins by placing the market ("in the middle of each quarter") and concludes by displacing the vice of pride, which has in Utopia "no place at all." In reading this passage, we experience firsthand the translation from the "eutopia" (good place) to the "utopia" (no place) of the island's hexastichon. The description of the marketplace exchanges the good place for the placeless, the machine of regulated desire for the sin of avarice.

What connects Utopia's centralized markets to the disciplinary system of improvement I have been discussing is a shared concern with the conversion of value, whether it pertains to capital or to character. I have already suggested that certain values within Utopia are shown to be socially constructed rather than innate—courage on the battlefield, for example, or enthusiasm for edifying literature. In economic terms, "value" becomes especially problematic in More's commonwealth. Just as the need to regulate the population leads to the establishment of colonies on the mainland, destabilizing the very boundaries the Utopians have worked so hard to construct, the desire to store "treasure not as treasure" creates two separate economies on the island: a domestic economy (communist) and a foreign economy (capitalist). What has no value within Utopia has immense value outside its borders, so that gold, which we are ambiguously told no Utopian values "more highly than [its] true nature deserves," is both despised and treasured: despised in the commonwealth, where it is associated with childhood, excrement, and slavery to debase its value, and treasured in the sense that it is deliberately stored in order to bribe mercenaries during times of war. "For these military reasons," Hythlodaeus explains with further ambiguity, "they keep a vast treasure, but *not as a treasure*" (151). Like the storehouses in the marketplace, these treasuries both represent and complicate the idea of plenty. Gold in Utopia becomes the most overdetermined of signifiers, scattered rather than hidden, making it least visible by overexposure. Dissociating gold from any use other than holding waste ensures that the ore will always be available but never desired. Ironically, the officials organize this devaluation precisely because they recognize the value of gold in foreign markets. In the island's other economy, gold allows the commonwealth to import and export, to make profits, to accumulate wealth, to manipulate prices abroad, to establish colonies and to wage (and win) wars. Like the school, the market defines value by demonstrating that it is unstable, that it can be manipulated, augmented, or decreased, that it is not absolute but part of a sequential chain of relations. The same ore which as a child's bauble, slave's chain, or chamberpot is a mark of stigma is at other times treasure not kept as treasure. Similarly the student chosen one year as monitor may the next year resume his position as monitored, and what he learns in the transition is the instability of his own status. What is stable—what controls the treasure, the plenty, ensuring its use—is the state; without its firm control, plenty becomes shortage, need becomes greed, the good place becomes no place.

Under the watchful eyes of utopian officials a citizen can work his way up into the class of learning, but he can also be subject to slavery if he commits a crime. In Utopia these possibilities of conversion rigidify structures rather than relax them. It is because promotion is possible that everyone must be watched; it is because gold sometimes has value and sometimes does not that its use must be regulated so strictly. While the possibility of promotion or conversion may appear empowering to the individual, its promise in More's commonwealth in fact empowers the state, justifying authorities of enforcement, promotion, and supervision. On the definition of this authority *Utopia* is vexingly silent. Who determines when an artisan has improved enough to be promoted or a slave has shown enough goodwill to be set free? Or is the promise of such conversion used only as a lure to exact loyalty from its citizens and never realized? Promotion and demotion, after all, are forms of payment and of debt, of what Pierre Bourdieu has called the "symbolic violence" of exchange.[32] In More's commonwealth, the market teaches its citizens a lesson: in the hands of the state, need and want can be eradicated; left to individual control, "the fear of want" regains its place.

Instituting Utopia

Utopia advertises itself from the outset as self-consciously and impressively novel, despite its rich amalgamation of sources, from Plato, Plutarch, and Lucian, from Amerigo Vespucci's and

Peter Martyr's accounts of the New World, and from contemporary debates among humanists on education, law, penal codes, and political service. The word *new* in More's subtitle is placed in apposition to the word *best*, heralding the emergence of a new form as well as a new subject. *Utopia* distinguishes itself from its models and sources in several important ways. First, it is unique in bringing together two kinds of literature (the wisdom-dialogue and the traveler's account) in treating the subject of the ideal commonwealth. Treatises on government were common enough in the late fifteenth and early sixteenth centuries, but the representation of an ideal commonwealth based on fictional travels was something new. Second, *Utopia* frames this representation with a truth-claim, an elaborate hoax about the veracity of Hythlodaeus's account, using fictions about truth to destabilize the differences between romance and history. Finally, *Utopia* incorporates into its description of the "best" and the "new" an ironic, skeptical voice, a voice whose rebuttals interrupt not only the narrator's personal philosophy but also the practices he describes. By using the figure of Morus to represent this voice of negation, *Utopia* transforms the static wisdom-dialogue (something like five hundred of which were published in England just between 1500 and 1550) into a fictional debate in which ideology is censured, qualified, or rejected even as it is introduced. In *Utopia* the real and the fictional displace and destabilize each other, like a film that mixes animated characters with real actors. Cardinal Morton's table, like Vespucci's voyage, is a diagram in book 1 for this aesthetic, organizing a cast of fictional characters whose voices are arranged and controlled by the supervising authority of an actual historical figure. The character of Morus is the point at which the historical and the actual intersect and are ironized; Morus is and is not real, just as he is and is not the author of *Utopia*. Wanting to know what Morus really thinks of Utopia and being unable to is built into the text. It is just one example of the way Utopia doubles back on itself. It is both Eutopia (good place) and Utopia (no place), a representation of the ideal and its cancellation. As a discursive and didactic form, *Utopia* offered its readers a new subject for reform as well as a new structure for its expression.

Unlike the Utopian students Hythlodaeus praises for their "ready imitation," however, More's metafictional prefaces extravagantly praise the text for its brilliance and originality. *Utopia*'s value is said to reside in being better than anything that preceded it, chiefly, better than Plato's *Republic*. This competition is further established within the text between the characters Morus and Hythlodaeus. Part of the joke elaborated by the packet of commendatory letters preceding the 1518 edition of *Utopia* is that the text has not one author but two. Within the fiction Raphael Hythlodaeus, the Portuguese mariner who discovered Utopia on the fourth of Vespucci's voyages, tells the "real" story, and More has only to act as his amanuensis. Each of the humanists who appends commendatory letters to the 1518 edition embroiders this hoax, but at the same time each takes pains to point out that it is really More's part which deserves the highest praise ("Beyond question it is More who has adorned the island and its holy institutions by his style and eloquence." "I am even disposed to believe that in all the five years which Raphael spent on the island, he did not see as much as one may perceive in More's description." "*Utopia* owes much to Hythlodaeus who has made known a country unworthy of remaining unknown. Its debt is even greater to the very learned More whose pencil has very skillfully drawn it for us.") Throughout this prefatory material runs the suggestion, counter to Hythlodaeus's praise of the Utopians' "faithful reproduction" of Greek literature, that writing is competitive and that literary value is determined through that very competition. As in the "form" at Colet's school, there can be only one head boy or captain, one place of preeminence.[33]

For More, clearly both the writing and publication of *Utopia* provoked feelings of anxiety as well as of elation. *Utopia* was one of the first texts More wrote without Erasmus's collaboration, during a period of self-conscious and rapid political advancement for More at a time when his need to make a name for himself was particularly urgent. More's anxiety about writing alone is most fully expressed in his simultaneous insistence on collaboration and his rejection of it. His famous prefatory letter to Giles denies that he himself is the text's real author: "I had only to repeat what in your company I heard Raphael relate." On the one hand, this strategy seems delib-

erately to foreground the role of the author; the more vehemently
More denies his role, the larger that role becomes. In another
sense, More seems to be arguing for *Utopia* as a kind of authorless
text, a claim by no means a hoax: even if we are concerned only
with the actual production of the text, rather than the culture's
collaboration in it, *Utopia* was authored to some extent by a team.
The marginal glosses of the early editions were written either by
Erasmus or Giles; the prefatory letters, which may or may not
have been commissioned by More, were written by a long list of
humanists, including Erasmus, Budé, Lupset, Giles, and Schrijver.
Arguably, then, More's argument for collaboration is only partly
a measure for self-concealment, and it seems yet another of the
text's equivocal strategies for anticipating its own reception, its
own "authorlessness."

But if More is eager to represent the authorship of *Utopia* on one
level as teamwork, on another level he insists that the text is novel,
"better" than its models. The opening pages of *Utopia* foreground
More's competition with his "rival," Plato. In a six-line poem at the
beginning of book 1, the poet laureate of *Utopia* imagines the island speaking: "The ancients called me Utopia or Nowhere because of my isolation. At present, however, I am a rival of Plato's
Republic, perhaps even a victor over it. The reason is that what
he has delineated in words I alone have exhibited in men and resources and laws of surpassing excellence. Deservedly I ought to be
called by the name of Eutopia or Happy Land."

According to Peter Giles, More's *Utopia* is superior to Plato's *Republic* because "a man of great eloquence has represented, painted,
and set it before our eyes in such a way that, as often as I read it, I
think I see far more than when, being as much a part of the conversation as More himself, I heard Raphael Hythlodaeus' own words
sounding in my ears" (21).

More's reading of *The Republic* throughout *Utopia* (an instance of
what Thomas Greene calls "chronomachia" or subreading) is divided: he can only value Plato by devaluing him, and he can only
place his own text by displacing *The Republic*.[34] Yet the novelty and
comparative virtues of Utopia depend on Plato as a kind of ances-
tral monitor; it is as if More imagines himself measured, scruti-

nized, examined by Plato even as he claims to denounce him. To an extent, the competition More wages with Plato depends once again on a concealed doctrine of fair use. This may be why More identifies himself so explicitly with the character of Utopus, the founder/colonist who conquers the original land of Abraxa, severing it from the mainland and giving it his own name. In December 1516, More wrote to Erasmus about *Utopia*, expressing excitement as well as temerity about the publication of his text:

> Master Tunstal recently wrote me a most friendly letter. Bless my soul, but his frank and complimentary criticism of my commonwealth has given me more cheer than would an Attic talent. You have no idea how thrilled I am; I feel so expanded, and I hold my head high. For in my daydreams I have been marked out by my Utopians to be their King forever; I can see myself now marching along, crowned with a diadem of wheat, very striking in my Franciscan frock, carrying a handful of wheat as my sacred scepter, thronged by a distinguished retinue of Amaurotians, and with this huge entourage, giving audience to foreign ambassadors and sovereigns; wretched creatures they are, in comparison with us, as they stupidly pride themselves on appearing in childish garb and feminine finery, laced with that despicable gold, and ludicrous in their purple and jewels and other empty baubles.[35]

To be Utopus is to make something new through violence and conquest, for Utopus's creation of Utopia is also the desiccation of Abraxa and its people. More's work as an author, unlike the faithful reproducers of letters he describes in *Utopia*'s second book, is solitary and self-promoting. More insists that writing cannot be original and must always be imitation or collaboration; on the other hand, the text needs to separate itself from the site of its own conquest, repeatedly attesting to its own novelty, to being "best." How could two such different visions of authorship be conjoined? How, in short, could More "own" *Utopia* without appearing to have produced it? More's solution for this problem is to claim that he did not write the text at all but found it—that is, that Hythlodaeus told the tale, and he had only to write it down. The brilliance of this denial of authorship, attributed variously by critics to political savvy, fear of censorship, or sprezzatura, is that it replicates Utopus's discovery of the ideal commonwealth. Utopus discovered Abraxa, a peninsular country of rough climate and rude inhabitants. Like More, he had only to perfect what he found. This representation of authorial production, like so many of More's institutions, would be taken up by every English utopist after More; many subsequent utopists would also embed within their narratives foundational fables, and many would similarly conjoin the creation of a commonwealth with that of its narration.

If *Utopia*'s prefatory letters introduce some of the complexities of instituting utopian authorship, book 1 introduces the complexity of constructing a new category of utopian readers and preparing them to receive this novel form. Once again the first book of *Utopia* is patterned on the schoolroom, its readers intended to be instructed. More referred to *Utopia* as a "libellum," or handbook, a guide not only to the interpretation of new lands and peoples but to the interpretation of the way Europeans were to transform their experiences of new places into narrative. I see book 1 of *Utopia* as a handbook, first, on how English readers were to learn from fiction and, second, on how they were to make use of foreigners and foreign experience. Two kinds of readers are described over and over in book 1: the first eager, attentive, hungry (if not greedy); the second dismissive, resistant, deaf. If the good listener has an open mind (and mouth), the bad listener has a closed ear. Morus and Giles appear to have the characteristics of good listeners, "greedy to hear" and "eagerly" inquiring, with a special appetite for hearing about nations "living together in a civilized way" (49, 53). Of course, Morus turns out to be considerably less open than he initially pretends; by the end of the second book he harbors secret objections to the "whole system" of the Utopians, nevertheless praising their way of life and Hythlodaeus's account of it despite his skepticism (85).

Book 1 is actually an anthology of anecdotes about the failure to understand utopian narratives or to make use of them. Throughout *Utopia*, the account of the ideal commonwealth is bounded by the record of its misinterpretation. As Louis Marin has observed,

Hythlodaeus describes three "micro-utopias" in book 1, each sited progressively closer to Utopia itself. He describes in order the habitation and customs of the Polyerites, the Anchorians, and the Macarians, in each instance hedging his account with all of the reasons why European audiences would reject them.

Descriptions of such failures of listening recur in Hythlodaeus's account of the dinner party at Cardinal Morton's, a party that is a mirror-reflection of the day in the Antwerp garden Hythlodaeus spends with Morus and Giles. At the center of Hythlodaeus's attack on English customs are two vivid images of hunger: the masterless man turned out of his home, forced to subsist on nothing or to be hanged for theft; and the greedy sheep so ravenous that "they devour human beings themselves and devastate and depopulate fields, houses, and towns" (67). In Utopia hunger is repeatedly conjoined with listening. Hythlodaeus's first failure of narration takes place at dinner; his description of Utopia proper is framed by lunch and supper. Like the rapacious sheep, audiences turn on Hythlodaeus (or he imagines that they will). Rather than listening, one auditor at Cardinal Morton's spent the whole time Hythlodaeus was talking "busily preparing himself to reply," becoming an open mouth rather than an open ear. Hythlodaeus rejects the idea of serving as counselor to a king because he believes he would not be understood: "What little regard courtiers would pay to me and my advice." "What reception from my listeners, my dear More, do you think this speech of mine would find?" "What if I told them the kinds of things which Plato creates in his republic or which the Utopians actually put in practice in theirs?"(85, 91, 101). In other words, Hythlodaeus would find only bad audiences; he would be eaten alive. Since he speaks the truth and refuses doctrines of tact or accommodation, there can be no place for him in Europe. Hence, as More speculates in his (fictional) letter to Giles, he may well by now be back in Utopia, literally "no place," where he had found an audience always receptive, always hungry.

Future readers and imitators of *Utopia* were to inherit from More the prescriptions for new institutions as well as the inability to represent them uncritically. As William Budé, one of More's contemporary readers, noted with approval, "Our age and succeeding ages will hold his account as a nursery of correct and useful institutions from which every man may introduce and adapt transplanted customs to his city" (15). In fact, Budé was uncannily correct. For generations after its initial publication *Utopia* was reprinted in anthologies of travel literature and taken on actual voyages of discovery, as Mandeville's travels had been taken by Columbus, serving as a kind of early English guidebook to the Americas. When a lawyer and humanist named Vasco de Quiroga was sent to New Spain in 1531 to assess colonial conditions and to propose the best method for reorganizing Indians scattered by the Spanish conquest, he turned to More's *Utopia* for inspiration for the "hospital pueblos" which he established several years later near Mexico City and Michoacan. Quiroga's Indian villages cast a shadow over Budé's prediction. Each of the institutions *Utopia* represents—the school, the workplace, the market—was to be reread and reinterpreted by utopists in the seventeenth century, each of whom selected one or more in his or her own utopia as the central mechanism for reform. In this way *Utopia* provided a model for seeing and understanding national identity through representations of worlds elsewhere. Ultimately, the colonialism of *Utopia* was to have its greatest consequence in the "Englishing" of people inside as well as outside "English" boundaries, people who were to be reshaped by its changing vision of what was "best."

Thirty-five years after the first edition of More's *Utopia* was published in Latin in Louvain, the text was translated into English by a goldsmith named Ralph Robinson. Robinson's text—the only English translation for over a century—came out in four editions: 1551, 1556, 1597, and 1624. Robinson, the son of poor parents, was the only member of his family to attend university. His translation of *Utopia* is significant not only because its editions connect the history of utopian writing in England between More and Bacon but because it marks Utopia's transformation from Latin to English, from aristocratic, international humanism to the English middle classes. In fact, Robinson's translation is described in his introductory epistle as a conversion. Unlike the Marian edition of More's *English Works* published by More's nephew, William Rastell, in 1557, Robinson's translation explicitly argues for More's value to an audience envisioned as staunchly and self-consciously Protestant.

In his epistle to the 1551 edition, Robinson praises More for the valuable lessons his *Utopia* contains for English readers. He apologizes repeatedly for the "ignorance" of his translation and for his "barbarous rudeness," adding that he only agreed to the task of translating when pressed into service by one "George Tadlowe, an honest citizein of London, and in the same citie well accepted."[36] In the opening passages of his epistle, Robinson makes clear that he sees his translation as a civic duty: "I thought it my bounden duetie to God and my countrey . . . to tourne and translate out of Latine into oure Englishe tonge the frutefull and profitable boke, which sir Thomas more, knight, compiled and made of the new yle Utopia" (17).

For Robinson, the "turning" of Utopia from Latin into English is an act of nationalism—an act borne out by his explicit patriotism ("my bounden duetie to God and my countrey") as well as his summoning up of what Balibar calls the "linguistic community" ("oure Englishe tonge").[37] He recognizes the political nature of his work, as is evident in his denunciation of More's Catholicism; he assures his readers that More has much to teach them despite "his willful and stubbourne obstinancie even to the very death." Robinson's translation is intended to reclaim More, to make his text accessible to audiences who could not read Latin, and to resituate his *Utopia* as a work appropriate for English (and Protestant) readers. As Robinson's most important editor, J. H. Lupton, points out, the translation shares many of the stylistic features of the first English translation of the *Book of Common Prayer*, published two years before it. G. R. Elton argues that it was between the publication of the first and second Prayer Books (1549 and 1552, respectively) that England became a Protestant country.[38] It was at this point that Robinson—a Protestant of humble origins—turned "the fruitful and profitable" *Utopia* of Thomas More into what was to become one of the great masterpieces of English politics and literature. It is a great irony that Robinson was a goldsmith, a worker in that metal whose value *Utopia* makes so riddlingly unreadable.

Utopia is a founding fiction in that it chronicles the planting and development of a country that identifies itself as a utopia, its people unified by language, customs, culture. But like many fictions, *Utopia* conceals as much as it expresses. One such concealment, despite its rituals of confession and exposure, is Utopia's genesis in violence. Subsequent utopists learned from More that culture itself is a construction, that statesmen are authors and authors are merchants, that nations are not discovered but invented. Most important, More's paradigm established the institution as the centerpiece of national reform. Whichever direction one turns in Utopia one sees the market, a mechanism for evening out if not eradicating desire. Through the education that the market provides, Utopians become "good citizens," capable of reconferring the values that have constructed them.

Claudio Guillen has remarked that new genres become "official" as they are incorporated into systems, imitated, and conventionalized.[39] In 1606, with the formation of the Virginia Company (of which Francis Bacon was one of the founding members), England officially consolidated colonialism and capital venture. For the seventeenth century, England's role in the New World would mean actual as well as potential or symbolic capital. This is the setting in which Bacon planted his New World laboratory, an institution, like More's market-school, that creates value as it is transformed. Ironically, the Englishman who gave his name to the first stock exchange, Sir Thomas Gresham, funded the series of scientific lectures that were to form the nucleus of the Baconian Royal Society. The conjunction between stocks and science would not have seemed strange to More's Utopians, who knew well the similarity of "exchange" in the market and at edifying lectures. As More drew on the model of the Tudor school for his way of "patterning a commonwealth," he seemed to recognize, as did Colet and Lily, the crucial role of education in the formation of national character. In his *Proheme* to his *Grammaticus Rudimentia*, Colet had prayed that his schoolboys would be an honor to God and a profit to their countrymen. "And lyfte up your lytell whyte handes for me," Colet concluded, "which prayeth for you to God."[40] These "lytell whyte handes" belonged to a new community: a group of school-boys trained, like More's Utopians, to obedience, discipline, and watchfulness, taught to be proud of their nation and to work toward its improvement. That their hands had been specially chosen to do God's deeds because they were "whyte" and "English" was a lesson still before them, and More's description of Nowhere was to become a crucial handbook in this instruction.

Laboratory. [f.L. *laborare*, to LABOUR.] 1. A building set apart for conducting practical investigations in natural science, orig. and esp. in chemistry, and for the elaboration or manufacture of chemical, medicinal, and like products. 2. *Mil.* "A department of an arsenal for the manufacture and examination of ammunition and combustible stores." Voyle, *Military Dictionary*, 1876

Scientific activity is not "about nature," it is a fierce fight to construct reality. The laboratory is the workplace and the set of productive forces which makes construction possible. Every time a statement stabilizes, it is reintroduced into the laboratory (in the guise of a machine, inscription, device, skill, routine, prejudice, deduction, and so on) and it is used to increase the difference between statements. The cost of challenging the reified statement is impossibly high. Reality is secreted. —Bruno Latour and Steven Woolgar, *Laboratory Life: The Construction of Scientific Facts*, 1986

2. A Land of Experimental Knowledge

FRANCIS BACON'S *NEW ATLANTIS*

Four years before Francis Bacon wrote his unfinished utopia, *New Atlantis*, a scientist named Cornelis Drebbel demonstrated his latest invention for James I in the Thames. A crowd of spectators, among them the king and a band of courtiers, watched with amazement from the riverbank as Drebbel lowered himself in his "little ship" beneath the surface of the water. According to Huygens's description, Drebbel and his crew

> calmly dove down under the water and thus held the king, his court, and several thousand Londoners in excited expectation.

For the most part the onlookers thought that he had had an accident in this work of art of his when he did not come up in three hours' time, as he had said he would, when at a great distance from the spot where he had submerged, he emerged again. He called upon the several persons who had undergone the experiment with him to bear witness that they had had no discomfort under the river, but that they had as they listed sunk to the bottom of the river and when they chose risen to whatever height they liked.[1]

Drebbel's submarine was one of a series of technological wonders dedicated to the honor of the English throne. Although Drebbel was a Dutchman, he lived most of his professional life in England, first in the service of James and then of Charles I. For James he invented, among other devices, a pump for draining the fens, a torpedo, fireworks, and a fountain in which the figures of Neptune, Triton, and nymphs darted in and out of a jet of water. Drebbel's innovations in military and industrial arts led James to establish a laboratory for him at Eltham Palace, where he was installed from about the year 1610. The laboratory at Eltham became a source of national pride, alluded to by both Peacham and Ben Jonson and much approved by visiting foreigners. At Eltham guests could see virginals that played by themselves, demonstrations of artificial weather systems, and incubators in which Drebbel could "at all times of the year, yes, even in midwinter . . . hatch Duck and Chicken eggs without any Ducks or Chickens by."[2] Most impressive were Drebbel's optical innovations, including cameras, magic lanterns, and light shows through which Drebbel could appear to spectators in the guise of a tree with fluttering leaves, a lion, bear, or pig. "Nor is this all, for I can change my clothing so that I seem to be clad in satin of all colors, then in cloths of all colors, now cloth of gold, now cloth of silver; and I present myself as a King, adorned in diamonds."[3] Like Jonson's court masques, Drebbel's light shows were a highly specialized kind of theater, displaying to Stuart audiences the power of science to alter and ennoble. At Eltham the scientist could re-create himself as king; outside the laboratory his inventions, like the "little ship" capable of staying beneath the water's surface three hours or more, would enlarge and defend the king's realm.

An alchemical laboratory with seven furnaces. From Elias Ashmole,
Theatrum Chemicum Britannicum (London, 1652). By permission of
the Houghton Library, Harvard University.

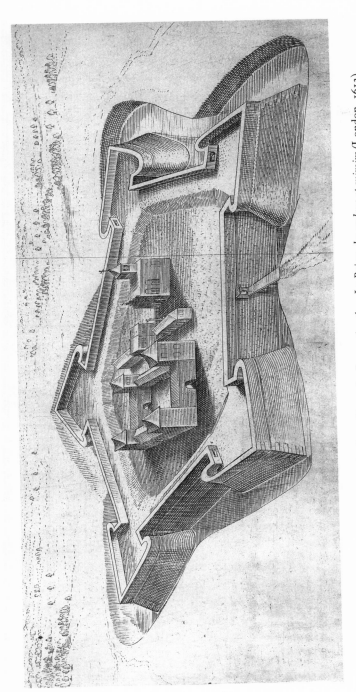

Plans for a pentagonal fortress by Salomon de Caus. From *La Perspective Avec La Raison des ombres et miroirs* (London, 1612). By permission of the Department of Printing and Graphic Arts, the Houghton Library, Harvard University.

The power of natural science to re-create and to contain the world greatly excited the imaginations of those who flocked to Eltham to see Drebbel's "Perpetual Motion" in 1610. The device offered admirers a world in miniature, immortalized in a descriptive dialogue by Thomas Tymme (credited by the *OED* with the introduction of the word *laboratory* into English). In the Perpetual Motion, Drebbel had invented "a glass or crystal globe, wherein he blew or made a perpetual Motion by the power of the four elements. For every thing which (by the force of the elements) passes in a year on the surface of the earth, could be seen to pass in this cylindrical wonder in the shorter lapse of 24 hours. . . . It made you understand what cold is, what the cause of the *primum mobile*, what the first principle of the sun, how it moves; the firmament, the stars, the moon, the sea, the earth; what occasions the ebb, flood, thunder, lightning, rain, wind; and how all things wax and multiply."[4] At Eltham Palace, guests could see the universe in a crystal ball.

Private laboratories like Eltham were relatively rare in Europe before the late seventeenth century. Emperor Rudolph II established a prestigious academy in Prague in the late sixteenth century, and in Denmark in the 1570s Tycho Brahe's Uranibourg, a research colony on the island of Hveen, drew especially great acclaim.[5] Given Bacon's early interest in establishing a national scientific institute, it is quite likely that he knew of Hveen, either through James or through correspondence from other English visitors.[6] But even if Bacon did not know Uranibourg, closer models could be found at home. In Elizabethan England, John Dee's library at Mortlake became an especially influential center for scientific inquiry. From 1570 until 1583, when Dee left Mortlake because of the crowds, his library attracted hundreds of scholars and tourists. Dee's was the most extensive scientific library in England; in 1583 his collection numbered close to four thousand volumes, as compared with a mere four hundred and fifty volumes at Cambridge University Library.[7] Dee had a laboratory at Mortlake, as well as a collection of astronomical instruments, including a "radius astronomicus," or cross staff.[8] A dedicated antiquarian as well as a mathematician and cartographer, Dee collected a wealth of Irish and Welsh genealogies and ancient seals. Visitors—including Queen Elizabeth (March 10, 1575), Sir Francis Walsingham, Philip Sidney, the earl of Leicester, and one "Mr. Bacon" (presumably Francis's father)—could see at Mortlake demonstrations of science's role in the development of what Dee called this "Incomparable BRYTISH IMPIRE."[9] A generation after Dee, Francis Bacon was to take up this conjunction between science and empire and make it the center of his career.

By 1608 Bacon had already begun to work on plans for an English institute dedicated to the study of nature. Unlike Drebbel or Dee, Bacon advocated an institute controlled by the state and run in its service. There was no real precedent for this kind of national institute in Stuart England. The closest model could be found in Gresham College, the "Invisible College" endowed by Thomas Gresham, a wealthy merchant who helped to fund the establishment of the Royal Exchange. The meetings that took place around these lectures came to be known as "Gresham College" or the "Third University," laying the foundation for the Royal Society in the 1660s. But Gresham College was closer to a university than to the experimental laboratory Bacon envisioned. In his diary in 1608 Bacon jotted down notes for the establishment of a new foundation, provided with "laborities and engines, vaults and furnaces, terraces for insulation," etc. Pensions would be granted to persons for research "to compile the two histories, of marvels and of mechanical arts." There would also be "two galleries with statues for Inventors past, and spaces, or bases, for Inventors to come. And a library and an Inginary."[10] Though Bacon died forty years before his vision of a state-run house of marvels and mechanical arts finally received the king's charter, he was to remain the spiritual founder of England's Royal Society. It was Bacon who was to contribute to modernity the conviction that a nation's strength depends on scientific and technological superiority.

During the decade in which Bacon was rapidly promoted from solicitor general in 1607 to lord chancellor in 1618, his scientific program remained his most ambitious proposal for personal and national "advancement." He continually urged King James to plot out "a new way for the understanding, a way . . . untried and

FRANCISCI
DE VERULAMIO,
Summi Angliæ
CANCELARIJ,
Instauratio
magna.

Multi pertransibunt & augebitur scientia.

LONDINI
Apud Joannem Billium
Typographum
Regium.

Anno.   1620.

Title page to Francis Bacon's *Advancement of Learning* (1620).
By permission of the Houghton Library, Harvard University.

unknown," articulating a desire for dominion over nature connected, overtly and covertly, to imperial aggrandizement (4:41). In 1609, the year after his plans for an English scientific institute were first put on paper, Bacon became a shareholder in the newly formed Virginia Company. At three separate points—in 1601, to Elizabeth, and in 1609 and 1616, to James—he appealed to the English throne to conquer Ireland as "another Britain," and in 1606 Bacon advocated strengthening England's colonial power in America as well.[11] Bacon was shrewdly aware of the economic gains and hazards of establishing new colonies far from home. Particularly striking is the advice he offered on dealing with native populations in his *Essays:*

> If you plant where savages are, do not only entertain them
> with trifles and gingles; but use them justly and graciously,
> with sufficient guard nevertheless; and do not win their favour
> by helping them to invade their enemies, but for their defence
> it is not amiss; and send oft of them over to the country that
> plants, that they may see a better condition than their own,
> and commend it when they return. (6:459)

This passage from "Of Plantations," with its string of qualifying and deconstructive phrases, spells out in small the paradigm of *New Atlantis,* reversing the customary roles of travel narrative so that the "planters" become the ones "used" or "entertained," sent back to "the country that plants" to learn of a condition better than their own. The plantation for Bacon is a carefully run experiment; in colonies, as in "laborities," "all depend[ed] on keeping the eye steadily fixed upon the facts of nature" (4:32).

Critics have begun to acknowledge how closely scientific and imperial goals were conjoined in the Baconian program.[12] The Great Instauration was mapped out during a crucial period of English expansion in the Americas and the West Indies; in the years in which Bacon was working out his great theory of method (1607–1627), English settlements were established in Guiana, Jamestown, and Massachusetts, as well as in St. Christopher and Barbados; an accompanying flood of propaganda was published defending the ventures of the two Virginia Companies, and the topic of colonialism was of greatest national concern. As one of the most prominent statesmen in the Stuart court, Bacon was necessarily involved in the overseeing of imperial ventures. Especially later in his career Bacon seems to have grown impatient with colonial misadventure, advocating instead the conjunction of empire and empiricism. For example, when Sir Walter Raleigh returned from his doomed second expedition to Guiana in 1617, charged with conspiracy and treason, it was Bacon who was asked to draft the commission's document sentencing him to death. Bacon scathingly charged in his report that the gold mine Raleigh had sought for so long in his elusive El Dorado was "not only imaginary, but moveable."[13] In 1618, at the height of his political career, it must have seemed to Bacon that science could provide the state with "the facts of nature" in such enterprises, rather than with the explorer's fancies. But ironically, gold was to be Bacon's undoing as much as Raleigh's. Rusticated to his house in Gorhambury in 1621 for accepting bribes while serving as lord chancellor, Bacon was abruptly shut off from the offices of power that he had sought so passionately throughout his life. Despite or perhaps because of this forced exile, Bacon's last five years were his most productive. His published works after 1621 include his *History of Henry VII*, his *Sylva Sylvarum, or A Natural History*, *An Advertisement Touching an Holy War*, an enlarged Latin version of *The Advancement of Learning* entitled *De Dignitate et Augmentis Scientiarum* (1623), *New Atlantis* (1624), a third edition of his *Essays*, and a translation of the Psalms. By the 1620s Bacon was exhorting English readers to prepare for real as well as symbolic battles. A strong nation required a people dedicated to defense: "For empire and greatness it importeth most, that a nation do profess arms as their principle honour, study, and occupation" (6:449). Periodic wars, especially "foreign wars," serve to keep the body politic healthy, as opposed to enjoying "slothful peace." Bacon deplores a "base and effeminate people," urging that "the breed and disposition of the people be stout and warlike" (6:450). His great contemporary model of empire is Spain, his classical example is Rome, and he praises both for their ability to enlarge dominion through naturalizing foreigners and through colonization, "whereby the Roman plant was removed into the soil of other nations . . . [until] you will say that it was not the Romans that spread upon the world, but it was the world that spread upon the Romans (6:448)." Ancient Rome and modern Spain were the models Bacon held up for England's emulation. So, it is not surprising that the laboratory at the heart of New Atlantis should number the invention of "instruments of destruction" as one of its chief goals alongside "the prolongation of life" (3:167–68). As Bacon saw it, a national scientific institute must function, as in Bensalem, both as the "eye" and "lantern" of a growing empire, defending and controlling what he was later to call "experiments of light" (4:95). The laboratory would act as a fortification for the burgeoning nation, bringing together the projects of empiricism and empire.

In *De Dignitate de Augmentis Scientiarum*, Bacon differentiated between proper and improper kinds of research. The scientist, he says, "may grope his way for himself in the dark; he may be led by the hand of another, without himself seeing anything; or lastly, he may get a light, and so direct his steps; in like manner when a man tries all kinds of experiments without order or method, this is but groping in the dark, but when he uses some direction and order in experimenting, it is as if he were led by the hand; and this is what I mean by Learned Experience" (4:413).

For Bacon, the ordered and directed experiment became the ideal social and linguistic form.[14] Even the failed experiment has special value, for "though a successful experiment may be more agreeable, yet an unsuccessful one is oftentimes no less instructive" (4:421). While Bacon's dedication to the experiment as an idea has become part of his myth (his death from pneumonia was a consequence of an experiment in refrigeration), too little attention has been paid to his use of the experiment as a discursive structure, a method for "directing and ordering" narrative as well as experience. Narratives are often organized around thematic quests or searches that allegorize the text's desire to find something: an ending, meaning or meanings. For Bacon this search always repeats or reinvents an earlier search; it is (literally and thematically) a *research*. Bacon's dependence on the experiment as a discursive model helps to elucidate the unfinished nature of his texts. Most if not all of Bacon's works remained "unperfected," a feature which more than one critic has suggested contributes to Bacon's "modernity."[15] An attraction to the fragmentary or incomplete may explain Bacon's delight in aphorisms, which he describes in *The Advancement* as "representing a knowledge broken, [and which] do invite men to inquire further" (3:405). As Freud suggested about Leonardo da Vinci, the reluctance to finish works may be connected to the initial compulsion to inquire.[16] In other words, Bacon's narratives may stop short because they have too closely skirted forbidden knowledge.

Like many of Bacon's texts, *New Atlantis* is a collection of broken or incomplete smaller literary kinds—aphorisms, dialogues, experiments, fables—adding up to a work unfinished, superseded by the task of the *Natural History* (3:127). The incomplete sea voyage that begins Bacon's utopia gives way to a series of dialogues or interviews, each curiously interrupted or broken off. Unlike More's *Utopia*, in which Hythlodaeus's narrative begins only after his return to Europe, his dialogue artfully framed in an Antwerp garden between a midday and evening meal, *New Atlantis* breaks off abruptly, before the mariners' return, with only Rawley's terse note for closure: [The Rest Was Not Perfected] (3:166). The original edition of *New Atlantis* ends with Bacon's catalog, *Magnalia Naturae*, in which the principal goals of the College of Six Days' Work are set forth in fragments: "The prolongation of life. The altering of features. Making of new species. Instruments of destruction, as of war and poison. Impressions of the air, and raising of tempests"(3:167–68).

New Atlantis breaks off in the middle of the circular and incomplete discourse of the experiment, a discourse central not only to Bacon's utopia but to his writing as a whole. Bacon's training in legal theory and rhetoric helped to structure his philosophical writing as a series of trials; even the new genre of the essay, which Bacon borrowed from Montaigne, is a literary "trial" or attempt, an "essai," and Bacon's "great instauration," never completed in his lifetime, was a monumental social and civic experiment. The perfection of the experiment seemed to lie in the opportunities it offered for revision and repetition, for searching again.

Against the experimental or fragmentary status of Bacon's writing runs a struggle for completion that emerges most clearly in his descriptions of the relationship between man and nature. For Bacon it is a feminized and eroticized Nature that becomes the body upon which the scientist must turn his eye. Nature must be searched out, inspected, and tried. Caroline Merchant has noted that Bacon's descriptions of Nature "strongly suggest the interrogations of the witch trials." As Merchant observes, Nature for Bacon must be "bound into service," made a "slave," and "put in constraint." The "secrets" of Nature are described as "holes and corners" which man must not scruple "entering and penetrating."[17] Bacon continually exhorts English readers to possess Nature, to "search out her secrets" and "storm her castles." Nature is not only a woman for Bacon but a woman bound and helpless, one who must be stripped and inspected, often by force. The more urgently Bacon feels the need for totality or completeness, the more vulnerable and erotic he makes his descriptions of the natural world. Reaching the "remoter and more hidden parts of nature" becomes an obsession for Bacon, who is dissatisfied with each trope for discovery he tries out (4:18). In his impatience with "the deplorably narrow limits of man's dominion over the universe," he sifts through increasingly violent imagery to emphasize the need for urgency, force, and will (4:57). So in 1623 in *The Advancement of Learning* he urges the English to turn "with united forces against the Nature of Things, to storm and occupy her castles and strongholds, and extend the bounds of human empire, as far as God almighty in his goodness may permit" (4:372–73). The enlargement of empire here becomes a mandate for siege.

But no exploration will suffice to uncover Nature's secrets, for the remoter and "more hidden parts of Nature" continually escape the scientist's eye (4:18). For this reason the maritime voyage, which Bacon repeatedly appropriates as a trope for scientific inquiry, is rejected as a metaphor even as it is invoked, for "before we can reach the remoter and more hidden parts of nature, it is necessary that a more perfect use and application of the human mind and intellect be introduced" (4:18). The mariners' failure in *New Atlantis* to complete their journey is part of a pattern of broken and incomplete procedures in Bacon's writing emblematizing and critiquing the inadequacies of human endeavor.

It may be this sense of Nature as intractable or elusive which led Bacon to the idea of the laboratory as the perfect institution for empirical containment and control. In the laboratory Nature can at last be fixed in place; here the scientist can transform as well as isolate and uncover his subjects. Aptly, Bacon appended *New Atlantis*, his representation of the ideal commonwealth, to his *Sylva Sylvarum, or, A Natural History*, an anthology of experiments (ten "centuries" long) that functions as a kind of discursive laboratory. In the *Sylva Sylvarum*, as in Drebbel's "Perpetual Motion," nature is at once re-created and "perfected": "Birds and beasts of strange colours" can be invented by experiments done to feathers and to skin (2:379); impure or salty water can be made pure through percolation; growing cycles of plants can be speeded up or slowed down, and plants can be molded into "curious" shapes (2:502). Animals can be stunted or perfected by stroking them, guiding the growth of limbs or features. In contrast with this fluidity, beer can be preserved by burying it underground, as can fruit or damask roses. Bodies, similarly, can be preserved "from change" if "no air cometh to them" (2:365). Bacon claimed that "this work of his Natural History is the world as God made it, and not as men have made it" (2:337). As his last work and to his mind the most important, the *Natural History* was a blueprint for "the erecting and building of a true philosophy" (2:335–36).

If the experiment for Bacon most closely approximated God's labor, the fragmented *New Atlantis* can be seen as an attempt to defray the necessity for limit, allowing for the sense of open-ended horizon Bacon wanted science to represent. "Therefore it is we cannot perceive of any end or limit to the world, but always of necessity it occurs to us that there is something beyond," Bacon wrote in his *Novum Organum* (4:57). The iterative pattern of *New Atlantis* is one of rupture and "interrupture," the experience of listening (and of reading) taken to pieces. These broken structures (the sea voyage, the interrupted dialogue, the ongoing experiment) function for Bacon as facets of an epistemological model. In the 1605 preface to *The Advancement of Learning*, Bacon defined *wonder* as "broken knowledge." Breaking knowledge becomes the central work of the laboratory in *New Atlantis*, a laboratory in which, as at Mortlake or Eltham Palace, visitors could see state secrets in the making. Harder to see either for guests or for the scientists themselves is the laboratory's power to invent myths about its own status as a "second world," divinely ordered and divinely overseen.

Seeing through More

In *New Atlantis* two ways of seeing collide. The narrator is one of a band of explorers sailing from Peru to China by the South Sea. They lose direction and give themselves up "for lost men, and prepare for death." Miraculously they discover "a land; flat to our sight, and full of boscage," and despite initial rebuffs ("straight-aways we saw divers of the people, with bastons in their hands, as it were, forbidding us to land"), they are cautiously welcomed on shore by the presiding officials (3:129–30). The mariners are relieved to learn that these people "had languages, and were . . . full of humanity" (3:130). Rather than a wilderness, the island that they find is technologically "perfect," governed by a group of scientific priests whose central institution, Solomon's House or the College of Six Days' Work, is dedicated to the scrutiny of nature. The mariners' initial quest (for gold and spices) is replaced through their "miraculous" displacement and discovery by exploration of a different kind, and their traffic for precious metals and spices is replaced by what the Bensalemites consider the barter for "light," or knowledge. Their prior search here becomes *research*. But the intersection of these two kinds of discovery creates uneasy resemblances between the two kinds of "traffic" that reverberate throughout the text. What has value? Who pays for knowledge, and what is its cost? Surveillance, inspection, and scrutiny mirror and double back on each other as the explorers are quarantined and kept for observation in Bensalem's Strangers' House for three days, then let loose, little by little, to explore the island and its inhabitants. By continuously reversing the positions of subject and object, *New Atlantis* complicates the panoptic model in which the subject suspects he or she may be under observation at all times.[18] In the

Strangers' House the narrator urges his men to stay on their best behavior, suspecting they are being watched not only by God but by the island's officials:

> Let us look up to God, and every man reform his own ways. Besides we are come here amongst a Christian people, full of piety and humanity: let us not bring that confusion of face upon ourselves, as to show our vices or unworthiness before them. Yet there is more. For they have by commandment (though in form of courtesy) cloistered us within these walls for three days: who knoweth whether it be not to take some taste of our manners and conditions? and if they find them bad, to banish us straightaways; if good, to give us further time. For these men that they have given us for attendance may withal have an eye upon us. (3:134)

The mariners' three-day confinement in the Strangers' House is a kind of experiment set up by the officials of Bensalem so that their behavior can be observed, judged, and recorded. This initial period of quarantine expires only to be replaced by another, for as the governor of the Strangers' House explains at the close of the third day, the state has granted the mariners permission "to stay on land for the space of six weeks," during which time, provided they stay within a *karan* of the city walls, they are (restrictedly) free (3:135). Only after they have sufficiently proven themselves can one of their party be invited to tour the island's sanctified scientific institute. And only after this carefully controlled tour can the final experiment of the colony be effected, as the Father sets the narrator the task of taking what he has learned back with him to Europe.

In these terms Bensalem's Strangers' House is an "entrance institution" in which the identity of "strangeness" is both metamorphosed and reinforced.[19] All social relations on this island work by the strict definition of boundaries, by sealing people off from each other, ritualizing communication and affect. The mariners, once out of the Strangers' House, find themselves in a country that strikes them both as peculiar and familiar, a land "beyond heaven and earth" inhabited by people who are (surprisingly) Christian and who speak (surprisingly) European languages, including "good

Latin of the School" (3:130). Here, in the middle of nowhere, the mariners find a technocratic city-state dominated by a central research institution, a state with an elaborate intelligence system, a complex government, and a highly ritualized culture, both patrician and patriarchal. It is the very familiarity of this colony which is most foreign in so remote a setting; as the mariners learn to their increasing discomfort, they are the ones considered strangers and primitive here, the subjects and not the guardians of this laboratory.

In Bensalem, strangeness is associated not only with portents, miracles, and conversion but also with danger and infection. In one of the carefully regulated interviews the mariners are granted with the governor, they learn that Bensalem has achieved its peculiar status (knowing Europe while remaining itself unknown) through strict "interdicts and prohibitions . . . touching [the] entrance of strangers" (3: 144). Bensalem's revered ancient King Solamona, the eponymous founder of its central scientific institution, feared strangers would allow "novelties, and commixtures of manners," diluting the race and ruining it as had already occurred in America.[20] Yet strangers *are* admitted into Bensalem, albeit guardedly; once admitted, they are absorbed into the culture, for few visitors ever return. "We have memory not of one ship that ever returned; and but of thirteen persons only, at several times, that chose to return" (3:145). Like James Hilton's Shangri-la, Bensalem culls from Europe "the best" of its culture (and population) over the ages.[21] Bensalem deals with foreignness by subsuming or nullifying it. Its institutions quarantine and transform difference so that no person who remains on the island for any length of time can effectively remain foreign. On the other hand, the "outsider" is necessary for conformity to have value. Joabin, one of the hosts who introduces the mariners to the island, is described as "a Jew, and circumcis'd," tolerated by the Christian citizens but kept apart (3:151).[22] Joabin testifies to the strict social categories manufactured and valued in Bensalem. The subject is necessarily inside or outside the laboratory, an institute that works largely to bolster such distinctions and to make them hold.

When the mariners try to reciprocate the information they have received by telling the officials something about their own country, they are told not to bother, for nothing the mariners tell them can possibly be new: the officials already know all about Europe through their system of secret intelligence, both what the mariners can tell them and more. For the mariners, then, the rite of first contact is disrupted and replaced by an uncanny sense of belatedness. Everything they have known or done has been foreseen by the Bensalemites; it is as if they have traveled to their own futures. Each excursion into Bensalem is more deeply marked by the uncanny.[23] The mariners initially fear that they have discovered an island of conjurers or magicians, and while this suspicion elicits laughter from the officials, the sense that Bensalem is too powerful—"a land of angels"—never entirely recedes.[24] Bensalem is clearly associated with higher powers, from its initial conversion to its present "perfection." If Bensalem dates its spiritual birth from its discovery of the ark, its birth as a nation derives from the realm of King Solamona, whom the citizens esteem "as the lawgiver of our nation" (3:144). Solamona's greatest bequest to his country was his doctrine of isolation. Fearing the example of America, reduced to a "poor remnant of human seed . . . [unable] to leave letters, arts, and civility to their posterity," the king, wholly bent "to make his kingdom and people happy," sought to make his island self-sufficient (3:143–44). As the island is large enough (5,600 miles in circuit) and uncommonly fertile, blessed with great fishing, its people are able to subsist entirely independent of foreign goods. Science, however, cannot develop without exchange. For this reason Bensalem regulates trips to Europe through a system of intellectual espionage, sending missions every twelve years to collect "knowledge of the affairs and state of those countries to which they were designed, and especially of the sciences, arts, manufactures, and inventions of all the world." These ships deposit carefully chosen spies (called "Merchants of Light," or "Lamps") somewhere in Europe, leaving them there as undercover agents until the next ship comes along in twelve years to drop off fresh spies and retrieve the old. "But thus you see we maintain a trade, not for gold, silver, or jewels; nor for silks; nor for spices; nor any other commodity of matter; but only for God's first creature, which was *Light*" (3:146–47). These covert trips provide Bensalem with a one-way mirror through which to observe the rest of the world, taking in knowledge without infection or risk. Their secret service constructs a model for epistemological as well as international relations, for in this way information can be absorbed without exposure or reciprocity.

This intellectual espionage closely parallels Bacon's description of reading in his essay "Of Studies," where he argues that "some books may also be read by Deputy, and extracts made of them by others" (6:498). So a deputy or "Merchant of Light" can bring back the information necessary for perfect knowledge without interrupting the scientist or taking him away from his work. This information, like More's treasure kept not as treasure, troubles the bounded status of the colony. To maintain their technocratic superiority, the Bensalemites must import information from overseas, consuming foreign knowledge in order to reproduce or transform it in the scientific factory which is at once the colony's eye and brain. Moreover, the value of their own innovations is impeded by their isolated status. Until their successes are "published," what value can they have?

The ambivalence surrounding the exportation of such transformed materials is explicitly associated for Bacon with the relationship between reading (consuming) and writing (reproducing). The extent of this ambivalence is understandable once we recognize that Bacon's literary career was largely that of a brilliant and entrepreneurial importer. Many of the genres with which he worked were new to English readers—his essays (from Montaigne), his *Natural History* (from Della Porta), and especially and most self-consciously his utopia were all reinventions of new literary forms. In *New Atlantis* Bacon's anxiety about such importation is thematized by the colony's suspicious foreign relations. Like More's *Utopia*, *New Atlantis* is highly protective of its own boundaries. Even its isolated position is not isolation enough from the threat of territorialist neighbors. In his essay "Of Empire," Bacon warned that the first threat to a king comes from possible annoyance by neighbors who have overgrown their bounds (6:420). This suspicion, reiterated by Solamona in *New Atlantis*, who dreaded "novelties, and commixture of manners" from barbarous neighbors, underlines the need for separateness, for freedom from the overgrown, overbearing, or dominant "neighbor" (3:144). For Bacon in *New Atlantis*, this concern must derive at least in part from his own keen sense of proximity to his closest literary and generic neighbor. In Claudio Guillen's words, Bacon officialized *Utopia* by imitating it, importing from it for his own needs.[25] Thus, the connection between spying, barter, and the remanufacture of knowledge may hold metaliterary significance for Bacon in *New Atlantis*. The tradition of the literary utopia in England formally begins with *New Atlantis*, whose belatedness in the 1620s was to enable nearly a dozen secondary or belated utopias in subsequent generations. Someone had to risk imitating More before imitation could be imitated. It is not the exemplars of a given genre who make the "contractual assumptions to familiarity with a tradition" that comprise generic history; rather, it is their imitators, those who come second in line, who solidify that "generic contract."[26] But Bacon is uneasy at best about intertextual exchange, even as he uses it to authorize *New Atlantis*. More's *Utopia* thus stands as a kind of Europe to Bacon's Bensalem—a place of origins from which to draw raw materials to be remanufactured, a covert return-point from the secret and lonely place "out there" from which the experiment of *New Atlantis* could be proffered.

More's *Utopia* is alluded to only once in *New Atlantis* and not by name. The allusion comes during the second of the long interviews or "magisterial dialogues" that structure the utopia. The narrator, having learned some of Bensalem's customs from the governor of the Strangers' House, is escorted by Joabin to witness a "Feast of the Vine," a highly ritualized ceremony in which the institution of patriarchy is celebrated and reinforced. Appropriately, it is after this ritual of reverence for the father that the allusion to More occurs.[27] After the Feast, the narrator has time to ask Joabin a few questions about social and civic structures in Bensalem. Comparing marriage in Bensalem with European marriage, Joabin alludes to Hythlodaeus's famous discussion of selecting mates in Utopia. Joabin rejects the mutual inspection described by Hythlodaeus and describes the superiority of Bensalem's "Adam and Eve's pools":

> I have read in a book of one of your men, of a Feigned
> Commonwealth, where the married couple are permitted,

before they contract, to see one another naked. This they dislike; for they think it a scorn to give a refusal after so familiar knowledge: but because of many hidden defects in men and women's bodies, they have a more civil way; for they have near every town a couple of pools (which they call *Adam and Eve's pools*,) where it is permitted to one of the friends of the man, and another of the friends of the woman, to see them severally bathe naked. (3:154)

This passage submerges an allegory of reading in its trope of inspection. What methods of scrutiny are permissible or advisable? What does it mean to conceal or to expose "defects"? It is no coincidence that this passage, which is explicitly about reading More's *Utopia*, should represent itself as a kind of primal scene. One must look obliquely, through a "deputy," as it were, at one's site of origins, one's "Adam and Eve." Otherwise one might see the father's body as defective or be seen as defective by the father, either permitting or being permitted "too familiar knowledge." For fear of looking too closely at his source or original, Bacon triangulates his reading of More through a mediated source or "deputy"—that is, through Plato. For Bacon's is a *new* Atlantis, a re-creation or research of Plato's fable of Atlantis, which appears in the *Timaeus* and in the *Critias*, as More's *Utopia* claims in its prefatory poem to beat Plato's *Republic* at its own game. Seeing More through the deputy of Plato (and vice versa) enables Bacon to import "light" without risk or consequence, to occupy a "solitary situation," to know while remaining himself unknown.

The allusion to *Utopia* in Joabin's passage suggests the complexity for Bacon of seeing origins versus seeing originally. More for Bacon becomes the absent presence, the father who must be (and can never be) shown something new. Novelty in *New Atlantis* thus becomes a quality which is used as a defense as well as an instrument for constructing and interpreting Nature. Bensalem exists outside and ahead of time, claiming its authority in antiquity, enshrining European inventors in its museum yet at the same time dedicating itself to newer inventions in its College of Six Days' Work. This fetishizing of the new partly explains the aura of urgency in *New Atlantis*.

A Land of Experimental Knowledge 75

Interviews are no sooner granted than they are broken off and the officials are called away in haste. Something is always on the brink of happening, and the utopia's mood is one of anxious anticipation, if not of outright urgency. As Macherey suggests in his analysis of Verne's reading Defoe, this haste may derive from the sense that the journey being represented has already taken place.[28] In *New Atlantis*, "discovery" is continually deconstructed as the mariners find the future rather than the primitive past, a developed culture rather than an uncultivated Eden. They have, in fact, traveled to an island boasting a society more advanced than Europe, which has already been thoroughly explored, transmuted, and mastered. This is where *New Atlantis* is at once most peculiarly modern and most self-conscious of its own status as discourse—not so much in its preoccupation with novelty but in its awareness that novelty is already being depleted, that the expedition, however original, has already taken place.[29] Built into *New Atlantis*, with its central factory of inventions, is the uncanny sense that novelty is nowhere, that the "defect" in Nature's body is that somebody else has gotten to it first. Belatedness is thus built into this important second English utopia. With Bacon begins an acute sense of being late, of having to import the materials of knowledge from somewhere (or someone) else.

Enlarging the Bounds of Human Empire

Among the excellent acts of Bensalem's lawgiver, one above all "hath the pre-eminence," the mariners are told: "It was the erection and institution of an order, or society, which we call Solomon's House; the noblest foundation, as we think, that ever was upon the earth, and the lanthorn of this kingdom" (3:145). Solomon's House earns its second name, The College of Six Days' Work, from its imitation of the original six days of creation in Genesis. As the Father of Solomon's House tells the narrator in the lengthy dialogue that concludes the narrative, "the End of our Foundation is the knowledge of Causes, and secret motions of things; and the enlarging of the bounds of Human Empire, to the effecting of all things possible" (3:156). The scientists in Bensalem do not study nature so much as re-form it. In underground caves, they imitate "natural mines," producing "new artificial metals" (3:157). Pools of fresh water are turned into salt and vice versa, and great engines are used for the "multiplying and enforcing of winds." In great and spacious houses, meteors and weather systems are demonstrated, as are the "generations of bodies in air." In certain "large and various orchards and gardens" the scientists are able to alter plants and trees to hasten their growth and improve their taste:

> We have also large and various orchards and gardens . . . in these we practice likewise all conclusions of grafting and inoculating, as well of wild-trees as fruit-trees, which produceth many effects. And we make (by art), in the same orchards and gardens, trees and flowers to come up earlier or later than their seasons; and to come up and bear more speedily than by their natural course they do. We make them also by art greater much than their nature: and their fruit greater and sweeter and of differing taste, smell, colour and figure, from their nature. (3:158)

Science can improve if not "perfect" nature, hastening the growing cycles of plants, sweetening the taste of fruits, and making plants "by art much greater than their nature." For Bacon's scientists, the "grafting and inoculating" of Nature is not bastardization but enrichment. Even more striking and serious alterations are effected on animals and birds in New Atlantis's "enclosures," through the use of poisons "as well as physic":

> By art likewise, we make them greater or taller than their kind is; . . . and contrariwise barren and not generative. Also we make them differ in colour, shape, activity, many ways. We find means to make commixtures and copulations of divers kinds; which have produced many new kinds, and them not barren, as the general opinion is. We make a number of kinds of serpents, worms, flies, fishes, of putrefaction; whereof some are advanced (in effect) to be perfect creatures, like beasts or birds; and have sexes, and do propagate. Neither do we this by chance, but we know beforehand of what matter and commixture what kind of those creatures will arise. (3:159)

Here the scientists are able to instill procreative powers in barren species. Their Faustian capacity to stunt or enlarge living creatures testifies both to their own power and to the vulnerability of their subjects. Moreover, their zeal for transformation reminds us that it is *this* population (plants and animals) that is native to the island. Here, then, as on H. G. Wells's island of Doctor Moreau, the battery of experiments run by the scientists becomes a homology for colonialism. What is native cannot be left alone but must be altered, both from its own genus and from its environment, until the machine of science, like the Strangers' House, confers strangeness on every object it touches.

As the secrets of Solomon's House are revealed to the narrator, the interlocutor in the dialogue is increasingly silent; the narrator listens without saying a word until the interview, like all communication in this narrative, is abruptly broken off. What is his place in the experiment? Is he a scientist or a subject? Solomon's House is described as an elaborate factory of transformations in which, in every corner, nature is reinvented, reordered, and recorded. Here "all multiplications of light" are represented, as are "all delusions and deceits of the sight" and "all demonstrations of shadows" (3:163–64). Rainbows, haloes, and circles about light are invented, while in sound-houses "all articulate sounds and letters, and the voices and notes of beasts and birds" are imitated. In perfume-houses the scientists "multiply smells," and in engine-houses "new mixtures and compositions of gunpowder" are created: "We imitate also flights of birds; we have some degrees of flying in the air; we have ships and boats for going under water, and brooking of seas; also swimming-girdles and supporters. We have divers curious clocks, and other like motions of return, and some perpetual motions. We imitate also motions of living creatures, by images of men, beasts, birds, fishes and serpents" (3:163–64).[30]

From its double name to its battery of experiments, Solomon's House is a factory of reinvention, its experiments dedicated to the estrangement and re-creation of what is rather than the creation of what is not. What comes under scrutiny in Bacon's fictional laboratory is not merely the effects and consequences of manipulation, then, but the procedures of manipulation itself—what is, in

Bacon's utopia, reform as a machine. The narrative, including its readers within its own experimental rubric, asks us to wonder how transformation is effected: how does a mariner become an inmate? a father? a patriarch? an interview? a lecture? Who constructs the experiments or frames the questions? What complicates *New Atlantis* is that just as its roles seem most firmly established they are suddenly altered, even undermined. Throughout the final interview the narrator remains frozen, silenced, "caused to sit down" while the Father of Solomon's House gives him "the greatest jewel" he has, "a relation of the true state of Solomon's House." For the duration of this exchange the narrator doesn't move, and even when the relation is finished, he shifts only from one position of deference to another: "And when he had said this, he stood up; and I, as I had been taught, kneeled down; and he laid his right hand upon my head, and said, 'God bless thee, my son, and God bless this relation which I have made'" (3:166).

Just at this moment of revelation, when the Father's power and that of his institution should be at its apex, the roles are abruptly transformed as the Father suddenly reveals his own power and that of his country to be abridged. With no warning he breaks off the exchange, telling the narrator, "I give thee leave to publish [this relation], for we are here in God's bosom, a land unknown." Bensalem's isolation, previously held as its greatest strength ("We know, but are ourselves unknown"), is abruptly revealed as a limitation, for how can the experiments of Solomon's House be of use if they remain unpublished and unread? "And so he left me," the narrator concludes, "having assigned a value of about two thousand ducats, for a bounty to me and my fellows" (3:166). The explorers, who have been rebuffed each time they offer the officials money ("What? Twice paid?") cannot themselves refuse to take payment, for their position has now been fixed. They have been hired as European Merchants of Light, and their office is to bring back to Europe "books, abstracts, and patterns of experiments of all other parts" (3:164). Experiment, like narrative, is incomplete until it finds an audience, for what is the point of "breaking knowledge" without the wonder it produces in those who watch? Whether this particular experiment ever finds its audience remains undetermined, for we do not know whether the mariners complete their expedition, either to China or back to Europe. The utopia breaks off, "unperfected" by the experiment of its narration.

In 1659, the year before Charles II was restored to the throne, Thomas Bushell proposed building a Solomon's House in Somerset. His idea was that "six exquisite, lucre-hating philosophers" should study mining and observe underground treasure, using debtors and prisoners as a labor force, allowing "trade increased and customs augmented . . . [and] new arts discovered for the universal good and honour of the nation."[31] Bushell's proposal to employ debtors and prisoners as a workforce raises an interesting question about *New Atlantis*—who is it who does the real work of science? As Julie Solomon has suggested, Bacon's *New Atlantis* seems to formulate a "science of production without producers."[32] On the one hand, the utopia is clearly a paean to labor. Nature works, in the sense described by Cyrus Smith in Verne's *Mysterious Island:* "My friends, this is iron ore, this is pyrites, this is clay, this is chalk, this is coal. Look at what nature gives us, this is her part in the common labor."[33] Science, moreover, works to appreciate nature. Paolo Rossi points out that critics "too easily forget that Marx applauded not only the radical criticism of civilization in Rousseau's first *Discours* but also the celebration of work and technical skill in Francis Bacon's *New Atlantis*."[34] But while it is true that *New Atlantis* celebrates trial and effort, it is also true that the utopia distances "works" from labor, describing the ends of procedures rather than the procedures themselves. In fact, the Father of Solomon's House describes its achievements not as works but as possessions, using the phrase "we have" to form an anaphoric chain of ownership: "We have also precious stones of all kinds . . . we have also sound-houses . . . we have also perfume-houses . . . we have also engine-houses . . . we have also houses of deceits of the senses" (3:162–64). Only at the very end of his catalog does the Father include a generalized workforce in his list of "haves," and once again, these workers are described through the language of possession: "We have also, as you must think, novices and apprentices, that the succession of the former employed men do not fail; besides a great number of servants and attendants, men and women" (3:165).

The place of these "employed men," novices, and apprentices within New Atlantis is left deliberately obscure. Is their labor experimental? Who watches them—and who alters or "perfects" them should their energies subside? For such reformers as Gabriel Plattes and Samuel Gott who were to see the laboratory of *New Atlantis* in the middle of the century as a model for a new kind of English workhouse, these questions would have special concern. For if the English were by "nature" especially suited to the study of science, as Thomas Sprat was to argue, science might be used in the defense of that nature or to improve it if it should slacken. Here is Sprat's description in his *History of the Royal Society* (1666) of the English nation's ideal situation for philosophical and scientific inquiry:

> If there can be a true character given of the Universal Temper of any Nation under Heaven: then certainly this must be ascrib'd to our Countrymen: that they have commonly an un- affected sincerity; that they have love to deliver their minds with a sound simplicity; that they have the middle qualities, between the reserv'd subtle southern, and the rough unhewn Northern people: that they are not extreamly prone to speak: that they are more concern'd, what others will think of the strength, than of the fineness of what they say: . . . which are all the best indowments, that can enter into a *Philosophical Mind.* So that even the position of our climate, the air, the influence of the heaven, the composition of the English blood; . . . seem to joyn with the labours of the *Royal Society,* to render our Country, a Land of *Experimentall Knowledge.* (114)

When Sprat wrote the history of the Society, his frontispiece revealed the extent to which he saw Bacon as its spiritual founder. The figure of Scientia or knowledge—pictured as a woman— is crowning a statue of Charles II, flanked on one side by the Society's president, and on the other by Francis Bacon. Bacon and Charles II appear to gaze together here, sharing the solemn view before them. Bacon's influence on the institution of experimental science has long been recognized, but his influence on the institution of experimental discourse was in many ways to be as profound. In the thirty-three years between the publication of *New Atlantis*

Frontispiece to Thomas Sprat's *History of the Royal Society* (1666).
By permission of the President and Council of the Royal Society.

and the founding of the Royal Society in 1660, over a dozen utopias were published in England, many of them mentioning Bacon
in their prefaces or opening passages. During these years, "experiment" was not really the province of science in England but of
politics, and its trials were not contained in laboratories but were
effected on the battlefield and in Parliament. Bacon would hardly
have approved of the experiments of the Civil War or Interregnum. Nevertheless, utopists as different from Bacon (and from
each other) as Gabriel Plattes, Samuel Gott, and Gerrard Winstanley can all be seen in the 1640s and 1650s, like the Royalist "R.H."
in 1660, as working to "perfect" *New Atlantis*, to hammer out the
"frame of the commonwealth" Bacon's own experiment had left incomplete. Such revisions were to refashion *New Atlantis* as a colony
or outpost, a site for bringing together the pursuits of science and
of nationhood. For the generation of utopists working around the
Civil War in England, Bacon's vision of the scientific institute as a
homology for the state was taken with a new kind of literalness. Increasingly, the focus of English reformers was turned from the re-
creation of knowledge to the reform of English workers, those
"novices and apprentices" Bacon had barely mentioned, and upon
whose efforts the vision of England perfected seemed increasingly
to depend.

So that now the question is not whether this Land, and so consequently other Kingdoms may live in worldly happiness and prosperity for ever hereafter, but whether they will do so or not; for if they be willing, they will show the same by their actions, and then I am sure there is no doubt to be made of the possibility thereof; whereby *Utopia* may be had really, without any fiction at all.—Gabriel Plattes, *Samuel Hartlib His Legacy*, 1655

3. Houses of Industry

UTOPIAS IN THE COMMONWEALTH, 1641–1660

By the 1640s in England the term *utopia* was increasingly associated with real-life reform. At one extreme, utopianism could be seen as dangerously radical, at the other, disappointingly ineffective.[1] In 1642, for example, Charles I nervously complained that his subjects were threatening to turn England into Utopia, whereas in 1644 Milton dismissed utopias as inefficacious, emphasizing in *Areopagitica* the necessity for intervention in "this world of evil" rather than sequestering "out of the world into

Atlantick and Eutopian polities, which never can be drawn into use, [and] will not mend our condition."[2] Even here the king and Milton disagreed; for the former, utopia was a realizable threat, while for the latter it was a mere chimera in an age demanding prompt and radical reform. The production of utopian literature in this period was prodigious, not to be equaled again before the early nineteenth century in France. This was partly due to the sectarian nature of reform in the Civil War and Interregnum; there were as many as two hundred different sects in England in the middle of the seventeenth century, and almost every sect produced a utopia. Relative freedom from censorship during the Interregnum meant that utopias could actually be printed and distributed after they were written.[3] Through the new medium of print some believed radical ideas could spread rapidly enough so that England really could be turned into Utopia—and for many, despite Charles I's alarm at the prospect, this was becoming a widespread dream.

The printing press clearly helped to make new kinds of political vision available to new parts of the population, and in this period utopias were rapidly becoming the province of "the people." As Gabriel Plattes optimistically concluded in his *Description of the famous Kingdome of Macaria* (1641), "The art of Printing will so spread knowledge, that the common people, knowing their own rights and liberties, will not be governed by way of oppression; and so, little by little, all Kingdomes will be like to Macaria." To some extent, Plattes's prediction proved true. Experimental communities proliferated in the period, along with pamphlets, platforms, and programs, and as Charles Webster points out, "designs for utopian communities became a hallmark of the Puritan Revolution."[4] Three years before he published his communist utopia, *The Law of Freedom in a Platform* (1652), the Digger Gerrard Winstanley established a communist colony in Surrey, thus becoming the first English writer to precede his utopia with an actual experimental society. Peter Cornelius Plockhoy followed his full-employment utopia, *A Way Propounded to make the poor . . . happy* (1660), with the establishment of a society along the lines of his prospectus in New Netherland, or what is now Delaware. Communities and plans for communities multiplied, both in England and in America, where

John Winthrop's visionary "city on a hill" inspired others to follow suit. In 1635 John Winthrop Jr. established a utopian community at Saybrook; John Eliot set up nineteen Algonquin "praying towns" in New England based on a model he claimed to have found in Exodus; and for some years Samuel Hartlib and his followers had serious intentions of establishing a utopia called Antilia somewhere in the New World, possibly Virginia.[5]

As connections were strengthened between reformist tracts and communities, English authors tried to make their utopian programs more realistic. One way of doing this was to reject the utopia's distant or exotic setting in favor of a realizable location. Before the 1640s and after 1660 utopists in England favored the paradigm established by More and Bacon, choosing settings for their ideal commonwealths that were at once remote and unfixable. Robert Burton had made fun of this practice in his brief utopia embedded in Democritus Jr.'s "Preface to the Reader" in *The Anatomy of Melancholy*, which went through five editions between 1621 and 1638. After scorning the "witty fictions" of More and Bacon, Democritus went on to say that his own utopia would be situated at a latitude of 45 degrees, "in the middle of the Temperate Zone, or perhaps under the Equator, that Paradise of the World, . . . where is a perpetual spring: the longitude for some reason I will conceal."[6] But utopists in the Commonwealth were not very interested in paradisical or idealized settings. Gabriel Plattes's *Macaria*, described in a dialogue between a Schollar and a Traveler who brings news of Macaria "like merchandize" from across the sea, is not given a setting at all. *Macaria* is addressed to the Long Parliament and is explicitly set forth as an "example" or program; as Plattes's Scholar approves, "I have read over Sr. Thomas More's *Utopia*, and my Lord Bacon's *New Atlantis*, which he so called in imitation of Plato's old one, but none of them giveth me satisfaction, how the kingdom of England may be happy, so much as this discourse" (9). In *Nova Solyma* (1648), Samuel Gott situates his utopia in New Jerusalem; the utopia ends with the symbolic weddings of the English travelers to the twin daughters of the city of Zion, signaling the larger marriage of New Jerusalem and England, which are to be symbolically conjoined. In the 1650s,

English utopists (such as James Harrington) continued to restructure the utopia as a literary form, rejecting the distant geographic setting, reshaping and internalizing the utopian dialogue, and shifting from a romance paradigm to a political platform. By the 1650s, the idea of a distant geographical setting seemed anathema to English utopists, who were much more interested in the political and spiritual transformation of their own nation.

Despite the new pragmatism of Civil War utopias, the impact of millenarianism on alternative societies blends realism with fervent mysticism. Throughout the 1650s the belief intensified that the end of time was at hand, and English utopists combined their visions of ideal communities with representations of the New Heaven and Earth. Samuel Hartlib claimed in *Clavis Apocalyptica* that the world would end in 1655. "Farwel (welmeaning reader!)," Hartlib wrote warmly, "and bee patient for a short time, thou shall see the end of these distractions in great Revolutions both in Church and State, within and without Europe."[7] Millenarians were not dissuaded when time and the world kept going after 1655. In 1660 John Sadler published a utopia entitled *Olbia*, which used mystical numerology to argue that the Second Coming would occur in 1666, a prognosis that garnered strong popular support.[8] Millenarians and utopists alike drew heavily from the Book of Revelation and from the Old Testament Book of Daniel, whose widely quoted verse, "Many shall run to and fro, and knowledge shall be increased," was used to support the belief that the reform of earthly institutions, particularly those governing education, would restore man's dominion over nature, allowing the New Jerusalem to be built in England.[9]

The utopias written during the 1640s and 1650s drew together diverse kinds of puritan reform literature, redefining reform through industry and discipline. Rather than a New Model army, these utopists envisioned a civilian corps of trained and zealous workers dedicated to the ideals of industry, cooperation, and productivity. The greatest common theme of these utopias is that the nation must be strengthened through economic improvements. In the 1640s a series of tracts proliferated urging reforms in agriculture and education, subjects linked both by the desire for in-

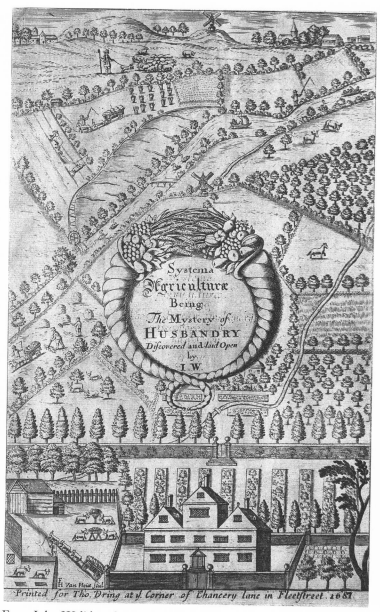

From John Wolidge, *Systema Agriculturae: The Mystery of Husbandry Discovered* (1698). As the accompanying poem emphasizes, "Plenty unto the Husbandman, and Gains / Are his Rewards for's Industry and Pains." By permission of the Houghton Library, Harvard University.

creased utility and by the dread of waste. Plattes and Winstanley, for example, each wrote tracts suggesting how the English could better utilize the land, both in mining and in agriculture. In Plattes's *Macaria*, the first of five civic councils is a "Council of husbandry," which in Winstanley's *Law of Freedom* is also the first of five "fountains" of training; for Winstanley, in his utopia as well as in many of the Digger tracts, civic freedom consists quite simply in free (and appropriate) use of the land.

Tracts on husbandry and on educational reform covered similar subjects and shared metaphors; as gardening had been a stock trope in humanist tracts on education for the training of the soul, agriculture and husbandry dominated the imagery of educational reform literature in the middle of the seventeenth century. Puritan reform literature sharpened earlier emphases on utility, industry, and cooperation. In 1642 Hartlib translated Johann Comenius's essay "A Reformation of Schools" into English, remarking in his preface that education was "for the general good of this nation" and that "serious exercises [must be] the preparations of serious employments" (20). Hartlib's *Reformed Husband-Man* (1651) describes itself from the outset as a "good and public work" intended to advance English "prosperity, health, and Plenty." Essentially a how-to manual, Hartlib's *Reformed Husband-Man* promises that all men may improve by "Experimentall Industriousness," that all men have "the meanes of all Plenty and Riches," and that despite recent complaints that "Trade doth decay, and that the poor are multiplied for want of employment" (which Hartlib sees as "a natural consequence and result of civil warres"), "the State may recover itself, and flourish."[10] Education was increasingly seen as a means of training a corps of able workers and of mitigating two grave (and interrelated) national threats: poverty and idleness.

A new emphasis on the recovery (or establishment) of English prosperity is one of the most striking features of utopias written during and after the Civil War. But there are other important common features of these texts as well. In the utopias I treat in this chapter—Gabriel Plattes's *Macaria* (1641), Samuel Gott's *Nova Solyma* (1648), Gerrard Winstanley's *Law of Freedom in a Platform* (1652), Milton's *Readie & Easie Way To Establish A Free Com-*

monwealth (1660), and the anonymous *A Commonwealth Defended* (1660), a clear shift from monarchy to the republic as the model utopian government is discernible. While Burton in 1638 and Plattes in 1641 are still in favor of the Crown, the authors of the commonwealth tracts in 1659 and 1660 see the monarch as the people's enemy. In Winstanley's *Law of Freedom* only monarchists (and women) are denied franchise. These utopias also demonstrate a generic shift from romance to platform, from fiction to political theory. This raises important questions about the utopia as a narrative form. Later in this chapter I will discuss what happens to the utopia's "two voices" when the dialogue form is internalized or abandoned; similarly, I will consider whether the travel paradigm leaves a residual structure in texts designed as platforms.

Each of the utopias I discuss in this chapter isolates labor and industry as the panacea for social ills. If the laboratory was the model utopian institution for Bacon, for the civil war utopists it is the workhouse or "college of experience" which is seen as having the power to transform the raw materials of humanity into a productive labor force. After Gott's millenarian utopia in 1648, utopists increasingly turned their attention to the problem of the poor in England, trying to determine how they could be rehabilitated and which of their numbers could be salvaged or transformed into a national resource. Idleness and poverty were argued to be interrelated. It is telling that the poor in this period should so often have been compared to American Indians. Since the publication of Montaigne's 1580 essay "On Cannibals," Europe's poor had been compared (often unfavorably) with "primitives" and savages from the New World.[11] At various times in the 1630s and 1640s England's poor were packed off to America and left to starve on another shore.[12] More subtle and continuous colonization of the poor took place in England, under English rule. Increasingly reformers, despite and in some instances in contradiction to their pleas for unity, divided the poor into two strata or "nations," those who could be "converted" through industry and hard work and those whose idleness condemned them as unsavable. This splitting of the poor into separate classes was yet one more division in a country whose civil war ran along lines much deeper than those supported by organized parties or armies. Appropriately, it was the disjunctive nature of utopian representation which gave that division its fullest (and at times, most painful) expression.

The College of Experience: Training the Labor Force in *Macaria* and *Nova Solyma*

In the 1640s two utopias were published in England: Gabriel Plattes's *A Description of the Famous Kingdome of Macaria* (1641) and Samuel Gott's *Nova Solyma* (1648). At first the two works seem to have little in common. Plattes's utopia is a spare fifteen pages long, addressed to Parliament, and though it claims to follow More and Bacon in choosing to fashion its utopia "as a fiction," the text reads much like a political address. Only the barest sketches of Macaria's fictional government are provided. *Nova Solyma*, on the other hand, is a dense two-volume romance. Its descriptions of Nova Solyma's institutions and policies are interspersed with philosophical and theological debate, digressions on topics such as theology, dueling, platonic and romantic love, and philosophy, its interwoven subplots describing such complexities as piracy and bandits, cross-dressing, mistaken identity, and unrequited love.

Oddly, the two utopias share a complicated history of reception. For centuries Plattes's *Macaria* was attributed to Samuel Hartlib, to whose alleged authorship the text owes what little interest it has received; only in recent years has it been reattributed to the less illustrious Gabriel Plattes. Gott's *Nova Solyma* sank into obscurity soon after its publication, enjoying a brief resurgence of interest when Walter Begley edited it in 1902, painstakingly annotating the text to support the thesis that the text had been written by Milton at Cambridge—a thesis that generated little if any scholarly support.[13] But aside from their authorial misattributions, these utopias have a more intrinsic connection. Both *Macaria* and *Nova Solyma* elaborate a new fictional form—the utopia of industry. In each, the college praised as its central institution works like a bank or "treasure house" to enlarge capital, promote plenty, and train up model citizens. With their systematic programs for economic advancement, these utopias effectively conjoin the Morean marketplace with the Baconian scientific institute. In these new utopias, the treasure not kept as treasure is neither gold nor nature but the labor force itself.

The title of Plattes's utopia is an intertextual allusion, derived from More's micro-utopia of Macaria, "not far from Utopia," described by Hythlodaeus in *Utopia*'s book 1. According to Hythlodaeus, Macaria is praiseworthy for its frugality. The king takes a vow upon entering office to limit his own treasury in order to enrich that of his people. This law "was aimed chiefly at keeping the king in check, but he also wanted to ensure an ample supply of money for the daily business transactions of the citizens." The word *Macaria* comes from the Greek *makarios*, meaning "fortunate." For Plattes, as for many utopists in the 1640s and 1650s, fortune is increasingly equated with industry. Treasure must be regulated and balanced, distributed among the middle classes who, through industry and labor, will leverage it and ensure its growth. Like gold in Utopia, industry preserves the nation through *use*.[14]

Aptly, Plattes's *Macaria* was written in a period of increasing attention to the balance sheets of other countries. The Dutch were a favorite symbol for the English of industry and successful commerce, and if the Dutch excited English envy, they also prompted imitation. As the English struggled to redefine themselves as a nation during the Civil War, they turned increasingly to an idealized image of labor as the panacea for social and political shortcomings.

Little is known about the life of Gabriel Plattes. He was associated with Hartlib and his circle in the 1630s and early 1640s, and he wrote three texts other than *Macaria: A Discovery of Infinite Treasure, Hidden Since the World's Beginning* (1639); a manual on mining entitled *A Discovery of Subterraneal Treasure* (1639); and *The Profitable Intelligencer* (1644?). His interest in mining and husbandry were part of his ardent desire to eliminate waste and to discover methods for employing the poor. In his preface to *A Discovery of Infinite Treasure* (75–76), Plattes claims he "put out this Booke" due to "a greife of mind to see some indifferent well disposed persons" lying and stealing "for very hunger," due to unemployment "at least answerable to their nature and education." His hope was to set out a program, elaborated in *The Profitable Intelligencer*, so that "all the inhabitants of England will recover the wealth of the kingdom now so miserably wasted." In his preface to *A Discovery of Subterraneal Treasure*, Plattes praised Christ, capable of multiplying loaves and fishes, as supplying a commendable "pattern of frugality." He promised that if his book were "diligently perused" and its plans "industriously practised," a cure might somehow be found for the maladies of poverty and want. Almost two generations before Bunyan was to immortalize the labor of "buying truth" in *Pilgrim's Progress*, Plattes was advocating a very similar economics of salvation, linking morality and diligence, the husbandry of the land with the husbandry of the soul.

What Max Weber was to call the ethics of frugality and the shoring up of capital are emphatically advocated in *Macaria*, where Plattes's Traveler promises that "any man may be rich that is industrious" (11).[15] The promise of prosperity for the working and middle classes is the greatest treasure of Macaria. Plattes's full title reads *A Description of the Famous Kingdome of Macaria; Shewing its Excellent Government: Wherein the Inhabitants live in Great Prosperity, Health, and Happiness; the King Obeyed, the Nobles Honoured; and all good men respected, Vice punished, and vertue rewarded*. In Plattes's prefatory letter to the Long Parliament he adds, "I have delivered my conceptions in a Fiction, as a more mannerly way, having for my pattern Sir Thomas Moore, and Sir Francis Bacon once Lord Chancellour of England." If in fact Plattes meant his representation of Macaria to be an elaboration of Hythlodaeus's remarks on the micro-utopia of Macaria in *Utopia*'s book 1, his "advice" to the Long Parliament can be read ironically, for More's Hythlodaeus had used the example of Macaria to prove to Giles and Morus that a philosopher's counsel falls on deaf ears:

> "What if I then were to put before them the law of the Macarians, a people not very far distant from Utopia? Their king, on the day he first enters into office, is bound by an oath at solemn sacrifices that he will never have at one time in his

coffer more than a thousand pounds of gold or its equivalent in silver. . . . To sum it all up, if I tried to obtrude these and like ideas on men strongly inclined to the opposite way of thinking, to what deaf ears should I tell the tale!"

"Deaf indeed, without doubt," I agreed. (97)

Sadly, as Hythlodaeus might have predicted, Platte's tract did indeed fall on deaf ears. But the urgency of his utopia suggests he was determined (and unironic) in devising a program for the eradication of "want."

Plattes's Macaria is described in a dialogue between a Schollar, or "Master of Arts," and a Traveler who, like one of Bensalem's Merchants of Light, commodifies his narrative, comparing it to merchandise: "I am a Traveler, and can tell you strange newes, and much knowledge, and I have brought it over the sea without paying any custome, though it be worth all the merchandize in the kingdome" (2). Though Plattes describes this commonwealth only briefly, he establishes several critical ideas for subsequent utopias of industry in the 1640s and 1650s. Macaria has a "great council" and five "under councells," governing "husbandry, fishing, trade by land, trade by sea, and a councell for new Plantations"(3). The country is strictly governed by what Plattes calls "principall Lawes." Civic and self-regulation are of paramount importance. In Macaria no man is allowed to "hold more land than he can husband," for waste is an offense resulting in eventual banishment (4). The council of trade strictly regulates the number of tradesmen. There are no religious sects in Macaria; Christianity there comprises "infallible tenets, which may be proved by invincible arguments" (7). A policy of censorship is enforced, and anyone opposing the king is an enemy and a traitor (7).

Macaria may sound grimly overregulated to modern readers, and it is hard at times to share in Schollar's enthusiastic and uncritical reception of this "brief and pithy" example of "how the kingdome of England may be happy." But in Macaria, where most citizens are tradesmen rather than nobles, English working- and middle-class readers saw for the first time a glimpse of "their own rights and liberties," as Traveler promises in his conclusion. *Macaria* is an artisanal utopia, promising utopia not to the patrician classes, like Bacon's *New Atlantis*, but to ordinary laborers.

In Macaria, industry itself ensures prosperity. Husbandry is held in the highest esteem, and citizens are taught to internalize the commonwealth's strict laws of regulation in Macaria's "House, or College of Experience," in which skills in Husbandry, Physick, and Surgery are established. Though details concerning this College of Experience are scant, the institution seems to have been intended, like Solomon's House, to epitomize Macaria and its aims. As a kind of national laboratory, the College of Experience would collect "any experiment for the health or wealth of men." It would study the "transmutation of sublunary bodies" and publish important books, such as the text on husbandry and trade on which Plattes himself was at work, entitled *The Treasure House of Nature Unlocked*. Where the scientists in Solomon's House worked to transmute or re-create Nature, in Plattes's College of Experience the emphasis would be put instead on nature's control, regulation, and utility. Nature in Macaria is a great "treasure house," and Macaria's College of Experience is a kind of vocational school to teach the way to mine and utilize those riches. In Macaria, earth's treasure is meant to be balanced and saved, not hoarded, wasted, or spent.

Michael Walzer has argued that for the new class of people left without position or "masters" in England as the feudal system gave way to capitalism, self-mastery became more and more important.[16] Plattes's emphasis on regulation in Macaria lends support to this claim. In Plattes's texts the regulation of the self is projected onto the kingdom, which must be plumbed to its depths, scrutinized, inspected, mined, and measured, every inch of land used, every gram of ore utilized or transmuted. The vision of earth as a treasure house persists throughout Plattes's writings, accompanied by a touchingly sanguine sense that industry could transform England from a place of dearth to a place of plenty. In 1641, Plattes predicted that England was not far from becoming a Macaria, a wish that seems painfully ironic in light of his own fate. Three years after he published *Macaria*, Plattes was found dead from "meer want" (starvation). In England in the 1640s, industry and effort could not guarantee subsistence, let alone the enjoyment of the "treasure house" that was the earth.[17]

In comparison with Plattes's artisanal utopia, Samuel Gott's 1648 utopia, *Nova Solyma*, is resoundingly bourgeois, reflecting the ethos of what was rapidly becoming a new English middle class. Gott, the son of a successful ironmonger, was trained at the Merchant Tailors' School, then at Cambridge and the Inns of Court, acquiring an education that several generations earlier would have been reserved for the aristocracy. *Nova Solyma, the Ideal City; or, Jerusalem Regained*, is the account of the New Jerusalem, restored to its "present wonderful prosperity" some fifty years back, after the Jews recognized "the true Messiah" and were promptly transformed from misery to bliss.[18] Two Englishmen, Eugenius and Politian, are invited to visit Nova Solyma by one of its inhabitants, Joseph, whom they meet during a grand tour of Italy. Nova Solyma is set on a mountain slope, built on the ruins of the Old Solyma; it is a walled city with twelve gates, all of solid brass, on which are carved the names and images of the Patriarchs. In the public hall, the principal tenets of Nova Solyma are inscribed for all to read. The inscription is a doctrine of industry and frugality in the name of the state. Here "the necessaries of life are stored up as occasion requires, but honestly always, and each one is occupied by his own work for the commonweal, while the happy spirit of union breaks forth in songs of mutual joy" (83).

Jacob, Joseph's father, is cordial to the English visitors, for in Nova Solyma "it is a national duty to treat strangers with kindness." He explains to them that in Nova Solyma they take "special care of the young" as is true "in every true republic." Nova Solyma is especially concerned with improvement, a value pursued by its citizens with zeal: "We try to improve by art and culture in every way the gifts of body and mind with which kindly Nature endows our race" (90). Nor are the poor excluded from such improvement, for, as Jacob explains, "children of the poor are heartiest" and males from all classes in Nova Solyma are educated, using prizes and "trials of strength" to winnow out the most able. Even less able students are looked on with favor here, as they "may prove more tractable" than their more gifted peers. Jacob goes on to explain how values (such as moderation) can be inculcated. In a passage remarkable for its intricate horror he describes how "disgust" can be constructed through the manipulation of appetite and desire: "We put special restrictions on eating and sleeping too much; all must rise early and eat what happens to be set before them. Hardly ever do they get the chance of delicacies; but sometimes, to create disgust, we allow them to gorge to repletion" (92).

This enforced nausea is the most striking but by no means the only method by which the state constructs value in Gott's utopia. It is no coincidence, for example, that schoolboys are taught math first, priority being given to the "calculation of figures and weights and measures." From the earliest years, theirs is a course in business, on the weighing up of profits. Even their theology is represented in terms of economics: "viz. that God's Providence is the best provision for life's journey, and a good stock of really useful knowledge the safest patrimony to start with" (128). In literature as well as math citizens of Nova Solyma are taught to turn "mere idle tales" to profit by extracting morals and meaning, using the tales for introspection. Idleness is everywhere to be abhorred, and profit everywhere encouraged and pursued.

Nova Solyma is dominated by a central college or institution of learning, in this case the Public Academy, which Joseph's younger brother is preparing to enter as Eugenius and Politian are welcomed to the city. The public school buildings stand not far from Nova Solyma's Public Hall or Merchants' Exchange, a structure dominated by a great clock that calculates and makes public the passing of time, as if to illustrate that time governs the Exchange, and vice versa:

> In front a square tower rose from the roof, having on each of
> its four sides a clock face to draw attention to the passing
> hours, while the clock within ever and anon sounded forth the
> time for all to hear. . . . Below this were little stores filled with
> merchandise and necessaries of all kinds, while on a higher
> level there was what might be called the Ladies Bazaar, an emporium of all articles of feminine adornment, a "tiring house"

of which they never tired. . . . The buildings were roofed with
lead, and the walls that faced the central area were all blank.
(201–2)

Gott's Exchange anticipates Bunyan's Vanity Fair, a "tiring house"
of which the people never tire, suggesting a certain futility in the
relation between the passing hours, the accumulation of merchandise, and the endless displays in "little stores."[19] The blank walls of
the Exchange contrast with Nova Solyma's Public Academy, where
boys between the ages of ten and seventeen years are separated
from the townspeople "as if they had been banished." In the Public
Academy the buildings are decorated with "statues of men of old"
celebrated for life or learning, like the narratives embossed on the
gates in Campanella's *City of the Sun* (231). But the Exchange is the
institution these students must be prepared to enter. Thus, education in Nova Solyma involves strict training in state history and
policy. Allegiance to the republic is taught from an early age, so
that the boys "learn the habit of mind by which they would willingly, in their own interests, keep inviolate the laws of God and
their country, and put the advantage of the republic before any private or personal benefits whatever." As Alphaeus, the schoolmaster,
explains:

> The founders of our republic, in their zealous enquiry how
> best to establish it on a sound basis, put the education of the
> rising generation in the very forefront of all means to that
> end. They held the opinion that good laws, an effective army,
> and all the other defenses of a State, were of comparatively no
> avail if obedience and benevolence and the other virtues
> which tend to the well-being of mankind were not early im-
> planted in the minds of the young. (235)

The Public Academy is the spiritual and intellectual mirror of
the Merchants' Exchange in Nova Solyma, teaching the acquisition
of knowledge rather than goods, the exchange of ideas rather than
money and objects. The two institutions share methods as well as
values. Alphaeus includes an entire chapter defending the use of
material prizes to spur schoolboys on by rivalry. Literary competi-

tions, for example, are held for the acquisition of "symbolical prize pens" of bronze, silver, or gold for various levels of excellence in various genres. In athletics, cash prizes are given "as a spur to . . . exertions and a token of victory" (250). Like the Merchants' Exchange, the Public Academy in Nova Solyma is an elaborate storehouse in which knowledge itself becomes a commodity, and its attainment teaches citizens that they must compete, that the best goods are in short supply, and that excellence is rewarded with gain.

This incipient capitalism pervades all aspects of life in Nova Solyma, where even the vineyards have account books. Joseph's description of "the true life" connects Puritan asceticism and capitalist values:

> The true life that we should embrace is one of solid reality
> and severe earnestness; not a course of life that promises the
> greatest gain, or the most luxurious ease, nor yet one leading
> to mere fame or successful ambition, but rather that way
> should be chosen which, from a careful consideration of all
> things, seems most likely to tend to the glory of God and the
> service of our fellow-citizens. Such a life, when chosen, is of
> ever-increasing interest; nay, it is well worth our while to de-
> vote our leisure time and holiday intervals to the same great
> aims. (2:96)

Nowhere is the Puritan need for self-regulation described more tellingly than in the public lecture Politian and Eugenius attend entitled "The Well-Regulated Mind," in which the lecturer explains that the mind is like a kingdom to be properly governed, ordered, and improved. "The man who can rule himself," the lecturer tells them, "is the greatest of all commanders." A "well-regulated and temperate body" is the best home for the soul: "and the whole man, body and soul, should be ordered that, like a perfect machine thoroughly wound up, he may be ready with every move and limb that he can use to serve God, to help his country, and to save himself" (2:129). Three years later in *Leviathan*, Hobbes would also compare man to an engine or machine: "For what is the Heart, but a Spring; and the Nerves, but so many Strings; and the Joynts, but so many Wheeles, giving motion to the whole Body, such as was intended by an Artificer?"[20] In suggesting man train himself "like a perfect machine" for God's service, Gott's utopia uneasily predicts the totalitarian visions of manufactured classes in Huxley's *Brave New World*. But in *Nova Solyma*, only the middle class is manufactured by the twin institutions of the Public Academy and the Exchange. How, then, were the poor and working classes to be incorporated into such a vision of the commonwealth? Jacob assured his English visitors that the poor were not left out of Nova Solyma's educational system, as they were "heartier" than other classes and thus more suitable for rigorous training. In this belief, Jacob articulated a point of view widely held by English readers. *Nova Solyma* was written during one of the most severe harvest failures England had experienced since the devastating famine of 1623, and Gott was apparently not the only English reformer to believe the poor were hearty enough to pull through. But as poverty worsened in England in the middle of the century and the numbers of unemployed or destitute increased, concern for the "lower orders" became more pressing. In 1649, one year after *Nova Solyma*'s publication, the first public workhouse was established in London, and increasingly the focus of reformist and utopian literature in England became the rehabilitation and control of the poor. In most cases they were to be saved not through education but through labor. Like Gott's "well-regulated man," the poor were to be retrained "like a perfect machine" to serve their country. Paradoxically, the enemy plaguing the poor was seen as their own idleness, and even the most dedicated and radical of the reformers, such as Gerrard Winstanley, condemned to "meer want" those who could not or would not work for themselves and their country.

Utopia and the Institution of Labor

In the years following the Civil War, poverty intensified in England both in reality and in popular perception. This was partly an effect of protracted war, which caused an "acute, albeit relatively short-lived economic and social dislocation in many areas."[21] Particularly for those who worked on the land, the war exacerbated the deterioration of feudal ties, which meant displacement, vagrancy, and potential starvation for an increasing sector of the peasant population. Between 1570 and 1640 the portion of English peasants who lost rights to the land and had to work for wages rose by 40 percent.[22] While historians now believe the mortality caused by failed harvests or "dearth" had dropped off in England by the middle of the century, some regions (especially in the North) continued to suffer, and in the late 1640s three consecutive years of bad harvests (1647, 1648, and 1649) forced grain prices higher, intensifying poverty and starvation throughout the country. Despite rigid Poor Laws tying the poor to their own regions, London remained a magnet for the destitute, helping to create "a highly visible sub-stratum to urban society, living in cellars, divided tenements, and hastily erected cottages, and surviving by begging, prostitution, and crime."[23]

The belief that unemployment was the fault of the unemployed was almost universal in England, and almost all reformers decried idleness as a sin.[24] Poor Laws and relief bills were used both to rehabituate and to control the lower orders, for with relief came, almost ubiquitously, severe restrictions: those receiving charity were often required to wear pauper's badges, which became compulsory everywhere after 1697. Accepting the "gift" of charity meant that one's attendance could be required at church or forbidden at alehouses, and stringent restrictions could be placed on the recipient's social behavior and companions.

The most organized expression of this control could be found in the new workhouses, established in Norwich in the 1570s and in Salisbury in 1623. In 1647 Parliament established a London Corporation for the Poor, which was to receive one thousand pounds annually and to build two houses for the "rehabilitation" of the needy. The architectural space of the enclosure coincided with the distribution of individuals "in a space in which one might isolate and map them."[25] For Puritan reformists like Hartlib and Petty, the workhouse provided a model for what could be developed into an entire city of industry, rather like the factory-town owned by Mr. Trafford in Disraeli's *Sybil*, where the "spreading factory" provided a moral as well as an economic habitation. In *The Parliament's Reform* (1646), Hartlib set forth an elaborate plan for a system of workhouses for "the imployment of the poore, the suppressing of

idle Counterfeits; and the education of all poore Children." Hartlib believed children's labor should go hand in hand with children's
education and that, as they learned to read and write, poor children
should learn to "doe some worke to help relieve them."

Vocational training schemes were enthusiastically proposed by
a host of reformers, such as Rice Bush, Hugh Peter, Henry
Robinson, and Balthazar Gerbier.[26] One of the most interesting
was William Petty's proposed system of *Ergastula literaria*, or literary workhouses, intended to employ all children over the age of
seven, instilling in the young respect for manual labor while ensuring that they earned enough money to survive. By harnessing so
many able (and tractable) workers, Petty promised that "all Trades
will miraculously prosper." His "literary workhouses" proposed to
teach reading, writing, "artificial memory," drawing, mathematics,
crafts, and (if aptitude was apparent) music or languages. The curriculum consisted largely of trades: watchmaking, art, optics, bot-
any, music, ship design, confectionery, and anatomy, developing a
model for trade and vocational programs in successive generations.[27] Such schemes continued to grow in popularity, culminat-
ing at the end of the century in John Bellers's *Proposals for Raising
a College of Industry* (1695) and John Carey's *House of Industry*
(1696). What reformers envisioned was "laborious knowledge"
(Winstanley's phrase), a vocational training that would equip every
citizen to share in the utopian enterprise of rehabilitative labor.
Winstanley took the vocational schemes of Hartlib and Petty one
step further by actually establishing a full-employment utopia in
Surrey. But Winstanley's digging experiment, like his communist
utopia addressed to Cromwell in 1652, was considered a failure. It
was one thing for the poor to be reformed in institutions set aside
for them and controlled by the state; it was quite another when the
poor tried to build their own community dedicated to labor, with
its own manifesto and defense. The Diggers' experience in Surrey
suggests that the worst victims of the new English war on poverty
were the poor themselves.

IN APRIL 1649, soon after Parliament's funding for the London
workhouses came through, Gerrard Winstanley, William Everard,

and half a dozen other men began ploughing what they claimed was waste or common land on St. George's Hill in Surrey. Their intention was to plant crops on the unused land for their own subsistence. The community of Diggers (or True Levellers) was small at first, but they recruited others, inviting all "poor men" at a neighboring market to join them and publicly predicting their numbers would soon swell into the thousands. Neither the Council of State nor Lord Fairfax intervened, believing the matter would best be left to local property owners, who maintained that the land which the Diggers wanted to use lay within the bounds of bordering manors.[28]

In all likelihood the Digger community never amounted to more than a hundred people, but from records of disputes with local residents, they were clearly seen as a threat. The Diggers built makeshift houses on the eleven acres of land they claimed was "waste." Like More's Utopians, they acted on the principle of fair use, believing unused land should be available to anyone willing to husband it. Apparently local landowners felt differently. At the end of April a few Diggers were dragged off to a local church and held as prisoners. After a local justice set them free, their harassment intensified: about a hundred local men stormed their community, stole their tools, and dragged another few Diggers off to jail. Twice in the spring of 1649 members of the Digger community were attacked and beaten, their crops trampled, their spades and other tools broken, and their houses torn down or "fired." In a June raid, led by "lesser" neighbors (some of them apparently disguised as women), a few of the Diggers were severely beaten and one was left close to death. Local landlords, disliking the publicity, took the Diggers to court where they were found guilty of trespassing, and five members were jailed. But the Diggers hung on through the winter. Winstanley was optimistic about their first real harvest, for "they have Planted divers Acres of wheat and Rie, which is come up and promises a very fruitful crop."

By spring, animosity between local neighbors and the Diggers had worsened. The Diggers moved their colony to land bordering on the property of the rector of the local church, John Platt, who keenly resented the Diggers' reliance on "scriptural authority" to defend their actions. Platt led a number of fierce attacks on the Diggers. In the first, "divers men" pulled down a poor man's house and "kikt and struck the poor man's wife, so that she miscarried of her Child." On Good Friday Platt and his men burned down five or six of the Diggers' houses, destroying or scattering their possessions. That night the Diggers slept on the open common, determined to keep the community intact. But Platt and his small local army returned and attacked the Diggers once again, this time appointing guards to keep them from rebuilding. Platt's men, according to Winstanley's account, were instructed to "beat [the Diggers], and to pull down their tents or houses, if they make any more; and if they make only caves in the earth, they threaten to murther them there" (6).

At this point even Winstanley had to admit defeat, though in his account ("An Humble Request") he represents the Diggers' final eviction as a moral victory: "The poor have striven with them 12. moneths, with love and patience: The Gentlemen have answered them all the time with fury." The clash between the Diggers and the citizens of Surrey was a grave, albeit small-scale, civil war in a country whose larger civil war had not much benefited the destitute, even those, like Winstanley, who believed it was kingly government which oppressed the people and commonwealth government which would ensure their liberation.

Not much is known about Winstanley before 1649 or after 1652. He was born in Lancashire, probably in 1609, the son of a wool-trader, apprenticed to a merchant tailor's widow and married in 1640 to a woman named Susan King. After some small success in business he apparently suffered bankruptcy in the Civil War, and by 1643 he was living in Surrey, pasturing a neighbor's cattle. At one stage he may have been a Baptist, but by the time of the Digger tracts he was dissatisfied with all existing churches, believing God's spirit was extant in all human beings. As he wrote in *The Saint's Paradise*, "I do not write anything as to be a teacher of you, for I know you have a teacher within yourself (which is the Spirit)."[29] Winstanley's native Lancashire suffered severely in the depression of 1648–1649, and he became increasingly concerned about the poor, whom he saw being destroyed by what he called "that cheating art of buying and selling." In the Diggers' manifesto, *The New Law of Righteousness* (1649), Winstanley recounted experiencing a trancelike vision in which a voice instructed him that people need to "work together, eat bread together." It was this vision that engendered the community on St. George's Hill. By the time he was working on his utopia, addressed to Cromwell in 1652, Winstanley knew how unlikely it was for such a community to actually establish itself in England. Nonetheless, *The Law of Freedom in a Platform* is written as a real prospectus for the reformation of England under commonwealth government. The utopia is preceded by two prefatory letters, one to Oliver Cromwell and one to "the Friendly and Unbyassed Reader," both of whom are exhorted to join him in the labor of reformation. Winstanley's utopia abolishes the cheating art of buying and selling that he associated with kingly government. "When Mankinde began to buy and sell, then did he fall from his Innocency," he remarks, and "this buying and selling did bring in, and still doth bring in, discontents and wars, which have plagued Mankinde sufficiently for so doing" (59).[30] True freedom, Winstanley argues, lies in free use of the land, or labor: "Every Freeman shall have a Freedom in the Earth, to plant or build, to fetch from the Store-houses any thing he wants, and shall enjoy the fruits of his labours without restraint from any; he shall not pay Rent to any Landlord, and he shall be capable to be chosen any Officer, so he be above forty years of age, and he shall have a voyce to chose Officers though he be under forty years of age" (597).

The central institution in Winstanley's utopia is the common storehouse, which, like the exchange at the center of More's utopian cities, provides plenty and rectifies dearth while eliminating currency: "There shall be Store-houses in all places, both in the Country and in Cities, to which all the fruits of the earth, and other works made by Tradesmen, shall be brought, and from thence delivered out again to particular Families, and to every one as they want for their use" (582). There are two types: general storehouses, which provide people with raw materials, and particular storehouses, like shops, where hats, shoes, gloves, stockings, and the like can be had. People simply take what they need without buying and selling and without money and without "exchanging the Conquerers picture or stampe upon a piece of Gold or Silver, for the fruits of the earth" (584).

This is not to say that some people will be given a free ride. "If you say, Some will live idle; I answer, No: It will make idle persons to become workers, as is declared in the *Platform;* There shall be neither Beggar nor idle person" (513). Winstanley is particularly hard on the idle. In his utopia, everyone works. "Every man shall be brought up in Trades and labours, and all Trades shall be maintained with more improvement, to the inriching of the Commonwealth" (526). "Idle persons and beggars will be made to work," he says (527). Idleness is to be punished, first by admonishment, then by public reproof, then by whipping, and finally by forced labor for one year, or until the offender submits to "order." Labor is so integral to Winstanley's utopia that the very offices of government are broken into categories called "works"—such as "the work of a Father or Master of a Family" and "the work of a Peace-maker" (545); of an overseer, a postmaster, etc. Education is a facet of labor as well, for it is the work of officers, overseers, and fathers to see their young "broken" by education and correction: "Mankinde in the days of his youth, is like a young Colt, wanton and foolish, till he be broke by Education and correction. . . . Therefore the Law of a *Commonwealth* does require, that not only a father, but that all Overseers, and officers should make it their work to educate children in good manners, and to see them brought up in some trade or other, and to suffer no children in any Parish to live in idleness" (576).

Winstanley describes five "fountains" of training—training in husbandry, in manual employment, in "dairy" (which includes work in leathers, dyes, and weaving), in timber (which includes carpentry), and in natural science. What is desired is a "laborious Knowledg," patterned after God's works, not the impractical, "lazy contemplation" of traditional scholarship (579). Winstanley's utopia is unusual in providing education for both sexes, though he relegates domestic trades to "all maids," who "shall be trained up in reading, sewing, knitting, spining of Lynnen and Woollen, Musique, and all other easie neat works" (579). After attending school, all able members of his utopia work until they reach forty years of age, at which point they are free.

But freedom for Winstanley is never really freedom from work; as in Milton's Eden, freedom is defined consistently as freedom *to work*. Labor is so fundamental to Winstanley's vision that even Cromwell's task is defined by it, for what he has before him, Winstanley says, is the "Work of Reformation" (505), and Winstanley requests that his reading of his utopia should be similarly industrious: "be as the industrious Bee, suck out the honey and cast away the Weeds" (510). This emphasis on industry and utility leads Winstanley to a strict endorsement of laws and their enforcement. Like Hobbes, he believes human nature is difficult to control until it is "broken." Mankind's spirit is too "various within it self," for "some are wise, some are foolish, some idle, some laborious, some rash, some milde, some loving and free to others, some envyous and covetous." For this reason Winstanley recognizes that his commonwealth will work only if laws are strictly enforced. Though there are to be no lawyers, "there must be suitable Laws for every occasion, and almost for every action that men do" (528). Secondly, "there must be fit Officers" to execute those laws. Winstanley institutionalizes the Puritan principles of scrutiny and regulation in his office of overseer. Offices in general correspond to the basic model of the patriarchal family. In a private family, the father is officer. In a town, there is to be a peacemaker, a fourfold office of overseers, a soldier, a taskmaster, and an executioner. In the county there will be a judge, a court, boards of peacemakers, overseers, and soldiers, and in the nation, a parliament, a commonwealth's ministry, a postmaster, and an army. Winstanley believes that government exists for the common good and for self-preservation. Given the "variousness" of human nature, law and its enforcement are necessary: "therefore because of this was the Law added, which was to be a Rule and Judg for all men's actions, to preserve common Peace and Freedom." For Winstanley, this social contract exacts from citizens a pattern of obedience based on "the law of liberty which is the command of Christ" (585). Law in Winstanley's utopia is represented contradictorily, for while in one sense law would provide real protection for Winstanley's citizens (for example, in his utopia the crime of rape is punishable by death, provided there are two witnesses or the accused confesses), in another sense law becomes an institutional articulation of control, a method of regulating the population, eradicating its "variousness" without lessening productivity.

Robert W. Kenny, who edited *The Law of Freedom* in the early 1940s, remarks in the preface to his revised edition that Winstanley's utopia, "*by no means a literary utopia* in the tradition of Thomas More and Francis Bacon, . . . was designed as a blueprint for immediate and specific social reform" (1). While Kenny's use of the category "literary" is problematic, his remark raises important questions for *The Law of Freedom* and for subsequent utopias that eschew or remodel the traditional romance paradigm of More's and Bacon's texts. Kenny is right, I think, to draw attention to an important feature of *The Law of Freedom*. Like Gott, Winstanley makes no mention of literary antecedents for his utopia. Substantively, Winstanley's *Law of Freedom* has a good deal in common with More's *Utopia*—his communism, his rejection of currency, his strict social conformity, his central storehouses which transmute dearth to plenty. But it is hard to know whether or not Winstanley knew either More's or Bacon's utopias. *The Law of Freedom* is richly allusive, but its allusions are all scriptural, and like many of Winstanley's Digger tracts, the text comes out of a tradition of radical millennialism rather than classical or contemporary utopianism. Two stylistic changes signal that Winstanley's is a new kind of utopia, a blueprint, model, or platform rather than a romance. First, Winstanley rejects the travel paradigm in which a traveler describes his impressions of an ideal commonwealth from which he has recently returned. Second, Winstanley rejects the utopian dialogue in which an outsider (often a philosopher or student) questions the traveler on the procedures and possible shortcomings of the commonwealth.

These changes are significant both for Winstanley and for his successors. Winstanley's utopia borrows from the generic model of the jeremiad, in which a prophet or spokesperson informs the community that its covenant with God has broken down, that its prior glory has been diminished, and that it is necessary to fight to regain it.[31] The jeremiad restructures the travel paradigm, describing a spiritual progress (and return) rather than a navigation or sea voyage. For Winstanley, kingly government and commonwealth government are as vivid as places, and his utopia recounts the spiritual and political journey between them.

Even more strikingly, the two voices of utopian dialogue are retained in Winstanley's utopia. In his prefatory letter to Cromwell, Winstanley uses the rhetorical question to replace the questions of the visitor, outsider, or philosopher: "Do not the Ministers preach for maintenance in the Earth? . . . Doth not the soldier fight for the Earth? And doth not the Landlord require Rent, that he may live in the fulness of the Earth by the labor of his tenants?" (520). Winstanley represents an imaginary dialogue with Cromwell in which he scripts both voices: "It may be well you will say to me, *What shall I do?* I answer, You are in place and power to see all Burthens taken off from your friends, *the Commoners of England*. You will say, *What are those burthens?*" (503).

Winstanley occasionally scripts the voice of the Commoners as well as of Cromwell: "And is this not slavery, say the People, That though there be Land enough in England, to maintain ten times as many people as are in it, yet some must beg of their brethren, or work in hard drudgery for day wages for them, or starve, or steal, and so be helped out of the way, as men not fit to live in the earth, before they must be suffered to plant the waste land for their livelihood, unless they will pay Rent to their brethren for it? . . . And who now must we be subject to, seeing the Conqueror is gone?" (507). Scripting two voices, Winstanley imagines them always in concert rather than in disagreement. This internal dialogue covers up what was in effect a very real (and unpleasant) division in England. Winstanley's two voices always speak from the same vantage, inside the community that creates their accord as it secures their prosperity: "Shall every man count his Neighbor's house as his own, and live together as one family? No: though the Earth and Storehouses be common to every Family, yet every Family shall live apart as they do. Shall we have no Lawyers? There is no need of them, for there is to be no buying and selling" (512).

Winstanley's utopia creates what John Donne in "The Extasie" calls "a dialogue of one." Chapter headings are posed as questions, such as "What is Kingly Government or Monarchy?" (529),

"Where began the first Original of Government in the Earth among Mankinde?" (536), and "What are the Officers' Names in a Free Commonwealth?"(544) The dialogue (like the travel paradigm) is internalized in Winstanley's utopia, the residual voices of interrogation and response giving the utopia both its form and urgency. Stripping away the fictional personae who represent those voices in earlier works makes *The Law of Freedom* seem at once more universal and more "real"—as literary an effect as the assigning of characters and plot. Like the internalized office of master, dialogue's internalization establishes a new model for utopists in subsequent generations. While utopias had always made the relationship between fiction and nonfiction part of their subject, Winstanley's platform offered a new model for this balance as well as for a new model government. No dissenting voices challenge his vision inside the utopia, but Winstanley was well aware of the opposing voice most English readers would raise to his scheme for the abolition of private property and currency. In fact, Cromwell's response to the tract—total silence—was Winstanley's most crushing defeat. After *The Law of Freedom* Winstanley himself lapsed into silence and obscurity, and before his death he was apparently back to "the cheating art of buying and selling," working as a corn chandler and prospering enough to be sued by creditors before his death.

Winstanley's utopia is organized around strict oppositions. In *The Law of Freedom* no word is more important than *or:* "We must either be subject to a law, or to mens wils," he declares (507). There are two kinds of land: common or waste. There are two kinds of government: commonwealth or kingly. There is idleness or labor. There is free enjoyment of the land, or there is dearth. Perhaps the deepest internalization of utopian dialogue for Winstanley can be seen in the way he divided humanity and government into a yes and a no, an affirmation of life and its denial. Disturbingly and paradoxically, the *or* of Winstanley's utopia divides the poor from each other as well as from the rich. For the poor willing and able to work, Winstanley is a genuine advocate. But those condemned as "idle" become the other voice in the dialogue, the nay that makes the utopia's yea possible. They become the utopia's underclass, that vile and cankered part of the nation that must be cut out in order to heal the body of the nation, united less by common goals than by a common enemy.

Winstanley's goals in *The Law of Freedom* seemed less and less realizable as the initial idealism of Cromwell's Protectorate gave way to disillusionment and resignation in the 1650s. After Cromwell's death in 1658, popular opinion began to sway in favor of a return to monarchy, and it may have seemed wiser once more to intervene in "this world of evil" rather than to construct its utopian antithesis, even in a platform or fiction. The dark nostalgia of Republican utopias in the years before the Restoration may be the greatest testimony to the general spirit of defeat as England prepared to shift back to "kingly government," that other voice in the dialogue which Winstanley had so bitterly (and fruitlessly) opposed. In 1659 and 1660, Republicans watched two decades of political idealism end as England prepared to return to monarchy, fed up with the disintegrating commonwealth that Cromwell's son was struggling to hold together. For those who persisted in seeing the Commonwealth as utopia, or at least as the means to it, this "return" was particularly hard to accept.

Defending the Commonwealth: Prosperity Lost

The first edition of Milton's *Readie & Easie Way To Establish A Free Commonwealth* (1660) has generally been read as an anti-utopian or pragmatic defense of the commonwealth in the face of evident defeat. As James Holstun suggests, the *Readie & Easie Way* is a self-consuming text, a tract in which Milton undercuts his own proposals and withdraws from his community, rejecting institutional solutions or qualifying them "out of existence."[32] In several senses Milton's tract allies itself with the utopias of industry which it succeeds. First, Milton employs the idea of the "little commonwealth," linking it to improvements (real or imagined) in trade. Second, like so many of the economic reformers of the day, he engages English nationalism by comparisons with the Dutch, who, as Joyce Appleby has observed, demonstrated commercial prowess that "acted more forcefully upon the English imagination than any other economic development of the seventeenth century."[33] In the beginning of his tract, Milton reminds his readers of the great example England was to Europe after the abolition of monarchy. England became, he says, "the admiration and terrour of our emulous neighbors" (VI.112).

> After our liberty thus prosperously fought for, gaind, and many years possessd . . . to fall back or rather to creep back so poorly as it seems the multitude would to thir once abjur'd and detested thraldom of Kingship . . . not only argues a strange degenerate contagion suddenly spread among us fitted and prepar'd for new slaverie, but will render us a scorn and derision to all our neighbours. And what will they at best say of us . . . but scoffingly as of that foolish builder, mentioned by our Saviour, who began to build a Tower, and was not able to finish it. Where is this goodly tower of a Commonwealth, which the *English* boasted they would build, to overshaddow kings, and be another *Rome* to the west? The foundation indeed they laid gallantly; but fell into a worse confusion, not of tongues, but of factions, then those at the tower of *Babel*; and have left no memorial of thir work behinde them remaining, but in the common laughter of *Europ*. (117–18)

Now England, Milton claims, will become a joke, a degraded example unless its people find some way to rebuild that "tower of a Commonwealth." Milton proposes a system of "little commonwealths" united by a stable Grand Counsel, which should become "the basis and main pillar in every government." He urges the people not to fall prey to a false imagination of renewed trade and prosperity under monarchy, for it is not under monarchy where countries prosper but in the "free Commonwealths of *Italie*, *Germanie*, and the Low Countreys" (147). Like the utopias of industry, Milton justifies his political vision through economic improvement, claiming his little commonwealths "would soon make the whole nation more industrious, more ingenuous at home, more potent, more honorable abroad" (145).

Milton concludes the first edition of *The Readie & Easie Way* by framing his tract, analyzing his own authorial production in some senses as the swain had done at the end of "Lycidas." Here, however, the sanguine conclusion of "Lycidas" is inverted. It is an especially dark passage: "What I have spoken, is the language of . . . *the good Old Cause*: if it seem strange to any, it will not seem more strange, I hope, then convincing to backsliders. Thus much I should perhaps have said, though I were sure I should have spoken only to trees and stones; and had none to cry to, but with the Prophet, *O earth earth earth!*" (148). The stones Milton addresses could be, if God would raise them once more, "children of liberty." They are the scattered fragments of the "goodly tower of Commonwealth," which has fallen to ruin. Milton here can no longer locate a puissant commonwealth in England's present or future. Instead, England's strength has been repudiated. In 1659 and 1660 it seemed more feasible to represent monarchy as ill-advised than to enthusiastically represent any commonwealth as ideal, and liberty and bondage, even in utopia, began to feel more or less the same.[34]

One of the most passionate exhortations against the return to monarchy was written anonymously in a pamphlet entitled *A Modest Plea for an Equal Commonwealth Against Monarchy. By a Lover of His Country in order to the Healing of the Divisions of the Times*. Addressing the "High Court of Parliament," the author urges his readers to consider their power to create and fashion a commonwealth: "God hath put the nation like wax into your hands, that you may mould it and cast it into what Form your Honours please: We are now Rasa tabula, and your Honours may write what you please upon us" (A2). Like most authors on this subject, this writer reminds his readers that a king is only one person and may fail. The title of good, he continues, was never justly attributed to any king (5). He reminds his audience that in English *king* is a version of the older word *cunning*. He cites Scripture to authorize God's historically mandated breach with kings, especially with Nimrod. A council is a much wiser form of government, he advises, for "in the multitude of councellors there is safety" (16).

A Modest Plea concludes with "An humble motion on behalfe of the Poor." The author asks that workhouses be established "so that none may be permitted to eat the bread of idleness" (42). Like Milton, the author views the Netherlands as "a mirror of industry to all the world" and the Dutch as "the very Ants of diligence and industry" (43). "I am persuaded if a greater door of encouragement were opene'd to industry and diligence, nothing would prove a more effectual means to crowd out that Poverty and Penury, that hath so long dwelt among us"(43).

Poverty and penury, it would seem, were more enduring than models of government. In 1659 political instability exacerbated a severe depression in England. Trade was as bad as many could remember, and poor consecutive harvests in 1658 and 1659 once again drove grain prices higher. By the end of the year the depression had reached crisis proportions, and in December 1659 what little business there was in London was occasionally halted by riots. For many English people, monarchy was distant enough to be seen, if not nostalgically, at least as preferable to the hard times and confusion following Cromwell's death. In the late 1650s nostalgia for monarchy competed with nostalgia for the "good old Cause," for a kind of commonwealth that had not yet been established and that appeared now as if it never would be. In 1660 England, following the familiar utopian paradigm, prepared itself to go back to the place from which it had begun. As the author of *A Modest Plea* lamented, this England felt all too familiar:

> Was this our evil and was this our crime? . . . Is there not as
> unequal a distribution of the wealth and the Riches of the
> Land as ever? Is there not as much Pride, covetousness, Ex-
> tortion and Oppression now as ever? Do not men (notwith-
> standing all the light that had dawned upon the world, and the
> many Hazards and Casualties Riches are exposed unto) with
> as great travail both of mind and body, accumulate wrath as
> ever? . . . To proceed, after all our great expectations, are we
> not still in the wilderness, instead of being arrived at the Ca-
> naan of our Liberties, that good land we promised ourselves
> by our Reformation?

In 1660, a Royalist by the appellation "R.H." set himself the task of completing Bacon's *New Atlantis*. It is perhaps not surprising that utopists after the Restoration should turn back to Bacon to revitalize their representations of alternative worlds. But R.H. transforms Atlantis into a kind of institute of institutions, elaborating schemes for education, law, and the discipline of crime. Despite general prosperity in his utopia, every city would contain a House of Charity to care for the infirm, for orphans, and for those incapable of labor, as well as a House of Correction where the idle or criminals would be put to work by force. These two houses correspond to a division in part created (if not merely elaborated) by English reformers in the period before and after the Civil War. After 1660 utopists were to turn increasingly to fantasy, focusing more and more on the family and the individual and leaving "institutional" utopianism behind. The projects of utopian fiction and social and economic reform would not intersect again with so much energy in England until the late nineteenth century. If post-Restoration utopias feel different than those they succeeded, the rejection of this reformist rigor may be partly the cause. A case could be made, however, that the poor had never been the subject of the utopias claiming to take up their cause between 1641 and 1660, but had been used as a convenient (and sentimental) symbol for the necessity of state intervention and control. In these terms, the utopias of industry, like the first workhouses in England, offered the poor assistance, but only for a price. Like Bacon's "nature," the poor provided utopists a continuous source of raw materials to study, experiment with, and eventually transform. It may be that like "nature," which Baconian science created in order to take apart, the English poor were as much a construction of these early utopias as the subject of their benevolence.

[Women] are not made citizens of the commonwealth. We hold no offices, nor bear we any authority therein. We are accounted neither useful in peace, nor serviceable in war. And if we be not citizens in the commonwealth, I know no reason we should be subjects to the commonwealth. And the truth is we are no subjects.
—Margaret Cavendish, *Sociable Letters*

She [Margaret Cavendish] should have had a microscope put in her hand. She should have been taught to look at the stars and reason scientifically. Her wits were turned with solitude and freedom.
—Virginia Woolf, *The Common Reader*

4. "No Subjects to the Commonwealth"

NATION AND IMAGINATION IN
MARGARET CAVENDISH'S
BLAZING-WORLD

April 1667. Lincoln's Inn Theater, recently reopened after the ravages of the Plague and the Great Fire, was packed with spectators. Samuel Pepys had come to this performance of the duke of Newcastle's *Humorous Lovers* mostly for a glimpse of Margaret Cavendish, who he believed had really written the play. He was in luck. At the performance's end, the duchess rose from her box to pay "respects" to the actors and actresses. In an astonishing moment, the bodice of her "antic dress"—curtained, like a miniature playhouse—sprung open, revealing her bare breasts. As one observer relayed, the duchess "was all ye pageant now discoursed on: Her brests all laid out to view in a playhouse with scarlett trimd nipples." This "outrageous upstaging" revealed the conjunction for Cavendish between power, performance, and display. In a characteristic gesture, she had transformed herself from spectator to spectacle.[1]

Despite Cavendish's alleged identification with Charles II, her return to England after the Interregnum was in most ways an anti-Restoration.[2] She and the duke had lost much of their wealth and lands during the war; her requests for membership in the Royal Society had been denied, and her literary productions were earning her notoriety rather than a "glorious fame" in her native country. None of her several dozen plays had been put on stage, a fact which must have rankled as she watched her husband's latest production. In her epistle to her second volume of plays, Cavendish averred that "malice cannot hinder me from Writing, wherein consists my chiefest delight and greatest pastime; nor from Printing what I write, since I regard not so much the present as future Ages, for which I intend all my Books."[3] Indeed, Cavendish continually tried to "publish" herself through her flamboyant costumes and eccentricities, subverting the constraints of her "present Age." But in her writing Cavendish interrogated self-display and its limits. As Wendy Wall puts it, "If women were tropes necessary to the process of writing, with what authority could a woman publish? How could she become an author if she was the 'Other' against which 'authors' differentiated themselves? If she was the body of the text?"[4] For Cavendish, always the "body" of the text as well as its author, performance offered the rehearsal of specularity more than inwardness, the opportunity to animate "the self in front of the gaze of others."[5] On the one hand, the stage allowed Cavendish to play out fantasies of absolute power, transgression, and revenge; on the other, to valorize restoration, the containment and consequences of spectacle.

The opening of the theaters in 1660 was one of the identifying acts of Charles II's new reign. On August 21, 1660, the king gave Thomas Killigrew and Sir William D'Avenant a royal grant as well

Here on this Figure Cast a Glance,
But so as if it were by Chance,
Your eyes not fixt, they must not Stay,
Since this like Shadowes to the Day
It only represent's; for Still,
Her Beuty's found beyond the Skill
Of the best Paynter, to Imbrace,
Those lovely Lines within her face;
View her Soul's Picture, Judgment, witt,
Then read those Lines which Shee hath writt,
By Phancy's Pencill drawne alone
Which Peece but Shee, Can justly owne.

Margaret Cavendish, from the frontispiece to her book *The World's Olio* (1655). Her allure, as the poem here suggests, is so compelling that not even the architectural figures that flank her can resist casting "a glance" her way. By permission of the Houghton Library, Harvard University.

as "full power and authority to Erect two Companies of Players." The Red Bull, the Cockpit, and Whitefriars boasted elaborate new set designs, orchestral accompaniment, and improved lighting, according to Killigrew.[6] *Restoration* and *theater* were terms that came to be seen as almost inevitably conjoined, from the triumphant spectacles associated with the king's coronation to the tortuous revenges exacted on his enemies, such as those inflicted on the exhumed body of Oliver Cromwell. As Laura Knoppers has observed, "Charles II, like his predecessors, was acclaimed and fashioned by public spectacle—ceremonies that deployed pageantry, splendor, and ritual. But . . . Restoration spectacle was marked by self-consciousness, anxiety and ambivalence, by internal fissures as well as by dependence upon the theater of punishment as dark twin to the celebratory pomp."[7]

Long before Charles II's romance with Nell Gwynn, the Caroline court was worrying about and appropriating theatrical power. Helgerson has pointed out that the theater (both an inclusive and exclusive institution) had offered itself as a simulacrum for the nation since the Elizabethan period. The popularity, indeed the "barbarity," of the theater allowed the English to fashion themselves through self-alienation, "the way to an acceptable national self." Paradoxically, for all its social inclusiveness the English theater tended to isolate and exclude "the popular, the socially marginal, the subversive, and the folk," consolidating power for the aristocracy and the monarchy.[8]

On the Restoration stage a new kind of inclusiveness demanded new forms of exclusion and purgation. The opportunity to see women performing provoked anxiety as well as amusement, gendering spectacle in new and significant ways.[9] As Sophie Tomlinson recounts, actresses had been countenanced as well as stigmatized in England before the Civil War. The Puritan William Prynne attacked actresses as "notorious whores" in his *Histrio-Mastix* (1633), but Queen Henrietta-Maria had given a number of performances both inside and outside the genre of court masque—performances which Cavendish as one of her ladies-in-waiting would certainly have seen. With the onset of the Civil War, Henrietta often adopted the dramatic role of the "martial lady" or Amazon Queen, a role which was to become an important model for Cavendish's literary characters from Lady Victoria in *Bell in Campo* to the empress in *The Blazing-world*.[10]

Cavendish's self-display at Lincoln's Inn may have been an extreme example, but patrons of Restoration theaters were accustomed to finding spectacles in the audience as well as on stage. People came hours before the production to secure a seat, and the pit was notoriously jammed and noisy, exhibiting all the features of that new social body, the urban crowd.[11] Pepys complained that the duke and duchess of York showed "impertinent . . . and unnatural dalliances there, before the whole world" at a performance at Whitehall. At one production, a woman in the next row turned and spat on Pepys, "but after seeing her to be a very pretty lady, I was not troubled by it at all." Pepys's wife, suffering from an intestinal disorder, had to bolt in the middle of a play to relieve herself in the adjacent fields; at another, she complained that she was not as finely dressed as other ladies in the audience, and only a later shopping spree at "the Exchange" could pacify her.[12] The English went to the theater to watch and to be watched, to take part in as well as to witness performance.

For Cavendish, for whom authority was usually self-ironizing, the potentialities of female performance always turned back on themselves. Her writings are "infinitely regressive," as Gallagher suggests, like a hall of mirrors in which spectacle is endlessly multiplied, each self-image successively smaller and further away than the one it succeeds. In the preface to *The Blazing-world*, Cavendish describes an imaginative restoration in which creative power compensates for the deficits of female authority: "I am not Covetous, but as Ambitious as ever any of my Sex was, is, or can be: which is the cause, that though I cannot be Henry the Fifth, or Charles the Second; yet, I will endeavour to be, Margaret the First: and though I have neither Power, Time, nor Occasion to be a great Conqueror, like Alexander or Caesar; yet rather than not be a Mistress of a world, since Fortune and the Fates would give me none, I have made one of my own."[13] The restoration Cavendish envisions here is at once imperial and trivial, for the world she has made, however marvelous, is a toy or substitute for the world she is denied.

In book 2 of *The Blazing-world*, the duchess of Newcastle, imported as scribe for the empress when none of the male authors she requests will accept the office, begins to demand a world of her own to govern. "Why should you desire to be Empress of a material world," the attendant spirits wonder, "and be troubled with the cares that attend government? When as by creating a world within yourself, you may enjoy all both in whole and in parts, without controle or opposition, and make what you please, and alter it when you please?" According to the attendant spirits, the imagination is a colony waiting to be discovered, like an Abraxa or Bensalem: "for every humane creature can create an immaterial world, fully inhabited by immaterial creatures, and populous of immaterial creatures, such as we are . . . he may make a world of Ideas, a world of Atoms, a world of lights, or whatsoever his fancy leads him to" (50, 96–97). These pronouncements have often been read as evidence for Cavendish's unqualified defense of the imagination, but the duchess is in fact reminded here that the spirits are already "immaterial subjects" in the empress's "immaterial" world, as is the duchess herself. Cavendish would have been the first to acknowledge the limited nature of authority in a world constructed by and for others. For her, the imagination was a colony, not an empire, and even in her imaginary kingdom somebody else had already claimed the throne.

CAVENDISH, BORN Margaret Lucas, was the eighth and youngest child in a Royalist and staunchly Catholic family. When the war broke out, she joined the makeshift court of Henrietta-Maria in Oxford, traveling with the queen and her entourage first to Bath and then, after the battle at Marston Moor, to France. In Paris she met a number of other exiled English Royalists, among them William Cavendish, then earl and later duke of Newcastle. Cavendish was twenty; Newcastle (a recent widower) was fifty-three: "My Lord, having but two sons, purposed to marry me, a young woman that might prove fruitful to him and increase his posterity by a male offspring. Nay, he was so desirous of male issue that I have heard him say he cared not (so God would be pleased to give him many sons) although they came to be persons of the meanest fortunes."[14] Cavendish accepted his proposal, but failed to produce any children, a consequence, according to one of the doctors Newcastle consulted on her behalf, of her eccentric ambitions.[15] For fifteen years the couple lived in France and in the Netherlands, waiting for the reinstallation of the king. It was on the Continent that Cavendish slowly began to establish herself as a writer and scientific philosopher. In Paris she was introduced to Gassendi, Descartes, and Thomas Hobbes, but though she was ostensibly accepted in their circles, her critics hinted that this was only for the sake of her husband.

Cavendish received no formal education. In her autobiography she describes the frustration of watching her brothers study philosophy and literature while she and her sisters were taught only to dance, embroider, and play musical instruments. Having struggled on her own to compensate for this deficit through voluminous reading and writing, Cavendish found it as difficult to place her creative work as to place herself. Despite flattering letters from the universities to whom she dedicated texts—letters no doubt hoping that bequests from her husband would follow—Cavendish never felt she had garnered a real audience or a legitimate position as an author. As she observes in her preface to *The World's Olio*, women had no models who held position or property in either intellectual or artistic realms:

> It was not a woman that found out the invention of writing
> letters and the art of printing. What women were such sol-
> diers as Hannibal, Caesar, Tamburlaine, Alexander, and
> Scanderberg? What woman was such a chemist as Paracelsus,
> such a physician as Hippocrates or Galen, such a poet as
> Homer, such a painter as Apelles, such a carver as Pygmalion,
> such an architect as Vitruvius, such a musician as Orpheus?
> What women ever found out the Antipodes in imagination
> before they were found out by navigation, as a bishop did?
> Or whatever did we do but like apes by imitation?

Cavendish's desire to "find out" an invention increasingly led her to natural philosophy. In the late 1650s she began to reject poetry and fiction, "so suited to a lady's pen," in favor of philosophy and science.[16] Her *Philosophical and Physical Opinions* (1657) and *Observations On Experimental Philosophy* (1666) were the first scientific studies by a woman to be published in England. Of all Cavendish's eccentricities—her reclusiveness, her unusual costumes, her outspoken and unconventional views on women—it was her interest in science that struck her contemporaries as the most bizarre. When Cavendish wrote *The Blazing-world* in 1666, she appended her utopia, as Bacon had, to a document of scientific speculation. But for Cavendish, the scientific academy would remain private, an institute of the imagination and not the nation. Cavendish's exclusion from the Royal Society may have been the most painful denial of entrance she experienced after her return to England in the early 1660s. While Charles II could issue charters and grant foundations, Cavendish was not even allowed to join.

The Weighing of Air

May 1667. According to Pepys and Evelyn, London was buzzing with the news of Cavendish's request: an invitation to the Royal Society for a tour of its widely lauded experiments. Hot debates ensued, in Pepys's words, "many being against it." Cavendish's request enlarged her celebrity while furthering her estrangement from London society. Pepys had been pursuing her all spring, since she and Newcastle had come to the city from Wellbeck. "The whole story of this Lady is romance, and all she do is Romantick," Pepys noted in his diary on April 11: "There is so much expectation of her coming to Court, that so [many] people may come to see her, as if it were the Queen of Sweden." On several successive days in April and May he tried to catch sight of her. Nor was Pepys alone in this endeavor: "That which we, and almost all went for, was to see my Lady Newcastle; which we could not, she being followed and crowded upon by coaches all the way she went, that nobody could come near her . . . and so, back the same way and out to St. Jones, thinking to have met my Lady Newcastle before she got home, but we staying by the way to drink, she got home a little before us, so we lost our labours." On May 10 Pepys "drove hard to Clerkenwell thinking to have overtaken my Lady Newcastle, whom I saw before us in her coach, with 100 boys and girls running looking upon her: but I could not." What these hundred boys and girls wanted from Cavendish is hard to determine. For his own part, Pepys seems to have wanted to confirm his approbation. By the spring of 1668 he had made up his mind that Cavendish was a "mad, conceited, ridiculous woman" and her husband an "asse" to permit her to write what she did.[17] But Pepys consistently sought Cavendish out to confirm this negative review. When he learned she was to visit the Royal Society, he made sure he was part of the crowd in attendance.

Like the newly opened theaters, the Royal Society epitomized the cultural charter of the Restoration. Here, its apostles claimed, political schism and private interest could be reconciled in the performance of empirical labor. The Society, which comprised mostly well-to-do Londoners, some serious scientists, and some amateurs, saw itself as a bulwark of the new London, officializing experiment for a realm that had rejected experimental government. Like many single-minded organizations, the Royal Society prided itself on principles of democracy and debate. No voice should be excluded from its dialogue, not even the *foreign*, Sprat magnanimously claimed in his *History*. Like Bensalem, its spiritual model, the Society suggested it would willingly import all "inquisitive strangers" who could offer aid: "We are to overcome the mysteries of all the Works of Nature; and not only to prosecute such as are confin'd to one kingdom, or beat upon one shore. We should not then refuse to list all the aids that come in, how remote soever. . . . To this purpose, the Royal Society has made no scruple, to receive all inquisitive strangers of all Countries, into its number."[18]

For Cavendish's "country," however, the Society was ill-prepared. Though critics have largely dismissed Cavendish's scientific writings, the questions she explored in her *Philosophical Letters* (1664) compare favorably with the speculations of the Society's chief luminaries, such as Robert Hooke and Robert Boyle. While the Society pondered such questions as "whether diamonds and other Precious Stones grow again after three or four years, in the same place where they have been digged out?" or "Why Thunders and Lightnings happen, and what Effects they produce; as souring

Beer, turning Milk, killing Silk-worms, and etc.," they were dismissive of Cavendish's curiosity about why flame ascends in a pointed figure, whether there is sense and perception in matter, if it is possible to have an idea of God, why sound is louder in a vault than not, what composes colors, and what makes an echo.[19] These were apparently not subjects for women to explore. Fiction might be seen as decorative or entertaining, like music or embroidery, but science, like politics, belonged to men. The more strenuously Cavendish fought for admission to its society, the more foreign, the more a spectacle, she would appear.

The much-discussed visit to the Royal Society took place on May 27, 1667. Cavendish, Pepys noted with irritation, was late. When she at last arrived she swept into the building with a host of waiting women, "six being necessary to carry her train alone." A roster of experiments, recorded in the Society's minutes for that week, had been set up to impress her:

> 1. Those of colours. 2. The mixing of cold liquors, which upon their infusion grow hot. 3. The swimming of bodies in the midst of water. 4. The dissolving of meat in the oil of vitriol. 5. The weighing of air in a receiver, by means of the rarefying engine. 6. The marbles exactly flattened. 7. Some magnetical experiments, and in particular that of a terrella driving away the steel-dust at its poles. 8. A good microscope.

But the staging of these experiments was eclipsed by Cavendish's visit, itself a spectacle, like the weighing of air, which could provoke nothing more than "admiration." Here, as at Lincoln's Inn, Cavendish was both spectator and spectacle; whatever she was looking at, nobody else was looking at anything but her. John Evelyn observed that she arrived with "much pomp," and his ballad on the occasion anxiously mocks her masculine deportment: "God bless us! when I first did see her / She looked so like a Cavalier / but that she has no beard!"[20] Pepys found his distaste and disappointment confirmed:

> The Duchesse hath been a good, comely woman, but her dress is so antick, and her deportment so ordinary, that I do

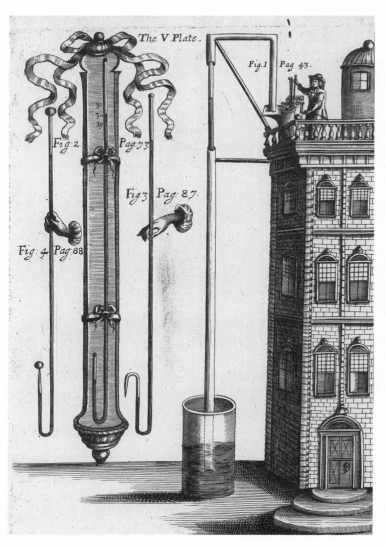

Weighing the air. From Robert Boyle, *A Continuation of New Experiments Physico-Mechanical Touching the Spring and Weight of the Air* (1669). By permission of the Houghton Library, Harvard University.

not like her at all, nor did I hear her say anything that was worth hearing, but that she was full of admiration, all admiration. . . . After they had shown her many experiments, and she cried out still that she was full of admiration, she departed, being led out and in by several Lords that were there. . . . She gone, I by coach home.[21]

Most displeasing to Pepys was how "ordinary" this celebrity proved up close. Why didn't she say "anything that was worth hearing" in front of so great a crowd? Pepys wanted Cavendish to perform, to provoke wonder rather than to experience it. His summary of her visit suggests that it worked, once again, to exclude the duchess, this time through a token visit. For once again it was Cavendish who was on display and Cavendish who was found wanting.

In book 1 of her utopia, Cavendish imaginatively transforms her visit to the Royal Society, turning what must have felt like a snub into a fantasy of acceptance and inclusion. In *The Blazing-world* the empress, like Charles II, is benefactor and patron of her own scientific society, and all her questions are taken seriously. "To increase the Powers of all Mankind, and to free them from the bondage of Errors, is greater glory than to enlarge Empire," Sprat had written to Charles II in his *Dedicatory Epistle*. In Cavendish's utopia women are given authority both to increase knowledge and to enlarge empire, restoring their status through science, religion, and battle. *The Blazing-world* revises and estranges history so that the mimetic and fantastic become intertwined, but Cavendish was not entirely able, in the words of Luce Irigaray, to "transform language's frontiers," to get beyond a representation that defined itself in opposition to masculine models.[22] Behind her utopia is an unarticulated but insistent question: did women have a Restoration? The answer, even in Cavendish's daring utopia, must be finally that they did not. It is true that women in the Blazing-world are able to borrow the role of monarch. But monarchy is a contested institution for Cavendish, a performance at times powerful, at others a mere toy.

Blazing Worlds

Cavendish wrote her utopia in 1666, that infamous year of calamity, self-scrutiny, and apocalyptic ruin. As Knoppers points out, the Plague and Fire exposed its horrified witnesses to unparalleled "spectacles of misery."[23] In four days in early September 1666, most of the city of London burned to the ground. Thirteen thousand, two hundred houses were destroyed, as were most of London's public buildings and over eighty churches, including the old Saint Paul's. The fire moved slowly enough so that spectators, like Pepys, were able to watch it like a morality play from the relative safety of the Thames:

> All over the Thames, with ones face in the wind you were almost burned with a shower of Firedrops—this is very true— as houses were burned by these drops and flakes of fire, three or four, nay, five or six houses, one from another. When we could endure no more upon the water, we to a little alehouse on the Bankside over against the Three Cranes, and there stayed [until?] it was dark almost and saw the fire grow; and as it grew darker, it appeared more and more, and in corners and upon steeples and between churches and houses, as far as we could see up the hill of the City, in a most horrid malicious bloody flame, not like a fine flame of an ordinary fire. . . . We stayed till, it being darkish, we saw the fire as only one entire arch of fire from this to the other side of the bridge, and in a bow up the hill, for an arch of above a mile long. It made me weep to see it. The churches, houses, and all on fire and flaming at once, and a horrid noise the flames made, and the cracking of houses at their ruine.[24]

Initially, the blaze did not cause undue alarm. Fires were common enough in English towns that during the Civil War and Interregnum William Gosling's "Seasonable Advice for Preventing the Mischiefe of Fire" was "thought very necessary to hang in every man's house, especially in these dangerous times." Bonfires were set regularly during celebrations, including the coronation of Charles II and days of victory during the Second Dutch War. Small fires were set deliberately during outbreaks of plague to disinfect afflicted households, and in 1665–66 such bonfires would have been particularly numerous.[25] In fact, the mayor of London first reacted to news of the Great Fire with scorn, insulted he had been awakened on its account and complaining that even a *woman* could piss out a blaze so small. But dry weather and strong winds accelerated the fire. Within four days over 100,000 people were without homes and five-sixths of the city was destroyed. As John Evelyn noted on September 7, the ground he walked on was so hot it burned his feet through his shoes, and for weeks smoke continued to linger in burnt-out buildings.[26]

While the fire first "took on the character of penal ceremony," Knoppers points out that Royalists eventually began to "reread the spectacle or to find a counterspectacle as sign of a divine hand." The Fire's punishment was thus seen as corrective, indicating "divine love as well as wrath" and confirming England's status as a nation-elect.[27] Two famous accounts link the Fire to the Restoration, praising Charles II's tactful and appropriate action during and after the disaster and suggesting a connection between architectural and political rebuilding.[28] John Evelyn's diary contains several descriptions of the king ministering to the needy and ceremoniously restoring order, providing a "little touch of Harry in the night" to his bereft subjects.[29] The Great Fire gave Royalists an opportunity to represent the new king's strength in a time of crisis. In the days and weeks following the calamity, nationalist sentiment was running high, and despite widespread belief that the fire was the result of God's wrath, suspects were being sought closer to home.[30] In 1666 England was at war with the Dutch and their French allies over trade disputes, and the court appears to have subtly encouraged scapegoating of French and Dutch suspects, sensing that the conviction of a political enemy would strengthen support for England's military efforts abroad. When a twenty-six-year-old French watchmaker named Hubert confessed to starting the blaze, he was hanged with great publicity at Tyburn, despite glaring inconsistencies in his testimony.[31] It did not hurt Charles II to renew English zeal against foreign enemies, however dubious allegations of arson came to seem.[32]

The domestic crisis of the Great Fire presented Charles with the material task of restoration, the great theme of his reign. This task called for political as well as architectural vision. If the fire was caused by insurrection, internal or external, Charles II's court would expunge it. If the old London (and its monarchy) had been frail and susceptible, the new London would be strong and enduring. On September 13 John Evelyn presented Charles with a "plot for a new Citty," matching the spirit of the new monarchy: this city would endure, where its predecessor had been vulnerable.[33]

It was John Dryden who brought the Restoration and the Great Fire together most closely in his utopian poem of 1666, *Annus Mirabilis*. For Dryden, the Great Fire was represented as purifying and ennobling, signaling the beginning of a new era. London, which Dryden represents as Phoenix-like and feminine,[34] is free now to rise up on her "new foundations":

> More great than humane, now, and more August,
> New deified, she from her fires does rise:
> Her widening streets on new foundations trust,
> And opening, into larger parts she flies.[35]

Dryden's poem is not nostalgic for the old London, but rather sees in the devastation of the fire the possibility, if not the necessity, for a restored capital, a kind of second temple. Like Evelyn, Dryden rereads ruin as a sign of national election.

Margaret Cavendish, unlike Evelyn, Pepys, and Dryden, produced no eyewitness account of the Great Fire. She was not in the city when the disaster struck, but she did return to London several times in 1666–67 and must have been impressed both by the extent of the devastation and the energies devoted to the city's renewal. Especially striking given the absence of any mention of the Fire in her *Sociable Letters* or her *Autobiography* is the title she chose for the utopia written in the disaster's aftermath. The Great Fire offered Cavendish a symbol bringing together spectacle and incendiary power. "Of all creatures, fire is the most ready to occasion the most Mischief; at least, Disorders; for where it can get entrance, it seldom fails of causing such a Disturbance, as occasions a Ruine," she wrote in her *Grounds of Natural Philosophy* (1668). In her utopia Cavendish

London in Flames, London in Glory. "In 1666, September 2, a Fire broke out in Pudding lane near Fish-Street hill, which in four days burnt down 13,200 Houses." From R. Burton, *Historical Remarks and Observations upon the Ancient and Present State of London and Westminster* (London, 1703). By permission of the Houghton Library, Harvard University.

sees "disturbance" both as an instrument and consequence of Restoration. Men may govern, but women are left to *blaze*.

The Description of a New World, Call'd, The Blazing-world (1666), seems to be one of those texts that will not allow itself to be read. It has been variously accused of being disjointed, hallucinatory, narcissistic, and vain. For some critics, *The Blazing-world* has been seen as sororal and benign, a corrective to the masculinist utopias it takes (partly) as models.[36] But Cavendish's politics have continually perturbed her most sanguine readers. Her feminism is quixotic, her Toryism, self-promotion, and self-interest troubling. *The Blazing-world* fluctuates between thinly veiled compliments for monolithic royalism and digressive pleas for the recovery of Cavendish jewels, money, and land. Her romance is less accessible to most modern readers than More's *Utopia* or Bacon's *New Atlantis*, populated with fantastic, cartoonlike creatures adapted from the classical satires of Lucian; long digressions on science distract the reader from the story of the Blazing-world as an ideal place; and in the second book the utopia abruptly shifts its focus from the advantages of the Blazing-world to the problems of Europe and of England, reversing More's paradigm by ending in the real world rather than in the ideal. Closer to Continental writers of science fiction like Kepler and de Bergerac than to English utopists, Cavendish's utopia has struck many readers as peculiarly solitary, a text outside genre or tradition.[37]

It is important neither to discredit Cavendish's position within the tradition of English utopianism nor to deemphasize her desire to alter that tradition. The science fiction in Cavendish's utopia, frequently condemned as ludicrous or psychotic, comes out of a rich tradition in the early seventeenth century, and Cavendish's speculations on space travel and worlds elsewhere could be interestingly compared with John Wilkins's *Discovery of a World in the Moone* and Francis Godwin's *The Man in the Moone* (1638). Cavendish's utopia—the first published by a woman in England—is concerned with estrangement, isolation, and the relationship between real and invented worlds. Like More, Bacon, Gott, and Winstanley, Cavendish participates in the English utopian tradition of privileging and interrogating institutional models. But Cavendish explicitly genders monarchy, the renewed institution she chooses as the organizing model for her ideal commonwealth. Monarchy for Cavendish is the site at which the sexual and the political come together, as Catherine Gallagher has argued.[38] "Female monarchy" in the Blazing-world is curiously self-canceling, as the empress borrows her authority from an emperor who is, however invisible, the commonwealth's real source of power. Arguably, his transfer of authority renders both figures impotent, revealing royal power to be performative rather than absolute. Cavendish moves back and forth in her utopia between the idealization of monarchy and its rejection. Her heroine is transformed to autocrat in utopia and redressed in empress's clothing, but her transformation has the quality of theater, of playing the lead in a necessarily finite production. To play monarch in this realm is to blaze, in the sense of shielding, shining, and blazoning as well as burning. But as the lessons of 1666 would have confirmed, the power of blazing could eventually be construed as the power of containment.

The Emperor's Clothes

Cavendish's *Blazing-world* is set not in this world but in a world supplemental to it, "too far off to be discerned by our optick perception," a world at once accessible and supernal. The supplementary relationship of this world to its neighbors is one of the text's most prominent and anxious subjects. The utopia itself, as Cavendish claims in her preface ("To All Noble and Worthy Ladies"), "was made as an Appendix to my Observations Upon Experimental Philosophy; and having some sympathy and coherence with each other, were joyned together as two several worlds" (5, 3). But as "most Ladies take no delight in Philosophical Arguments," Cavendish has fashioned a "philosophical" romance for their pleasure. The ladies' text supplements the men's; romance supplements science; the empress, the emperor; and the imagination, the nation. Perhaps most remarkably, the "founding" of the imagined nation is supplemented by a dramatic and powerful unfounding in the utopia's second book.

In the first book of *The Blazing-world* a young woman is seized by a man who wants her for her beauty. He drags her off with him in a boat, but luckily the boat is "forced into another world" beyond the North Pole, and the abductor and his assistants perish, "not being provided for so cold a voyage." Only the young woman miraculously survives. When she reaches the Blazing-world she is greeted by its peculiar inhabitants, mixed-genre creatures such as Bear-men and Fox-men, who take her to their archipelago-capital and introduce her to their emperor. Swooning over her beauty, the emperor insists on making her his wife, once he is assured she is mortal and not divine. As it is her beauty which secures this union, the emperor's proposal both redeems and repeats the romance's earlier abduction. No sooner are they married than the emperor makes her a gift of his power, allowing her to act as "absolute Monarch" in his stead. She is thus free to do what she pleases—to establish a private scientific academy, in which the Bear-men and Fox-men teach her all the natural secrets of that world; to convert the inhabitants of the kingdom to Christianity in her blazing chapels; and finally, to import the duchess of Newcastle to be her "scribe" as she prepares to write a cabbala.

The theatrical fantasy of the young woman's conversion to empress is marked by her change in costume. From the outset, blazing in the Blazing-world is both dazzling and frightening. It can be staged like spectacle, flashed like a weapon, or worn like clothing. From the empress's initial promotion at marriage, she is dressed in blazing clothes, clothes that signal terror as well as magnificence:

> On her head she wore a Cap of Pearl, and a Half-moon of
> Diamonds just before it; on the top of her Crown came
> spreading over a broad Carbuncle, cut in the form of the
> Sun; her Coat was of Pearl, mixt with blew Diamonds, and
> fringed with red ones; her Buskins and Sandals were of green
> Diamonds. In her left hand she held a Buckler, to signifie the
> Defenses of her Dominions; which Buckler was made of that
> sort of Diamond as has several different Colours. . . . In her
> right hand she carried a Spear made of white Diamond, cut

like the tail of a Blazing Star, which signified that she was
ready to assault those that proved her enemies. (10)

In the Blazing-world, diamonds are mined not from the earth
but from stars. Their blaze, like the blaze of starlight, is celestial,
poetic, associated with the best light of the blaze of this new
world. But there is a less benign quality to the empress's costume as
well; sometimes she blazes to entertain, sometimes to terrify. The
people she must subdue include the "unconverted" populace of the
Blazing-world, whom she sets out to convert early in book 1. With
great care she constructs a two-story chapel, paving the upper
chamber with "starstone" or diamond to provide brilliant light and
paving the lower with "firestone," a "certain stone, whose nature
was such, that being wetted it would grow excessively hot, and
break forth in flaming fire." The empress delivers sermons in these
chapels, appearing "like an angel" in the upper chamber, where the
light blazes without heat. But in the "chappel which was lined with
Firestone the Empress preached Sermons of Terror to the wicked,
and told them of the punishments for their sins, to wit, that after
this life they should be tormented in Everlasting fire" (33–34). In
this theatrical chapel, what Knoppers calls the dual "spectacles of
punishment and power" of the early Restoration are aptly demonstrated.[39]

Blaze is never defined in Cavendish's utopia, but it is alluded to in
an important passage early in the empress's scientific tutorial with
the spirits. She asks them what causes thunder and lightning. They
offer several explanations, concluding, "Some answer that it is sudden and monstrous Blaz, stirred up in the air" (16). This originary
force is incendiary and destructive as well as luminous or divine.
Blazing is contested and contradictory, like utopian discourse itself. The most important appearance of the term *blazing* comes in
the utopia's title, for the real blazing world, the place where the
opposing meanings of *blaze* most importantly conjoin, is in the
imagination. Here the duchess can finally rule, as Utopus ruled in
Utopia or Salomona in Bacon's *New Atlantis*. For Cavendish, then,
imagination becomes a kind of anti-nation, a place where power

can be restored and ruin eradicated. But the penalty of such power is the knowledge that it is merely a toy, that this is a realm, like the theater, where authority is temporary and artificial. Even in her utopia the duchess must be secondary, a scribe rather than a monarch, and the role does not fully appease her. Despite the intimacy between the empress and duchess (who become "Platonick lovers"), their relationship is strictly hierarchized. In the Blazing-world authority is borrowed rather than owned: the duchess borrows hers from the empress, who borrows hers in turn from the emperor. And even in this imaginary realm the source of authority, dormant or dominant, is male.

Native Countries

One of the most remarkable features of Cavendish's utopia is the fluidity with which it draws its borders. Avowedly nostalgic throughout, the characters in *The Blazing-world* often yearn for home, longing to restore their native countries to the splendors they now inhabit. The duchess in book 1 cannot forget the state of England, torn apart by civil war. She urges the empress to travel back to England with her through a kind of metempsychosis, and when they do, they survey the ravages of war and together lament the duchess's loss of property. This return visit ruptures the perfection of book 1's idealized court, offering an embedded theater of ruin within the utopian narrative. England is the "other" of the Blazing-world, a place where ownership and ruin still bear the names of "lord and husband." As the duchess explains to the empress, "There had been a long Civil Warr in that Kingdom, in which most of the best Timber-trees and Principal Palaces were ruined and destroyed; and my dear Lord and Husband, said she, has lost by it half his Woods, besides many Houses, Land, and moveable Goods. . . . I wish, said the Empress, he had some of the Gold that is in the Blazing-world, to repair his losses. The Duchess most humbly thank'd her Imperial Majesty for her kind wishes; but, said she, Wishes will not repair his ruins" (56).

"Ruin" is the thematic center of this passage, as of the whole utopia. What has occasioned it? What can repair it? War and destruction stand on one side of ruin, repair and wishes on the other. The empress and duchess transform ruin into a spectacle, separated from it by their present good fortune. But they recognize that none of their gold from the Blazing-world can be carried back to repair English losses. Their wealth, like their power, has value only in their imaginary realm. England for them remains the site of exclusion, of invisible and unusable power.

The second book of *The Blazing-world* envisions the boundaries between real and irreal worlds quite differently. The empress learns her native country is being attacked by enemies. With the duchess's counsel she forms an armada, bringing with her a special mineral called firestone mined from the "Burning-Mountains." Its property is "that it burns so long as it is wet" (66). With this substance the empress creates a spectacle of terror in which the enemy is subdued, and she is able to reveal herself as her country's savior. Once back in her native country, the empress reenacts the punitive spectacle of the Great Fire, teaching a lesson not only to her country's enemies but to her own skeptical countrymen, who refuse to believe she can assist them. Lining the enemies' homes and public buildings with firestone, she waits for rain to make the disaster complete. When it does, "upon a sudden all their Houses appeared of a flaming Fire, and the more Water there was poured on them, the more they did flame and burn; which struck with such a Fright and Terror into the Neighboring Cities, Nations, and Kingdoms, that . . . they granted the Empress's desire, and submitted to the Monarch and Sovereign of her Native Countrey" (71).

Cavendish's empress uses fire as spectacle to prove to her countrymen that she is powerful enough to save them. When a messenger asks her "country," she responds elliptically:

> I will appear, said she, to your Navy in a splendorous Light, surrounded with Fire. . . . The appointed hour being come, the Empress appear'd with Garments made of Star-stone, and was born or supported above the Water, upon the Fish-mens heads and backs so that she seemed to walk upon the face of the Water, and the Bird- and Fish-men carried the Firestone, lighted both in the Air, and Above the Waters (68).

This response might seem at first to beg the question of national identity, but instead it offers a revision. When the empress appears in this guise before her countrymen, they kneel before her and worship her with "all submission and reverence," in awe of her "garments of Light," which make her appear "like an Angel or some Deity." This is, in effect, the empress's Restoration. Transformed from an ordinary woman to empress in the court of the Blazing-world, she is now transformed for her "native countreymen," to whom she explains that she was once "subject of this Kingdom" but is now "a great and Absolute Princess" (68). Her role as empress is not to rule benignly in the Blazing-world but rather to come back to her own country and to destroy its enemies. "Blazing" now becomes part of a theater of heroism and acceptance. Cavendish congratulates the empress of her utopia for "firing a City" to demonstrate her power. Blazing, restoration, and ruin are brought together as the empress demonstrates that women can wield power, can indeed have a "country," but that their identity will always require the invention of new names, new arsenals, and new kinds of performance.

Ironically, the best-known myth of fire in Western culture—the legend of Prometheus—has often been interpreted as a myth of masculine transumption. Gaston Bachelard has seen in the Prometheus legend "all those tendencies which impel [men] to know as much as [their] fathers," tendencies he believes constitute no less than the "unconscious of the scientific mind."[40] For Bachelard, as for Bacon, the "scientific mind" is masculine; its struggles and achievements can be articulated only through competition, theft, and punishment. Freud also saw the Prometheus legend as the record of masculine struggle in which the theft of fire necessitated divine revenge. According to Freud, Prometheus' "hollow rod" (which he uses to steal fire) is matched in "ordinary men" by the phallus, which admittedly cannot carry fire but instead its opposite, water, "the means of quenching fire." (Male) dreams of putting out fires are so common, Freud claims, because the phallus's "two functions" (procreation and urination) are in this way united.[41] This is reminiscent of the mayor of London's scornful remark on being roused to hear that London was burning in 1666—that the fire was so small "even a *woman* could piss it out." What is grandiose and transcendent for men (for whom even urination is heroic) is degraded for women—ludicrous, weak, a mere trickle.

Cavendish's utopia—which, like the legend of Prometheus, is a narrative about the acquisition and control of fire—reproduces as it defies the kind of scorn recorded by the mayor. For despite the power of this text, which genders blazing to show that fire can be magnificent as well as terrible, Cavendish frames her utopia with self-deprecating dismissals. The duchess is keenly aware of coming second. Her role of scribe is descriptive, not active. Even her handwriting, she tells her readers, is poor. The littleness of her utopia makes it a kind of toy, a bibelot—a woman's weak trickle, something capable of putting out only a small fire, hardly of starting a great one.

Cavendish divides her representation of feminine power between the incendiary empress and the supplementary duchess. The duchess, though she advises the action, is not permitted to blaze. Instead, as in the biography of Cavendish's husband (to which her own autobiography is an appendix), hers is the task of the blazon, the chronicle of praise for someone else. Even if she could be restored to the reign of Margaret the First, in other words, Cavendish could never occasion ruin like the empress. Hers is a diminished realm, a guided tour rather than full membership. It is not Charles II with whom Cavendish identifies, then, or even (entirely) with her imaginary and harmful empress, for whom fire is not just an event, not something to spectate or to put out, but an instrument of transformation and of triumph. It is the fictional duchess of Newcastle, with her bad handwriting and self-deprecation, imported to write somebody else's story, to admire someone else's coronation, to tell her own story only as an appendix to the one that really matters. In comparison, the duchess's story (of lost name, lost property, and lost opportunity) is an "appendix," a bow from the stage rather than the play itself.

It is characteristic of Cavendish's writing that the epilogue to *The Blazing-world* is a disclaimer. Apologizing for her narrative's flaws, Cavendish reminds her readers that she has done "little harm," that only a few men were killed in her text and those in its first few pages. Witty as this disclaimer is meant to be, she reminds her readers in this way that the imagination can be as harmful a place as any, and though she retreats from it, she has represented the place of fiction not as pacific or unified but as potentially powerful and violent. Unlike the watchmaker who died claiming he had set a fire which he had not, Cavendish in her utopia starts a fire and then denies it. Its meanings are too complex, too harmful to own even within the transformative discourse of fiction.

It is a great irony of literary history, given the title and subject of *The Blazing-world*, that the one compliment Virginia Woolf should have had for Margaret Cavendish was that she had in her writing a "vein of genuine fire."[42] Few other readers have seen that vein or seen it with pleasure. Perhaps this is because of the peculiar mix of the mimetic and the fantastic in Cavendish's writing, a mix that can be attributed to her desire to overwrite her predecessors, to make forms new without losing the authority of extant formulae. The contradictory quality of "blazing" in Cavendish's utopia is part of the struggle she represents between the power and the limits of the "alter-nation." Women's role in Cavendish's utopia is divided between ruin and restoration, for while the empress blazes with jewels and weapons, stunning her enemies, the duchess cannot even hope to recover what she has lost—property, title, place. Cavendish's utopia dismantles the distinction between ruin and restoration, between the celebratory and punitive elements of theatrical power. Just as the women's return to England in book 1 affords ruin inside of restoration, the magnificent fire set by the empress in book 2 offers restoration inside ruin. In the theater of the English Restoration, these are two aspects of a single play.

For there is no Maxim more infallible and hold-
ing in any science, than this in the Politics, that
Empire is founded in Property.—Henry Neville,
Plato Redivivus

Do we not find that in every family the government of one is most natural?—Robert Filmer,
Patriarcha

5. Nation, Miscegenation

MEMBERING UTOPIA IN HENRY
NEVILLE'S *ISLE OF PINES*

In 1668, in the first phase of the Restoration when
self-consciousness about England's identity as a nation was particularly acute, the Republican Henry Neville published a remarkable utopia loosely based on the Old Testament legend of Noah.
Neville was not alone in this period in his interest in the biblical
patriarch. Robert Filmer, for example, the Restoration's most famous defender of patriarchal power, saw Noah as the archetypal
father and king, a source of the dispersal and subsequent "establishment of regal power throughout the kingdoms of the world."[1]

For others in early modern England, Noah was associated not only with the origins of paternal power but with the beginnings of racial difference.

In the 1570s a mariner named George Best circulated an account in which he claimed that dark skin color was caused not by over-exposure to sunlight, as Richard Eden had argued a generation before him, but by "natural infection" originating in ancient disobedience. According to Best's account, Noah's son Ham was punished for filial treachery by producing a "black and loathsome" son named Cush:

> When Noah at the commandment of God had made the Ark
> and entered therein, and the floodgates of heaven were
> opened, so that the whole face of the earth, every tree and
> mountain was covered with abundance of water, he straitly
> commanded his sons and their wives, that they should with
> reverence and fear behold the justice and mighty power of
> God, and that during the time of the Flood while they re-
> mained in the Ark, they should use continency, and abstain
> from carnal copulation with their wives: and many other pre-
> cepts he gave unto them, and admonitions. . . . Which good
> instructions and exhortations notwithstanding his wicked son
> Ham disobeyed, and being persuaded that the first child born
> after the Flood (by right and law of nature) should inherit
> and possess all the dominions of the earth, he contrary to his
> father's commandment while they were yet in the Ark, used
> company with his wife, and craftily went about thereby to dis-
> inherit the offspring of his other two brethren: for the which
> wicked and detestable fact, as an example for contempt of
> almighty God, and disobedience of parents, God would a
> son should be born whose name was Cush, who not only
> itself, but all his posterity after him should be so black and
> loathsome, that it might remain a spectacle of disobedience
> to all the world.[2]

For Henry Neville in the 1660s, the retelling of the legend of Noah, Ham, and Cush in *The Isle of Pines* allowed for the presenta-tion of a new kind of utopia—one in which national identity depends on the very act of interracial crossing established by the colony as most taboo. In *The Isle of Pines* three topics new to the genre of utopia are presented, topics which I will suggest are connected: African slavery, political insurrection, and English sexual desire. Through the convergence of these topics, Neville's utopia presents patriarchal superiority both as exemplary and as explosive, for while it is the subordination of the eroticized and racialized Other which defines "Englishness," that subordination is shown to conclude in violence.

Neville's utopia has attracted scant attention despite its role as a likely source for Defoe's *Robinson Crusoe*. The text has been available in only one edition in this century and is mentioned in almost none of the criticism on early modern fiction, utopianism, or colonialist literature.[3] *The Isle of Pines* is the "true story" of a Dutch sea captain's discovery of an island inhabited by a colony of English men and women, all deriving their ancestry from the island's eponymous founder, George Pine, and his four mistresses, three white women and one black slave. Philippa, the slave (she has no surname), is a female version of Cush; like Cush, she is doomed to bequeath her "loathsome" blackness to her progeny, reproducing her otherness as if to punish the Pines for their paternal and imperial greed. As a woman, her role in the narrative is especially complicated. Pine must be punished for allowing himself to engage in sexual relations with her, and their union is at once the site at which the utopian colony is created and at which it is destroyed. Philippa and her offspring point retrospectively to the vexed issue of utopian slavery, which dates back to More's *Utopia* in the early modern period and to Plato's *Republic* in the classical. It is not the institution of slavery which is new to utopias in this period, but rather the conjunction between slavery and racial difference. Utopias before Neville's were presented as racially homogenous. Some utopists, like the Italian Tommasso Campanella in *La Cita del Sol* (1623), had included strenuous eugenics programs in their colonies to minimize physical differences among citizens, like over- or underweight or unusual beauty or plainness.[4] While the desire to eradicate difference persists in *The Isle of Pines*, it runs parallel to a stronger desire to experience and racialize difference and, more-

A DESCRIPTION OF ᵉ ISLE OF PINES

How they were cast away

gathering there Ship wracke

Pine · Numbring his People

ᵉ Dutch ship taking ᵉ ‑writing ‑

Frontispiece to Henry Neville's *The Isle of Pines* (1668). By permission of the Huntington Library, San Marino, California.

over, to use the idea of difference to justify social and political hierarchies. Neville's utopia is the master's story. For Neville, the colonial utopia is presented as a political (and sexual) body that must and can be mastered but that breaks to pieces once its European visitors pull away. Aptly, Pine's "master's daughter" is called Sarah English, and the tribe descended from her is known by her surname. As I will suggest, Neville illumines the classifications in *The Isle of Pines* that most matter to him and to his culture, defining the English as masters and antagonists of a race they themselves have created.

Associations between national identity and race have a complicated history in seventeenth-century England. In the *Basilikon Doron*, James I's great manifesto of Jacobean kingship, the king gave his son Henry the following advice: "Lastly, remember to choose your Wife as I advised you to choose your servants: that she be of a whole and cleane race, not subject to the hereditary sicknesses, either of the soule or the body: For if a man wil be careful to breed horses and dogs of good kinds, how much more careful should he be, for the breed of his owne loines?"[5] By *race*, James seems here to have meant constitution and character as well as physiognomy; the best wife would be the one closest in breeding to Prince Henry himself, and her race would affect the "cleanliness" of her offspring.[6] For kings, such concerns had consequences not only for marital harmony but also for the strength of the succeeding line; as James admonished Henry in a digression on the ills of adultery, only chastity within the royal marriage could ensure the purity of England's future kings. By the late 1660s, after almost a decade of Charles's notorious sexual liberties, concerns about royal chastity were becoming part of the national consciousness. But the Restoration's responses to Charles II's promiscuity were not all censorious. If the dissemination of royal sperm meant a certain decentering of royal blood, it could also be seen as the strongest affirmation of royal authority or "race," multiplying rather than diminishing Charles's potency.[7]

The notion of the king as a patriarch and, accordingly, the patriarch as king or demigod reached its fullest expression after the Restoration in Robert Filmer's *Patriarcha*. As Filmer described it, king and father were bound in a mutual model of paternalistic power:

> If we compare the natural duties of a Father with those of a King, we find them to be all one, without any difference at all but only in the latitude or extent of them. As the Father over one family, so the King, as Father over many families, extends his care to preserve, feed, clothe, instruct and defend the whole commonwealth. His wars, his peace, his courts of justice, and all his acts of sovereignty, tend only to preserve and distribute to every subordinate and inferior Father, and to their children, their rights and privileges, so that all the duties of a King are summed up in an universal fatherly care of his people. (63)

According to Filmer, all English men shared at least some of the obligations of the king, and it followed that they must be encouraged to preserve their national identity through their choice of mates. This supposition was borne out by English concern over the consequences of mixed marriages in the colonies, which was more acute than that evinced by other groups of Europeans in the New World. In 1630, a dozen years after the first cargo of African slaves arrived in Virginia, an English man named Hugh Davis was sentenced to public whipping "before an assembly of Negroes and others" for "abusing himself to the dishonor of God and shame of Christians, by defiling his body in lying with a Negro." Early English colonists were warned against intermarriage; biblical authority was cited to support the claim that a "formidable nation" depended on "the law of marriage among themselves," as the Reverend William Symonds preached in 1609:

> Out of the arguments by which God enticed Abram to go out
> of his country, such as go to a Christian plantation may gather
> many blessed lessons. God will make him a great Nation.
> Then must Abram's posterity keep to themselves. They may
> not marry nor give in marriage to the heathen, that are uncir-
> cumcised. And this is so plain, that out of this foundation
> arose the law of marriage among themselves. The breaking of
> this rule may break the neck of all good success of this voyage,
> whereas by keeping the fear of God, may grow into a nation
> formidable to all the enemies of Christ and be the praise of all
> that part of the world, for so strong a hand to be joined with
> the people here and fear God.[8]

The establishment of a new colony in a new (and to the English, racially different) world mandated strict taboos against interracial relations. How else could the colonists ensure that national integrity would be maintained once citizens left England behind them?[9] Though Virginia did not officially prohibit interracial marriages before the 1690s, colonial courts viewed interracial relations as a form of perversion. In 1662, Virginia passed a law rendering the children of free men and black female slaves "according to the condition of the mother." Slavery, in other words, was seen as being passed down from a black woman to her children, and "any Christian [who] shall commit fornication with a Negro man or woman" was obliged to pay a strict fine.[10] This law ensured that female slaves could only replicate their position through childbearing, making slavery a sex-linked condition. The female slave was sentenced to condemn her own offspring to slavery.

Given the prominence of insurrection as a theme in Neville's utopia, it is worth reviewing the anxiety produced by the idea of colonial slave revolts in the late seventeenth century. At least in part, it was fear of insurrection that lay beneath increasingly strict laws surrounding relations between Africans and English in the colonies. One example of this was the series of "deficiency acts" and "antimiscegenation laws" instituted both in the American colonies and in the West Indies by the middle of the seventeenth century, demonstrating colonists' concern over changes in the ratios between whites, black slaves, and native Indian populations. By the year 1650 black slaves accounted for almost half the population of Barbados. European enthusiasm for slavery accounted for the speed with which white servants were replaced with black slaves in the West Indies, but the demographic realities accompanying the large-scale importation of slaves were met with ambivalence. As Aphra Behn's narrator remarks in *Oroonoko* (1688), "a Mutiny . . . is very fatal sometimes in those Colonies that abound so with Slaves, that they exceed the whites in vast Numbers" (46). White servants continued to be aggressively recruited (in Antigua, as in many of the other islands, rewards were given to every importer of Scottish, Welsh, or Irish servants), but by 1676 Governor Atkins of Barbados publicly remarked that three black slaves could work harder (and much more cheaply) than a single white servant. In Jamaica, which the English seized from Spain in 1655, the changing proportions of the population were pronounced enough that by 1672 a law was instated requiring every plantation to keep one "Christian servant" for every ten slaves. These "deficiency acts" were maintained in Jamaica throughout the eighteenth century, though they eventually devolved into mere fines.[11] English colonial life in the West Indies rapidly organized itself around the institution of African slavery, and the smaller the proportion of whites, the greater the interest became in how those slaves were to be mastered.

Historical records suggest that the English quickly became adept at controlling large slave populations. Nevertheless, anxiety over disproportionate numbers in the West Indies continued for two reasons. First, the English feared raids from the French, the Spanish, and the Dutch. The smaller the English population, the harder it would be to raise an army quickly enough to defend the colony in question, and slaves might be bribed to join forces with the invaders. Moreover, large populations of slaves increased the risk of insurrection from within. This is the spectacle described so vividly by Neville in *The Isle of Pines* and more famously by Aphra Behn in *Oroonoko*. By the Restoration the fear of slave revolts was becoming part of English lore about the West Indies. Throughout the seventeenth century insurrections continued to produce anxiety for colonists. In 1638 slaves revolted on Providence Island, and seven separate revolts took place throughout the colonies between 1640 and 1713. Unrest was particularly vigorous in Jamaica, where uprisings occurred in 1673, 1675, and 1678 and where one protracted insurrection continued for over a year beginning in 1685. As an example of colonial authority, rebellious slaves were often brutally (and publicly) executed. One historian has observed that what was striking about successive rebellions in the English colonies was how swiftly they taught the English to become more rigorous as masters.[12]

In the decades following the English Civil War, the English accelerated the slave trade and used it to bolster Cromwell's "Western Design" in Hispaniola, where the beginnings of English imperial policy were being set in place. It was not in Virginia and Maryland where the English were making fortunes overnight by exploiting the cheap new labor force purchased by the shipload from Africa. In the West Indies—in Barbados, in the Leeward Islands, and in Jamaica—the English found great resources (chiefly sugarcane and dyewoods) that they rapidly converted to great riches.

Not surprisingly, the establishment of real English colonies in the West Indian islands altered literary representations of utopia in the late seventeenth century. Nor is it entirely surprising that representations of utopia in this period should have included, or even have focused on, the topical subject of African slavery. What is surprising is the way Neville's utopia complicates and eroticizes the relations between master and slave, embedding colonial politics within the structure of the patriarchal family. I want to suggest that this is partly because English stories about African slaves in this period fall into the category of colonialist literature that Abdul Jan-Mohamed has called "specular fiction," whose real subject is not the ignoble or noble slave so much as the power, great or awful, of that new breed emerging in the 1660s: the English master.[13] Neville's utopia is a particularly interesting example of this kind of colonialist fiction, as Pine's island becomes a place where English identity can be preserved only through the experience and rejection of the Other. In this sense *The Isle of Pines* is a contradictory master-narrative, simultaneously legitimizing the power of the master and revealing that power to be dangerous, self-limiting, and artificial.

The Isle of Pines was published anonymously in 1668 in four parts, its fictitious author a Dutch sea captain named Cornelius Van Sloetten. The text was immediately successful. It came out almost at once in French, Italian, German, and Dutch editions, and it elicited much speculation over Van Sloetten's veracity and the legitimacy of his report. The romance was not Neville's only literary production. A staunch Republican who later translated works by Machiavelli into English, he also wrote two egregiously sexist satires on contemporary politics, *The Parliament of Ladies* (London, 1647) and *News From the New Exchange; or, The Commonwealth of Ladies* (London, 1650), as well as a dialogue on the decay of English government entitled *Plato Redivivus; or, Discourses Concerning Government* (London, 1698).[14]

The Isle of Pines is a framed narrative. Van Sloetten, the Dutch explorer, discovers an island inhabited by naked English people when his ship is blown off course somewhere around Madagascar. The Dutch are promptly invited to the island's palace, where a man named William Pine greets them, claiming to be the grandchild of the island's discoverer, George Pine. The history of Pine's settlement has been fortuitously preserved on "two sheets of paper fairly written in English," intended to "impart . . . the truth of our first planting here" by its author and delivered as the first part of the narrative. The utopian colony thus has two histories: an Elizabethan history of its founding, and a Restoration history of its dislocation and political unrest.

George Pine's narrative converts the Noah legend into a story of bourgeois advancement. In 1569, according to Pine's "paper," he was indentured to an Englishman planning to establish a factory in the East Indies. Their ship capsized in a violent storm, and Pine, who could not swim, was miraculously saved along with four women—his master's daughter, two maidservants, and a Negro slave. His master dead, Pine appointed himself his heir. The group washed up on a deserted island, which Pine, well trained in the procedures of improvement, proceeded to make habitable. Gradually, lulled by seclusion and "idleness" into a state of continuous desire, Pine began to have sex with each of the women: a maidservant first, his master's daughter next, the second maidservant, and finally the Negro slave. One by one the women became pregnant, each of them producing a brood of children whom Pine separated (by mother) into four tribes. Each tribe was named after its mother: the English, the Sparkes, the Trevors, and the Phils (after Philippa, who as a slave "has no surname"). Rather than the factory his master had planned in India, Pine thus established a factory of reproduction, "membering" the island until its inhabitants number 1,789. The community continued harmoniously until without warning the Phils rose up in insurrection, and a series of harsh laws had to be instated to keep the peace. This concludes the historical part of the narrative. The Dutch are then invited by William Pine to observe the monthly religious service of the island, which was to take place the following day. They do so, farewells are said, and just as the Dutch are leaving, a second insurrection breaks out, once again caused by the rebellious Phils. Again, this insurrection is squelched and the Dutch set off for Calcutta, the destination Pine's displaced master was never able to reach.

For George Pine, the island is a place of possessing bodies, both sexually and politically.[15] Pine's narrative begins with the language of commerce and calculation. His master's voyage had been engendered by "the great advantages arising from the Eastern Commodities, to settle a Factory there for the advantage of Trade" (61). Pine travels under his master as his bookkeeper on a ship called the *India Merchant*. After the ship capsizes, both the *Merchant* and master are ruined, but Pine clings to the office of bookkeeper, both in his compulsive interest in numbering his progeny and in his literal keeping of the Book of the Bible, which he uses to teach "some of my children to read," charging it should be read from once a month at a general meeting to help maintain order (69).[16] If Pine's tallying up of progeny is, like Crusoe's calendar, a numerical record of capitalist values, the guardianship of the Book is a demonstration of political authority, for Pine claims to be author of this island, first by sexual and second by narrative reproduction. The utopia tests the limits of this authority. Pine's sexual prowess is problematic: in fulfilling his "natural" desires, he creates both a good race and a bad, one representing the potential of civil obedience, the other, of instability, insurrection, and anarchy. These terms are unstable, for it is only in contrast to the Phils that the English appear "good." Each generation's ritual execution of an insurgent Phil consolidates the white community, creating an enemy against whom they can wage battle. As René Girard has suggested, the isolation of a scapegoat works to construct identity and community for those who ally themselves against him. On the Isle of Pines, the "black" Phils help to define the identity of the "white" English, Trevors, and Sparkes.[17]

Initially the island that Pine and the four women wash up on is represented as empty. Though they worry about "the wild people of that Countrey," they see none, "no footsteps of any, not so much as a Path" (63). The island appears to be deserted, "full of Briers and Brambles," as wild as the absent people Pine so fears. Even at the outset, dread of "the wild people" draws Pine closer to the three white women, who turn to him for protection. Ironically, it is Pine who will create "wild people" to answer his own fears. Like More's Utopus or Bacon's Solamona, the entrepreneurial Pine quickly stops assessing the island and begins working to change it. The land is empty: it is his job to fill it. At first this office consists of the rudiments of survival. Pine sets up camp and gradually carries from the hold of the ruined ship various life-preserving necessities that conveniently happen to be there, including English hens and cocks, which set at once to reproducing themselves. Fortuitously, Pine has in his pocket everything necessary for building a fire: "a little Tinder-box, and Steel, and Flint to strike Fire," Promethean ingredients for the remaking of civilization. With some canvas and poles he makes a tent, so that by nightfall he can sleep soundly with the three white women, leaving the slave to keep watch ("the Blackmoor being less sensible than the rest we made our Centry"). From this first night, Philippa's position is to safeguard the whites from the wilderness they dread. Her position at the boundary of the camp is set up for their protection, drawing them closer, separated from the potentially frightening island by the intermediary figure of the lookout/slave. In this office, Philippa becomes the whites' literal and figurative boundary, standing between them and what it is that they fear.

Like the women he finds himself with, the island for Pine fluctuates in its ability to fulfill his desires. It is variously described as full and empty. Gradually, as he grows accustomed to the landscape, its emptiness reassures him, as it is "wholly uninhabited by any people, nor was there any hurtful beast to annoy us" (65). The blankness of the island allows Pine the freedom to write on it what he will. But he is at the same time aware of what the island lacks—for instance, "skillful people" and "culture"—which keep it from being Paradise: "the countrey so very pleasant, being always clothed with green, and full of pleasant fruits, and variety of birds, ever warm, and never colder than England in September: so that this place (had it the culture, that skillful people might bestow on it) would prove a *Paradise*."

Pine's parenthetical description here of the island as lack overlooks the fact that Paradise itself lacked "culture" and "skillful people." Pine is interested in numbers; the island as arcadia has no particular attraction for him, although he dutifully remarks that it is well stocked, its forests heavy with nuts as big as apples, with ducks, and with eggs, and its rivers so full of fish that it is easy to catch them. This forest, in fact, provides its own factory of plenty, its creatures bringing out "two young ones at a time" so that they thoughtfully replenish themselves even as they give themselves up to be consumed.

It may be the very fecundity of this wilderness that first inflames Pine's "desire of enjoying the women." In this desire, Pine follows a careful schedule of seduction, taking pains to enjoy each of the women in order of their social rank. None of their names are revealed until the end of his narrative. His "Master's Daughter" enjoys a certain privileged status, described at various times both as the "handsomest" woman and as being Pine's "first Wife," though this title is occasionally conferred on "the first" of his servants as well. These women remain remarkably fixed in their social positions; his "Master's Daughter" retains this status until her death, when she is accorded the best gravesite (i.e., the closest to Pine's own). Her children bear the name of "English," becoming the island's master race. The servantwomen are always referred to as a pair, like socioeconomic twins. One is "somewhat fat" and less handsome than the other, but in personality they are not distinguished, as if their class mitigates against separate characteristics.

This fixity of female position serves as a foil for Pine, who grants himself a dizzying series of promotions, from indentured bookkeeper to patriarch and finally to governor of the island. His grandson William is actually referred to by Van Sloetten as a "prince." While Pine sees his own status as fluid and upwardly mobile, the women's remains static. Their fixity helps to illumine Pine's real subject—his own swift ascent into the office of the master he used to serve, as well as his new office as creator of the "English" tribe. The women's function is to be filled by Pine with the progeny who will become his populace. Once he begins having sex with them, all three of the white women are constantly either pregnant or in the process of giving birth, a procedure with which they companionably help each other. Their role, like the slave's, is to act as guardians or sentries for the young, fixed at the limits between fullness and emptiness. Their agreeable if not enthusiastic acceptance of Pine's desire allows him to become, by silent consensus, their master. Pine's description of his relations with them is curiously anti-erotic, in fact almost businesslike, reminiscent of his description of carrying provisions out of the hold of the ship. He seems more enthusiastic about the number of children he has fathered than relations with the women themselves. Numbering his children, like bookkeeping, is a way of making inventory real to a mind that marks reality with numbers.

The relations Pine has with his "Negro slave" are represented from the outset in different terms. To begin with, Pine claims that Philippa is less "sensible" or sensitive than the others. She does not feel pain, according to Pine, not even during childbirth. But he insists that she *does* feel desire—for Pine. Unlike the other women, she tries to seduce Pine, rather than vice versa. In the passage in which her seduction is described, agency and desire are particularly complicated: "none now remaining but my Negro, who seeing what we did, longed also for her share; one Night, I being asleep, my Negro, (with the consent of the others) got close to me, thinking it being dark, to beguile me, but I awakening and feeling her, and perceiving who it was, yet willing to try the difference, satisfied my self with her, as well as with one of the rest."[18] Pine's use of the word *beguiled* here, as well as the slave's attempt to "deceive" Pine under cover of night, suggest a loss of innocence that distinguishes this sexual act from his encounters with the other women. Pine represents himself as sleeping, vulnerable, rather like Eve in Milton's *Paradise Lost* (published the previous year) who was also "beguiled," also approached at night, asleep and vulnerable, by the Serpent who attempts to penetrate "the Organs of her Fancy," precipitating her fall by advocating difference.[19] The slave's seduction of Pine involves a similarly complex mixture of consensus and duplicity. Apparently she has sought and received permission from the other women before trying to get Pine to make love to her. She believes that the "cover of dark" will keep Pine from "knowing the difference" between her and the others. Once again, Pine's language in this passage is curiously antierotic, largely because it is so explicitly about power relations and so very little about desire. The Negro's attempt to "beguile" her master is upended in the middle of the passage as Pine outmaneuvers her, awakening just in time to reassert his own agency and control. Pine's cursory interest in the slave's intentions or feelings, crudely described in economic terms ("who seeing what we did, longed also for her share"), is immediately replaced with his real subject: his own satisfaction and power, and his ability to "master" her as well as the other woman he turns to afterward. He is in command, even though he has been initially surprised. His "Negro's" attempt to beguile him has in fact awakened him to his role as master, willing first to "try the difference" and then to exploit it.

Philippa's seduction induces Pine to set up a strict new set of rules surrounding sexual relations. From this point on, once any one of the white women becomes pregnant Pine "customarily" does not sleep with her until the others are pregnant, too. The Negro he does not sleep with at all after she conceives, which is "generally" after the first night. He also desists from contact with Philippa except at night "and not else, my stomach would not serve me," although he hastens to add "she was one of the handsomest Blacks I had seen, and her children as comely as any of the rest" (67). Philippa's transgression introduces law into Pine's utopia. It is as if the abyss opened up by their union requires law for its amelioration.

Pine's descriptions of Philippa always end in her erasure. The first child she gives birth to is a "fine white Girl" (67). Her children are "as comely as the rest"; in short, Pine's whiteness has so overmastered her that her children, like the English, Trevors, and Sparkes, take on his features and none of her own (67). Even Philippa's death is an erasure. She dies suddenly and mysteriously after twenty-two years on the island, not having been ill, merely disappearing from life as if she had been suddenly canceled. But this continual erasure does not undo the power of Philippa's initial seduction. In successive generations it is her sons who carry on the revolution she began in breaking a racial taboo. But as men, their intransigence is presented not as a seduction but as open revolt.

Neville's representation of Pine's relations with Philippa blends apocryphal and Old Testament legends with contemporary fantasies about black sexual prowess and fertility. As Joseph Tillinghast argued in *The Negro in Africa and America* (1902), people of African descent have long been seen by white Europeans as possessing unbounded "sexual proclivities" and "exceptionally strong reproductive powers." African women have been purported for centuries by

European whites to be both more libidinous and more fertile than European women. As one critic recently phrased it, "in no other area [are] there . . . so many stereotypes and myths, than that of Black female sexuality. . . . The image . . . is that she is the most sensual of all female creatures."[20] The black woman's allegedly heightened sexuality can be used to put her in direct collusion with the white male, who believes he can use her to reproduce his own values and misconceptions. The eighteenth-century Jamaican planter Bryan Edwards took it upon himself to defend black women on his island who had been charged with "incontinency," "licentiousness," and "debauchery." While Edwards was unusual in apportioning blame to these women's "keepers," it would not have occurred to him that their "wantonness" was an excuse for English abuse.[21] Centuries earlier Vespucci had described the native women he encountered on his first voyage as "very prolific" and possessing "inordinate lust," maintaining that "they shewed themselves very desirous of having connexions with us Christians." European myths connecting libido to racial alterity excused exploitative behavior in the New World while ensuring it would continue, finding itself inscripted within colonial practice and ideology.

Pine describes his desire to sleep with all four women on the island as *fullness*. Yet having his "fill" of Philippa becomes a curious pun, for the offspring she produces, the Phils, threaten to unfill his island, unmaking the government Pine has established. Before his death Pine numbers his progeny at 1,789, sorting them into tribes and commanding them not to do for pleasure what he was forced to do from necessity. (This apparently means marrying his children to each other, but it may also imply interracial union.) After Pine's death his son Henry succeeds him to governorship of the island, and the established order begins to disintegrate. First, as the people grow "more populous" they range "further in the discovery of the Countrey, which they found answerable to their desires" (71). Though no weapons yet are necessary for self-preservation, the island falls into disorder. Pine's "pure" (and empty) island is replaced by a grim, Hobbesian state of nature in which war becomes inevitable. Pine's grandson William records this as a fall: "But as it is impossible, but that in multitudes disorders will grow; no tye of

Religion being strong enough to chain up the depraved nature of mankinde, even so amongst them mischiefs began to rise, and they soon fell from those good orders prescribed for them by my grandfather" (71–72). Like Philippa's "seduction" of Pine, these mischiefs create the justification for punitive laws, in fact, for the establishment of government, which in turn establishes the island as nation. William Pine blames this general decline on neglect of the Bible. Its most serious symptom is sexual depravity, which Pine describes as follows: "The sense of sin being quite lost in them, they fell to whoredoms, incests, and adulteries; so that what my Grandfather was forced to do for necessity, they did for wantonness; nay not confining themselves within the bound of any modesty, but brother and sister lay openly together; those who would not yield to their lewd embraces, were by force ravished, yea many times endangered of their lives" (72).

"What my Grandfather was forced to do for necessity, they did for wantonness." William Pine's use of the word *forced* here is particularly interesting, recalling the word *beguil'd* used to describe Philippa's initial advances. What was it George Pine had been forced to do for necessity—sleep with more than one woman at the same time? sleep with a black woman? Only after Pine has described the depravity and wantonness of these citizens in some detail do we learn who they are—none other than the Phils, Philippa's descendants, who have devolved now into lascivious rapists. Their depravity unites the rest of the island in working to suppress them. A civil war breaks out, with Henry Pine leading an army against "the wickedness of those their brethren," marching against them with "boughs, stones, and such like weapons." Many of the offenders drown themselves to escape "their deserved punishment," but "the grandest offender of all" is captured. This rebel is John Phil, the second son "of the Negrowoman that came with my grandfather into this Island." Once he is captured, a public execution is engineered to serve as an example to the rest of the nation (72): "He being proved guilty of divers ravishings & tyrannies committed by him, was adjudged guilty of death, and accordingly was thrown down from a high Rock into the Sea, where he perished in the waters."

John Phil's execution marks a new phase of Pine's utopia. The Phils may look like the English, Trevors, and Sparkes, but they have "Phil's blood"—a genetic disposition for rebellion. To control them, a constitution is drawn up and a series of harsh laws instated, a more formal version of George Pine's early rules governing sexual relations. William Pine sees the rigidity of this new government as a blessing, claiming that just as "stinking Dung" improves corn by fertilizing it, so bad manners can produce "good and wholesome Laws for the preservation of Human Society" (73). Pine decrees six new commandments: 1. Blasphemy or irreverent talk about God is punishable by death. 2. Missing the monthly religious assembly is punishable for first offenders by four days of starvation and death for second offenders. 3. Rapists are to be burned to death by their victims. 4. Adultery is punishable by castration for men, blinding for women, and death for subsequent offenses. 5. Injury to one's neighbor is punishable in kind. 6. Speaking ill of the governor is punishable by "whipping with rods" and expulsion from the community. Having devised these six laws, Pine next chooses an officer from each of the four tribes to enforce them. This frame of laws transforms the island into a nation.

A new political system is subsequently installed to maintain what William Pine calls "peace": "The Countrey being thus settled, my father lived quiet and peaceable till he attained to the age of ninety and four years, when dying, I succeeded in his place, in which I have continued peaceably and quietly til this very present time" (74). These remarks close the second phase of the narrative. Van Sloetten narrates the third part, in which the Dutch are invited to join the religious service, where several marriages are celebrated. The Dutch enjoy this service, which after Bacon's *New Atlantis* seems a requisite ritual in English utopian fiction.

For six days the Dutch survey the island, praising its landscape, its streams, its minerals, and the simple life of its people, who live, Van Sloetten notes, entirely without weapons. Before they depart, the Dutch build Pine a "very Lordly" palace to commemorate his authority over the island's people. The erection of this palace marks the pinnacle of the Pines' authority; George Pine's empty island has now attained a European standard of cultivation. After repeated and prolonged farewells, the Dutch prepare to depart. But no sooner are their sails hoisted than they are "suddenly Allarm'd with a noise from the shore, the Prince, W. Pines imploring [their] assistance in an Insurrection which had happened amongst them, of which this was the cause":

> Henry Phil, the chief Ruler of the Tribe or Family of the
> Phils, being the Off-spring of George Pines which he had by
> the Negro-woman; this man had ravished the Wife of one of
> the principal of the Family of the Trevors, which act being
> made known, the Trevors assembled themselves all together
> to bring the offender unto Justice: But he knowing his crime
> to be so great, as extended to the loss of life: fought to defend
> that by force, which he had as unlawfully committed, where-
> upon the whole Island was in a great hurly burly, they being
> two great Potent Factions, the bandying of which against each
> other, threatened a general ruin to the whole State. (80)

Once again, the Phil's crime is the ravishing of a white, in this case "the Wife of one of the principal of the family of the Trevors." Philippa's initial seduction is being replayed over and over on this island. William Pine concedes that he can do nothing himself to "repress such Disorders," "for where the Hedge of Government is once broken down, the most vile bear the greatest rule" (81).

The Dutch, who have already impressed the natives with their firearms, arm twelve men and head to shore, certain of victory, for as Van Sloetten puts it, "What could nakedness do to encounter with Arms?" (81). After a brief attempt at diplomacy, the Dutch resort to violence, "for this Henry Phil being of an undaunted resolution, and having armed his fellows with Clubs and stones," is deemed to be a public menace. A battle ensues, but the Dutch and their shotguns prevail. Like John Phil, Henry Phil is "adjudged to death, and thrown off a steep Rock into the Sea" (81). This public retribution seems once again to consolidate the nation, but the sense is that the peace afforded by this Phil's execution will not last and that a new phase of revolution will replace this phase of retaliation. The Pines' rule will continually be ruptured, for it is a rule dependent on the spectacle of insurrection it claims to abhor.

The Isle of Pines describes a compulsion to install order in a nation that uses disorder to justify its own social and political categories. Each male Phil is a version of Philippa—libidinous and "insensible." Neville represents the Phils as having inherited Philippa's "bad blood," her sexual aggression and subversion. But as men, he sees them as harder to master or erase than Philippa. It is fitting that they embody her name but carry it forward as the surname she never had. The Phils are dangerous because they are able to raise their entire "tribe" in mutiny. But their danger is limited by the Pines' ability to rein them in. Particularly disturbing in Neville's narrative is the suggestion that even the Phils' roles of resistance have been determined for them by their masters, that their very revolutions have been scripted to refine the Pines' role as governors. The Pines use the Phils to justify the drafting of their constitutions, the building of their palaces, the bringing of arms to bear against nakedness. The Phils cannot even claim a separate paternity from their enemies. Their origins, like everything else on the island that contains them, come back to a white man's "fill." George Pine has authored them, and they are trapped inside his representation, a representation which simultaneously separates them as a "race" and renders them subordinate.

It is hard to determine Neville's conscious intention in writing *The Isle of Pines*. He may have hoped to comment on Anglo-Dutch animosities in the trade wars of the 1660s or to use the legend of the curse of Noah to create a vehicle for his own Machiavellian speculations on the need for political control. He may have intended *The Isle of Pines* as a political satire on the Civil War and Restoration. What is least likely, and yet what comes through most forcefully, is that Neville intended to represent interracial relations as dystopic. My sense is that Neville unconsciously chose the topical subject of black slavery in this text in an attempt to reconfigure evolving ideas about the bases of national identity. This is borne out by the conclusion of Neville's romance, which closes with an anecdote about an Irishman named Dermot Conelly "who had formerly been in England" but had "quite forgotten" the English language. Is Conelly a displaced Briton, like Pine, or is he rather, like John or Henry Phil, a liminal figure, not-English, an "insensible" sentry whose role is to serve as foil for the more legitimate Europeans with whom he travels? One of the questions Neville's utopia poses is whether it is blood that makes a citizen English or rather marriage, language, and customs. Neville's representation of the deterioration of racial and national integrity suggests that for him, and perhaps for most English people in the 1660s, stricter categories were desired for nationality, race, and gender. In *The Isle of Pines*, with its cyclical insurrections and executions, the repression and containment of one part of the population is used to illustrate the superiority of all others. William Pine's conclusion suggests that only violence—arms, militia, and capital punishment—can keep his nation intact. But as the end of *The Isle of Pines* demonstrates, the utopia's reliance on spectacles of violence foretells its own dystopic conclusions. The more rigidly the Pines struggle to master their island, the further from utopia it recedes.

The relation between imperial ideology and fiction is not unidirectional: the ideology does not simply determine the fiction. Rather, through a process of symbiosis, the fiction *forms* the ideology by articulating and justifying the position and aims of the colonialist.—Abdul R. JanMohamed, "The Economy of Manichean Allegory: The Function of Racial Difference in Colonialist Literature"

6. Out of the Mouth of History

MASTERING *OROONOKO*

For seventy-five years, between Raleigh's first Guiana voyage in 1595 and England's loss of its Surinam sugar colonies in 1667, the English struggled to "plant" in Guiana. English settlements there were begun in 1604, 1609, 1617, 1620, 1629, and 1643, but none succeeded.[1] Perhaps no other site held as much appeal or frustration as Raleigh's fabled land of El Dorado. It was at the mouth of Guiana's river Orinoco, after all, that Columbus believed he had found the Garden of Eden. Guiana came to epitomize the opportunistic and self-canceling visions of the Elizabethan age: George Chapman wrote a poem on the subject in 1596 (*De Guiana*

Carmen Epicum), imagining Elizabeth would become the country's "father, mother and her heire," and in *The Merry Wives of Windsor* Falstaff alluded to Guiana as a region of "all gold and bounty."[2]

Raleigh's first expedition to Guiana in 1595 resulted neither in gold nor dyewoods but in a piece of writing that characterized the powerful and contradictory strains of Elizabethan colonialism. In his tract he promised both "the discovery of a large, rich and beautiful empire" and "a relation of the great and golden city of Manoa (which the Spaniards call El Dorado)." Throughout the tract run competing and contradictory narratives of the found and unfound. The explorers revel in the ocular splendor Guiana offered, wistfully boasting that they did not touch what they saw: neither the "fat and well-formed women" nor the terrain itself. What they most wanted to see—gold—eluded them. But as Raleigh and his men traveled up the river Orinoco toward the city of Manoa, they were mesmerized by the beauty of the landscape:

> On both sides of the river, we passed the most beautiful country that ever mine eyes beheld. . . . I never saw a more beautiful country, nor more lively prospects, hills so raised here and there over valleys, the river winding into divers branches, the plains adjoining without bush or stubble, all fair green grass, the ground of hard sand easy to march on, either for horse or foot, the deer crossing in every path, the birds towards the evening singing on every tree with a thousand several tunes, cranes and herons of white, crimson, and carnation perching in the river's side, the air fresh with a gentle easterly wind, and every stone that we stooped to take up, promised either gold or silver by his complexion. (401)[3]

Despite these tantalizing signs of wealth, the explorers refrained from prospecting. Raleigh hinted that the chaste explorers modeled their restraint on that of the queen, deferring desire for the sake of their country. But chastity and deferral are deconstructed in Raleigh's tract as the "purity" of Guiana is turned into opportunity, an advertisement, like virginity, to adventurers: "Guiana is a country that hath yet her maidenhead, never sacked, turned, nor wrought, the face of the earth hath not been torn, nor the virtue and salt of the soil spent by manurance, the graves have not been opened for gold, the mines not broken with sledges, nor their images pulled down out of their temples" (408–9). Raleigh's tract ends with the contradictory logic of *carpe diem* poetry: Guiana is ripe for the picking, and if the English do not hurry, some other nation will win the prize. Raleigh promised (or warned) Elizabeth that the possession of this empire would ensure greatness to the nation that attained it: "If the King of Spain shall enjoy it, he will become unresistable"(410). Guiana would greatly enrich the nation that won it, its booty transforming its prospectors into masters.

Raleigh's second expedition to Guiana in 1617—belated, engendered by and delimited by its own narrative—closely corresponds to the utopian paradigm I have outlined in this project. For two decades Raleigh struggled for royal support to return to the legendary El Dorado, but not until 1617 did King James finally grant his request. The England Raleigh left in 1617 was greatly changed from the country he had departed in 1595. Queen Elizabeth had been dead for fourteen years, Raleigh was an old man, and the English quest for commodities overseas had become serious business rather than speculation. The East India Company had been formed in 1600, the Virginia Companies in 1607, and the Newfoundland Company in 1610. In Guiana, a thriving Spanish settlement had replaced the Edenic landscape Raleigh described in 1595, and King James granted Raleigh's request to return only on the strict condition that no Spaniard be injured during the search for the mine. The expedition was a disaster. With no more than the map of the mine he had drawn in 1595 to guide him, Raleigh was determined to find "the same acre of ground again in a country desolate and overgrowne which he hath seene but once, and that sixteene years since (which were hard enough to doe upon Salisbury Plaine)."[4] To make matters worse, Raleigh fell ill on the voyage and was unable to disembark in Guiana. He sent his son Wat in his place along with his longtime lieutenant, a man named Keymis. Disobeying orders, Wat ignored the search for gold and instead stormed the settlement of San Thomé, crying "these or like words. . . . Come on, my hearts, here is the mine you must expect;

they that look for any other mine are fools!"[5] Wat got himself killed in the conquest of the town, and Keymis never left it to find the mine, opening Raleigh to suspicion back in England: Had the mine been found and the gold stolen? Had Raleigh conspired with the Spanish against James? When Raleigh blamed Keymis for the debacle, the lieutenant shot and then stabbed himself, leaving Raleigh to return to England alone. By the time Raleigh reached England—exhausted, ill, and in disgrace—James had asked the council to draft a document accusing him of treason and conspiracy. Raleigh's passionate petition to Queen Anne did no good; this was a different queen and a different homecoming, and he was sentenced to death without pardon.

In a sense, Raleigh died a martyr to a site that was to remain a powerful symbol throughout the seventeenth century for England's idea of empire. For Raleigh's second voyage was powerfully anachronistic, an Elizabethan venture in a Stuart age. Several seventeenth-century accounts of Guiana were to share Raleigh's convoluted nostalgia and idealism, the sense that a different England might have mastered a colony increasingly represented as violent and unruly. In 1595, Raleigh argued that England had found its utopia in Guiana; in 1688 Aphra Behn chose Guiana as the site for a romance about utopia's impossibility. What these texts share, beyond a complicated sense of Guiana as England's mirror and "other," is an acute anxiety about the transfer of power back in England. For Raleigh, the "Discovery" was an exhortation to Queen Elizabeth to redefine empire in the final years of her reign, while for Behn, *Oroonoko* was at least in part a complaint about the collapse of power in the court of James II.[6]

In 1667, BETWEEN the publications of Cavendish's and Neville's utopias, Guiana was visited by George Warren, who published his impressions of it in a tract called *An Impartial Description of Surinam upon the Continent of Guiana*.[7] For Warren, the Edenic Surinam was a fallen site, its lushness and beauty "swarming with so many severall kinds of Vermin," including "Snakes, Crocodiles, Scorpions, Bats, Ants, Musketoes, Toads, and Frogs" (20). Surinam's Indians were "a People Cowardly and Treacherous," its women "naturally

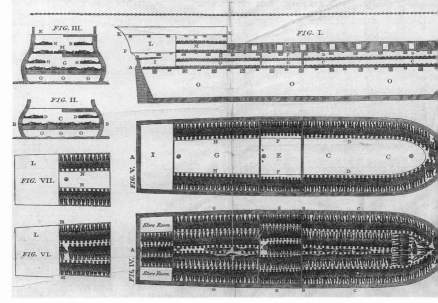

The Brooks, a ship well known in the trade of slaves between Liverpool and Africa in the early eighteenth century, allowed each man as little as nine inches of space in which to lie. By permission of the Houghton Library, Harvard University.

lascivious, and some so truly handsome, as to Features and Proportion," that the colonists would have needed more "than *Joseph's* continency" to avoid their embraces.[8] Warren was especially critical of the way slaves were treated in the English colony. In the eighth chapter of his tract, "Of the Negroes or Slaves," he objects that they "are most brought out of Guiny in Africa to those parts, where they are sold like Dogs, and no better esteem'd but for their Work sake" (19). The conditions under which the slaves lived resulted in attempts to escape or rebel: "These wretched miseries not seldom drive them to desperate attempts for the Recovery of their Liberty, endeavouring to escape, and if like to be re-taken, sometimes lay violent hands upon themselves; or if the hope of Pardon bring them alive again into their Masters power, they'l manifest their fortitude, or rather obstinacy in suffering the most exquisite tortures can be inflicted upon them, for a terrour and example to others without shrinking" (19). The wording of Warren's final phrase in this passage makes it difficult to determine who is served by this "terrour and example to others." Is it the master's power or the slaves' stoicism that is turned into a spectacle, or both? Warren was drawn to the colony by its familiarity as well as its sinister exoticism. Surinam, as he notes in his analysis of colonial government, was a little England, a microcosm of English manners and mores. "The Government is Monarchical, an Imitation of ours, by a Governor, Council, and Assembly; the Laws of England are also theirs, to which are added some by constitutions, no less obliging, proper to the Conveniences of that Country" (6). This colony, for all its cruelty and unpleasantness, was for Warren the "master's" country, a colony modeled on English customs and governed by English law.

As a physical and moral terrain, Aphra Behn's Surinam is closer to Raleigh's than to Warren's:

'Tis a Continent whose vast Extent was never yet known, and may contain more Noble Earth than all the Universe beside; for, they say, it reaches from East to West; one Way as far as *China*, and another to *Peru*: It affords all things both for Beauty and Use; 'tis there Eternal Spring, always the very Months of *April, May,* and *June;* the Shades are perpetual, the Trees, bearing at once all degrees of Leaves and Fruit, from blooming Buds to ripe Autumn; Groves of Oranges, Lemons, Citrons, Figs, Nutmegs and noble Aromaticks, continually bearing their Fragrancies. The Trees appearing all like Nosegays adorn'd with Flowers of different kind, some are all White, some Purple, some Scarlet, some Blew, some Yellow; bearing at the same time, Ripe Fruit, and Blooming Young, or producing every Day new. The very Wood of all these Trees has an intrinsick Value above common Timber; for they are, when cut, of different Colours, glorious to behold; and bear a Price considerable, to inlay withal. Besides this, they yield rich Balm, and Gums; so that we make our Candles of such an Aromatick Substance, as does not only give a sufficient Light, but, as they Burn, they cast their Perfumes all about. . . . But it were endless to give an Account of all the divers Wonderfull and Strange things that Country affords. . . . All things by Nature there are Rare, Delightful, and Wonderful.[9]

But this Eden, like Neville's, contains a serpent. Behn's narrator first reports that the English live in harmony with the native Caribs, a people so pacific and loving that they "represented to me an absolute *Idea* of the first State of Innocence, before Man knew how to sin. . . . Religion wou'd here but destroy that Tranquillity, they possess by Ignorance; and Laws wou'd but teach 'em to know Offence, of which now they have no notion" (8-9). These people are utterly innocent. They do not know the word for one who lies. They live unhampered by desire, with "no Wishes . . . [and] nothing to heighten Curiosity" (7). Among them, the English live "in perfect Tranquillity, and good Understanding" (11). But this apparent goodwill derives not from generosity, but from self-interest. The Caribs outnumber the English, the narrator explains; moreover, they are the ones who know where the best food is "and the Means of getting it" (11). "So that they being, on all Occasions very useful to us, we find it absolutely necessary to caress 'em as Friends, and not to treat 'em as Slaves; nor dare we do other, their Numbers so far surpassing ours in that Continent" (12). "Caressing" here is unfolded as just another species of exploitation.[10]

For Behn, Surinam is an unstable site, fluctuating like Neville's *Isle of Pines* between the description of utopia and its loss. By 1688, the year in which Aphra Behn published her romance, *Oronooko; or, The History of the Royal Slave*, England no longer held its colony in Surinam on the "continent" of Guiana. That colony, as Behn's narrator notes with evident regret, had been lost through mismanagement, through the English failure to "master." This is a loss that the narrator equates with the death of Charles II. She remarks of Guiana, "In a word, I must say thus much of it; that certainly had his late Majesty, of sacred Memory, but seen and known what a vast and charming World he had been Master of in that Continent, he would never have parted so easily with it to the *Dutch*" (149).

The narrator occupies a peculiar position in this colony. As a woman alone, she is both vulnerable and separate from the various camps in Surinam. Her identification with the slave at the center of her narrative is heartfelt and passionate; in this sense, her own stay in Surinam, like Oroonoko's, is a privileged captivity. But the narrator's loyalties are complex. As the daughter of the colony's lieutenant-governor-to-be, who has died en route to Surinam, she is granted (and unquestioningly accepts) the "best house" in the colony, waiting for the next ship to take her back to England and in the meantime enjoying herself by touring Indian villages, telling romantic stories, and observing the tragedy of Oroonoko and his bride. Her agency is equivocal, and her nostalgia for powerful English leaders is especially strong.

Behn's *Oroonoko* is a romance rather than a utopia. But it is a romance that takes the idea of utopia as part of its subject, and as such it represents an endpoint for a certain way of thinking about the English colony in the seventeenth century. By naming her romanticized hero Oroonoko, Behn associates the figure of the "noble slave" with the utopian terrain mythologized by Raleigh in the 1590s. Raleigh in his "Discovery" had included the description of Spaniards buying women and children from the "cannibals" to become their slaves, an event he had situated at "the mouth of the Orinoco."[11] These words are echoed by Behn's narrator in the opening paragraphs of her narrative as she declares that her entire report is founded on "truth," for what she herself did not witness she received "from the Mouth of the chief Actor in this History, the Hero himself," that is, from the Mouth of Oroonoko, the site where the body of the utopian colony and the body of the slave come together.[12] In Behn's romance, the fantasy of "possessing" Oroonoko (the "royal slave") runs parallel to the fantasy of possessing the Orinoco promised by Raleigh to the collective English imagination, the place where utopia could be charted, entered, transformed into England's "mine." Behn's romance chronicles the defeat of these desires. Like *The Isle of Pines*, *Oroonoko* uses the story of a slave revolt both to demonstrate and to justify the power of English colonial government. For Behn, this power is cruel rather than legalistic. Behn is more critical than Neville, albeit unevenly so, of England's position in the Indies. Her romance criticizes the English for allowing the Dutch to overmaster them as well as for overmastering the Coramantien slaves. Two questions preoccupy Behn's narrator: who is governing Surinam, and who is serving Surinam as slaves? Oroonoko's paradoxical status as royal slave makes him an emblem both of monarchy and slavery, a conflation of the most powerful and degraded signs of royal power. In 1688, on the eve of the "Bloodless Revolution," this simultaneous devaluation and valorization was especially apt.

OROONOKO IS THE story of an East African prince and his lover, Imoinda, who are tricked into slavery by a jealous patriarch. As luck would have it, the separated lovers turn up on the same plantation in Surinam. Both are bought by a Cornish planter named Trefry, a "witty" and amiable young man who is the apparent model for Behn of the ideal English master. Trefry recognizes Oroonoko's superior intellect and European education at once. He banters affectionately with Oroonoko, treating him "like a brother" and keeping him as a slave in name only: "he was receiv'd more like a Governor, than a Slave" (109). Confident that royal blood exempts this couple from real slavery, Trefry behaves throughout as if Oroonoko and Imoinda's captivity were nothing more than a diplomatic embarrassment to be cleared up after the long-awaited arrival of the new governor. In the meantime, Oroonoko is exempted from base labor, though he is treated in servile and humiliating ways, his strength and beauty publicly exhibited and his company clamored for by the "English ladies" as they tour the Guianan jungle or visit Indian towns. Oroonoko and Imoinda marry, she conceives, and the couple become increasingly impatient for their release, which is repeatedly deferred as the colony awaits its still-absent governor. Despairing, Oroonoko organizes three hundred or more slaves into a fugitive body, convincing them to flee the plantation with him and form a "new colony" beyond the river until they can capture a ship and return home. To contain them, the planters form an army of six hundred men, which Trefry joins "as a Mediator." All but three of the slaves are coaxed out of insurrection, and Trefry persuades Oroonoko to come back, insisting he will then be set free. Without Trefry's knowledge, the island's corrupt acting-governor, Byam, has already condemned Oroonoko to death as an example to the rest of the slaves.

The narrator's response to these events is complicated. She both identifies and competes with Oroonoko and the "loyal" Imoinda.[13] From the outset Behn's narrator has been a great champion of Oroonoko, enchanted by his royal blood, his European education, his striking good looks, and perhaps mostly by his enormous strength and physical courage. Overtly she is horrified by the thought of Oroonoko (and to a lesser extent, Imoinda) being kept as slaves. Like Trefry and the other "good" colonists, she doesn't give the rest of the slaves much thought; most of them had been sold into slavery in the first place by Oroonoko, who only bothers with them himself when they can help him plan an escape for his own family. But the narrator's empathy for Oroonoko extends only so far. She likes Oroonoko best when he isn't being "sullen" about slavery and is willing to chaperone for her and the other English women, who fill their time with "sport," such as touring Indian villages and shrinking from tigers and other exotic beasts. As their bodyguard and mascot, Oroonoko both provides and facilitates the English women's "entertainment."

Implicit in the narrator's treatment of Oroonoko is an undisguised fascination with his exotic looks, especially his black skin. That she finds him attractive may be meant (and has often been read) as a sign of her enlightenment.[14] But the narrator's lengthy blazon for Oroonoko regenders Petrarchan conventions in which, as Nancy Vickers has pointed out, the beloved's features are anatomized by an admirer, so that eyes, lips, cheeks, teeth, etc., are dismembered rather than integrated.[15] In the narrator's initial description of the noble Oroonoko, his eventual execution is prefigured as he is categorically taken to pieces by her admiration:

> He was pretty tall, but of a Shape the most exact that can be fancy'd: The most famous Statuary cou'd not form the Figure of a Man more admirably turn'd from Head to Foot. His Face was not of that brown, rusty Black which most of that Nation are, but a perfect Ebony, or polish'd Jett. His Eyes were the

most awful that cou'd be seen, and very piercing; the White
of 'em being like Snow, as were his Teeth. His Nose was rising
and *Roman*, instead of *African* and flat. His Mouth, the finest
shap'd that cou'd be seen; far from those great turn'd Lips,
which are so natural to the rest of the *Negroes*. (20-21)

In the narrator's blazon Oroonoko's European features are distinguished from those of the African he is not—the "brown rusty
Black" with a flat nose and "great turn'd Lips" who is far more
arrestingly described in this passage than the refined Oroonoko.
Oroonoko has two names—he is Oroonoko in Africa and is re-
named Caesar by Trefry when he is delivered as a slave to Surinam. Similarly, he has two faces: that of the attractive, digni-
fied man who is as civil, educated, and refined as any "well-bred
great Man," i.e., as any European; and a violent, unpredictable
side. Like Neville, Behn represents blackness as a contradiction,
seeing it simultaneously as noble and savage, masterful and un-
mastered.

Behn's narrator can go only so far in defending Oroonoko. Like
Trefry, she sees herself as a mediator, not as a governor. But like
Trefry, she is at the same time aware that she has power she doesn't
always wield. Trefry claims to be Oroonoko's champion. It was his
idea to turn Oroonoko's life into a romance, a task from which he
was prevented by his mysterious and untimely death after the
Dutch conquest. While he lives, Trefry is the text's consummate
master, however much he prefers to play the gentleman, emphasizing his skills as a linguist and a "Gentleman . . . of great Wit, and
fine Learning" (102). Only in one passage does Trefry acknowledge the extent of his own power. When Trefry first tells Oroonoko about the beautiful "She-Slave" everyone on his plantation
adores, he admits he himself has made advances to her, though they
have been rebuffed. Not knowing that the woman in question is
Imoinda, Oroonoko wonders, in a sly, man-to-man way, why Trefry doesn't just go ahead and take her if he wants her so badly; after
all, she is his slave. Trefry, relaxing, cheerfully admits that the
thought had crossed his mind, and in fact only the woman's bash-

fulness and tearful protestations had prevented him from making use "of those Advantages of Strength and Force Nature has given me" (132).

Behn's narrator, like Trefry, is similarly cognizant of her natural and native advantages. She is, after all, the former lieutenant governor's daughter, and she is treated with the respect she believes her due. When Oroonoko becomes "sullen" after a lengthy period in which his request for liberation goes unanswered, the narrator acts as Trefry's agent, trying first to cajole Oroonoko out of his anger and then resorting to threats, telling him that unpleasant behavior will only lead to his confinement. She backs away when Oroonoko becomes tragically ensnared in Byam's plot. Too late she "supposes" she might have come to his aid, preventing his brutal whipping and subsequent death by using her influence when it was needed. But like Trefry, she holds back, witnessing the travesties Byam and his corrupt council devise, celebrating Oroonoko's tragedy rather than preventing it.

For Behn, the role of bad master in Surinam is filled by Byam, a deceitful, ruthless man with a council "which consisted of such notorious Villains as Newgate never transported; and possibly, originally were such who understood neither the Laws of God or Man, and had no sort of Principles to make them worthy [of] the Name of Men; but at the very Council-Table wou'd contradict and fight with one another, and swear so bloodily, that 'twas terrible to hear and see 'em" (214-15).

It is Byam and his corrupt council who are overtly responsible for Oroonoko's death. But Trefry and the narrator are implicated as well, for when the slaves revolt, they side at once with the English. After the colonists discover that Oroonoko has "sacrificed" Imoinda, the narrator huddles with the rest of the women, frightened he will turn on them next. Oroonoko's strength, which the narrator has admired and put on display for public "entertainment," now becomes a subject of shared (English) terror. Like Milton's Samson, also enslaved and paraded as a trophy of national strength, Oroonoko is reduced to a sign, terrifying as well as thrilling. Now he is called a "monster." The English hint that

The frontispiece to Thomas Southerne's adaptation of *Oroonoko* (1735) illustrates the extent to which interpreters elided the roles of Behn's narrator and Imoinda. By permission of the New York Public Library.

Oroonoko, like the wild tiger he destroyed to the women's fascination, is a beast rather than a man. His dismemberment and execution are the acts on which the English idea of "civilization" depend, for the royal slave's potency is a threat that the colonists cannot allow. He becomes, symbolically and literally, a body of resistance that must be brought down.

Oroonoko's execution is meted out not as punishment for his sacrifice-murder of Imoinda but for organizing into revolt Surinam's slaves, many of whom had been subjects to Oroonoko in his native Coramantien. Raising an insurrection is seen by the colonists as unpardonable, and it continues to haunt them even after the rebellious slaves are coaxed to lay down their arms. In the first phase of his punishment, Oroonoko is brutally whipped, and perceiving for the first time the permanence of his enslavement, he determines to escape, first to seek revenge and subsequently to end his own life. First, however, he kills his wife, whose beauty he fears might lead to her ravishment after his own demise. Her death holds within it the death of their unborn child and hence their royal lineage. Imoinda's death by Oroonoko's hand is, like his own will be, a dismemberment; a "loyal and devoted wife," she begs for death faster than Oroonoko can suggest it (221). When she kneels before him, Oroonoko cuts her throat, then severs her head, her face still smiling, from her body. For days he weeps over her head, a terrible trophy of his desire to possess her, to make her his own in a way possible only when she is dead. Like Oroonoko's death, Imoinda's seems for its Royalist author to recall the "nobility" of Charles I, executed by an insensitive mob, and at the same time provides an eroticized theater of horror, an "entertainment," for its English audience.[16]

At the conclusion of the romance, Oroonoko is tied to a stake and burned to death while his executioner cuts him to pieces, throwing parts of his body into the fire one by one before the audience of English colonists. The body of the "mangled King" is intended to be a warning to the mutinous slaves. The colonial government decides that Oroonoko "ought to be made an example to all the Negroes, to fright 'em from daring to threaten their Betters, their Lords and Masters; [for] at this rate no Man [is] safe from his Slaves." According to Behn's narrator, Oroonoko behaves admirably throughout this grisly ordeal. She notes with approval that eventually he gives "up the Ghost, without a Groan or Reproach," still smoking tobacco from his pipe (238). Oroonoko's mouth, which she had always so expressly praised, is admired to the last. What the narrator most explicitly admires is his stoic resignation, the preservation of his dignity as his body is dismembered. But, as I have suggested, her admiration of his self-mastery conceals a deeper admiration for mastery in general, specifically for English colonial power. Oroonoko's execution is a spectacle in which the unruly political body is taken (literally) to pieces. Like the Pines' executions of the Phils in Neville's utopia, this execution is part of a continuous theater of power in which punishment is ritually acted and re-acted, a "terror and example" to the English as much as to the Coramantien slaves. Even Oroonoko's mouth—that source of history and romance—is silenced here.

In the last paragraphs of the romance, pieces of Oroonoko's mutilated body are sent off to various officers in Surinam to serve as signs of terror to their slaves. Behn, unlike Neville, is critical of the cruelty with which Oroonoko has been punished. But her narrator is unable to intervene or to offer an alternative other than the "reasonable" slave owners, like Trefry, who are able to govern their slaves without terror. This is the office Behn finally seems most concerned to define—a reasonable and "just" mastery, and a reasonable and "just" colonial government that might control its slaves without terror. But no sooner have the English overmastered Oroonoko than the English are themselves overmastered by the Dutch. Slaves, Behn's narrator remarks early in the story, had always been sold off in separate lots in Surinam, "lest Rage and Courage should put 'em upon contriving some great Action, to the ruin of the Colony" (101). Despite this precaution, and despite the colonists' brutal spectacle "of a mangled King," Behn's narrative ends in the very ruin the English had labored to prevent. *Oroonoko's* plot circles around the spectral figure of the absent English leader, whose arrival might have prevented tragedy and restored order, an arrival which is deferred until the Dutch conquest renders it inconsequential. The figure of the absent governor haunts the narrative as much as the figure of the rebellious slave.

In 1688 James II lost more than the colony of Surinam. For Behn, as for George Warren, the colony in Surinam was a small-scale model of England. At least in part, the story of Oroonoko for Behn recounts the end of the Restoration, the king "mangled," the seat of government empty. Both in *Oroonoko* and *The Isle of Pines*, the figure of the slave is set against the figure of the colonial governor. But for Behn these two figures are at least temporarily conjoined. Behn shared with Neville a sense of the slave revolt as spectacle, a crucial (if tragic) act in a drama whose central theme was the reestablishment of English control. But the Royalist Behn, unlike the Republican Neville, mourned the diminishing power of "governor," relegating the figure of the heroic leader to history and romance. The English had their chance to construct utopia in Guiana, Behn's *Oroonoko* suggests, but they lost it. Behn makes the utopian paradigm elegiac as she equates the golden place of Guiana with mismanagement and tragedy. As she transforms surveillance and punishment into spectacle, she reveals a fissure that had always been present in English utopian fiction. The ideal depended on inaccessibility. Utopia offered a space in which fantasies and anxieties about colonialism could be played out, but its story, like Oroonoko's, had to be silenced so that the story of mastery could take its place.

AFTERWORD

I have argued that utopias are founding fictions, narratives that delineate the origins and charters of emergent nationalism. Appropriately, the first phase of English utopianism (sometimes called "classical utopianism") came to a close as two great new discursive forms developed in England at the end of the seventeenth century. As Walter Benjamin suggests in "The Storyteller," the novel and the newspaper effectively revolutionized the transmission of "information" and created a new bourgeois community of readers in the modern period.[1] The utopia, situated midway between these two new forms, necessarily altered as newspapers and novels unbraided characteristics that until the 1700s had been indistinct.

Historians of the novel have tended to overlook the utopia as a protonovel or early form of fiction. Even Michael McKeon's encyclopedic study of fictional prose in the seventeenth century neglects to mention the imaginative narratives of such writers as Bacon, Gott, Winstanley, Cavendish, Neville, and Behn. This omission is puzzling, given the obvious utopian features of such novels as Defoe's *Robinson Crusoe* and the manifest connections between seventeenth- and eighteenth-century representations of other worlds (Mary de la Rivière Manley's *New Atalantis*, to name just one example). This omission has been especially distorting given the complexity and metafictional quality of sixteenth- and seventeenth-century fictional prose. The hybrid nature of utopian narrative—its various claims to be history, political theory, polemic, satire, romance—offers special insights into fiction writing in this crucial period before the English novel became institutionalized. The utopia is always, at least in part, an allegory of authorship, a metagenre concerned with the artificial, isolated status of the imaginative act. For many English utopists in this period, including Bacon, Plattes, Winstanley, and Neville, the utopia was the author's sole exercise in fictional prose. Utopias in this period and beyond offer important insights for narrative theorists as well as for historians of the novel.

After Behn's *Oroonoko*, the "speaking picture" of the ideal commonwealth became increasingly ironized for English authors. One has only to compare the narrator's sojourn in Bacon's *New Atlantis* to Gulliver's exile with the Houyhnhnms to recognize the extent of the change. In part, the new irony discernible in early eighteenth-century utopias is a result of the defeat of absolutism Laura Brown has described in the seventeenth century.[2] The period of classical utopianism in England witnessed the transfer (and fragmentation) of power from the monarchy to a series of modern organs or institutions. As the Restoration witnessed the development of national institutions on an even greater scale, the tone of utopianism became correspondingly skeptical.

One such institution, the first English daily newspaper, had its beginning three days after the succession of Queen Anne in 1703. *The Daily Courant*, written by Samuel Buckley, was to last for thirty-three years, and by the time it folded, the daily newspaper was an established English tradition. The lapse of the Licensing

Act in 1695 enabled a sudden flurry in newspaper production, a watershed Thomas Babington Macaulay was to romantically designate the emancipation of English literature from government control.[3] It is hard to overestimate the complex effects of newspapers on literacy rates, community ties, and changing ideas of what constituted news and dailiness in England. In fact, it is likely that no other discursive form would go so far as the newspaper in ritualizing the new mass ceremony of reading.[4]

The early modern utopia also depended on the categories of news and information, often beginning with claims to be a documentary, advertising itself as news (More's *New State of a Commonwealth*, Bacon's *New Atlantis*, Gott's *New Jerusalem*, Cavendish's *New World, called The Blazing-world*). The seventeenth-century English utopia, like the eighteenth-century English novel, was a perfect creole, in the words of Nancy Armstrong and Leonard Tennenhouse, "characteristically claiming to begin as another kind of writing, as a diary, a journalistic account . . . a travel narrative."[5] Often the utopia begins by claiming to be news, only gradually transforming itself into a romance of origins. Unlike the newspapers (read because they were true) and the novels (read because they were not), utopias deliberately confounded the truthfulness of fiction, the untruthfulness of fact. Overlaying fiction and information, the utopia exposed as it necessitated the demand for a new kind of readership, a membership in the unisonance of English reading.[6]

As early as 1595, Philip Sidney recognized More's *Utopia* as a national treasure. In his attempt to valorize the utopia as a "speaking picture," Sidney may have sensed how instrumental this new form would be in creating and conferring values for English readers. In assigning origins, rituals, and sacred spaces to imaginary commonwealths, utopias repeatedly demonstrated the value of what Ernest Gellner has called the three chief traits of the modern nation: homogeneity, literacy, and anonymity.[7] The utopia taught the preeminence of the state, the need for supervision, surveillance, and control. Perhaps most important, utopias demonstrated that institutions, not individuals, had the capacity to manufacture and transform values. Despite the utopia's distant setting, its lessons have felt increasingly close to home. As Homi Bhabha has re-marked, the other is never outside or beyond us; it emerges force-fully, within cultural discourse, when we think we speak most intimately and indigenously.[8] In seventeenth-century England, national identity took shape in crucial ways through representa-tions of alterity, and in their nascence, the fictions of utopia and of England were crucially intertwined.

NOTES

Introduction

1 Cited by Timothy Brennan, "The National Longing for Form," in *Nation and Narration*, ed. Homi K. Bhabha (London: Routledge, 1990), 51.

2 Homi K. Bhabha, "DissemiNation: Time, Narrative, and the Margins of the Modern Nation," ibid., 311. The phrase "imagined community" comes from Benedict Anderson, *Imagined Communities: Reflections on the Origin and Spread of Nationalism* (London: Verso, 1983).

3 Miriam Eliav-Feldon's monograph on Renaissance utopianism is an important starting place for a study of connections between Continental and English texts. See her *Realistic Utopias: The Ideal Imaginary Societies of the Renaissance, 1516–1630* (Oxford: Clarendon Press, 1982). Frank and Fritzie Manuel's *Utopian Thought in the Western World* (Oxford: Basil Blackwell, 1979) is a helpful source for this as for most questions.

4 Liah Greenfield, *Nationalism: Five Roads to Modernity* (Cambridge, Mass.: Harvard Univ. Press, 1992), 54, 52, and 67.

5 Richard Helgerson, *Forms of Nationhood: The Elizabethan Writing of England* (Chicago: Univ. of Chicago Press, 1992), 8.

6 Ernest Gellner, *Nations and Nationalism: New Perspectives on the Past* (Ithaca: Cornell Univ. Press, 1983), 57.

7 Peter Ruppert, *Reader in a Strange Land: The Activity of Reading Literary Utopias* (Athens: Univ. of Georgia Press, 1986). Eugene F. Rice claims that by 1500 European printing presses had issued about six million books. See his *Foundations of Early Modern Europe, 1460–1559* (New York: Norton, 1970), 1–10, and Lucien Febvre and Henri-Jean Martin, *The Coming of the Book: The Impact of Printing, 1450–1800*, trans. David Gerard (London: Verso, 1976).

8 Robert Burton, *The Anatomy of Melancholy* (1627), 2 vols., ed. Holbrook Jackson (London: Dent, 1932) 1:97.

9 Philip Sidney, *The Defense of Poesie*, ed. Albert Feuillerat (Cambridge: Cambridge Univ. Press, 1923), 3:15; John Milton, *Areopagitica* (1644), *The Works of John Milton*, 18 vols., ed. Frank Patterson (New York: Columbia Univ. Press, 1931), 4:318.

10 See Karl Mannheim, *Ideology and Utopia: An Introduction to the Sociology of Knowledge*, trans. Louis Wirth and Edward Shils (New York: Har-

court, Brace, 1936); Herbert Marcuse, *Eros and Civilization: A Philosophical Inquiry into Freud* (Boston: Beacon Press, 1955); Raymond Ruyer, *L'utopie et les utopies* (Paris, 1950); Roger Mucchielli, *Le Myth de la cite ideale* (Paris, 1960); Ernst Bloch, *Prinzip Hoffnung* (*The Principle of Hope)*, trans. Neville Plaice, Stephen Plaice, and Paul Knight (Cambridge: MIT Press, 1986). Northrop Frye discusses utopianism in greatest detail in an article entitled "Varieties of Literary Utopias," in *Utopias and Utopian Thought*, ed. Frank Manuel (Boston: Houghton Mifflin, 1966), 25–49. For Williams's remark, see "Utopia and Science Fiction," in *Problems in Materialism and Culture: Selected Essays* (London, 1980), 199. Louis Marin has written extensively on the subject of utopias. See "Theses on Ideology and Utopia," trans. Fredric Jameson, *Minnesota Review* (spring 1976): 71–75; "Towards a Semiotics of Utopia," in *Structure, Consciousness, and History*, ed. Richard H. Brown and Stanford M. Lyman (Cambridge: Cambridge Univ. Press, 1978), and *Utopics: Spatial Play*, trans. Robert Vollrath (Atlantic Highlands, N.J.: Humanities Press, 1984). For Fredric Jameson, see *Marxism and Form: Twentieth-Century Dialectical Theories of Literature* (Princeton: Princeton Univ. Press, 1971), 145–46 and *The Ideologies of Theory*, 2 vols. (Minneapolis: Univ. of Minnesota Press, 1988), 2:81. Darko Suvin discusses utopianism and estrangement in *Metamorphoses of Science Fiction* (New Haven: Yale Univ. Press, 1979), 53–55.

11 "What sets [science fiction] apart from older forms of fiction seems to be its new use of metaphors. . . . Space travel is one of these metaphors; so is an alternative society, an alternative biology; the future is another. The future, in fiction, is a metaphor." Ursula K. LeGuin, *The Left Hand of Darkness* (New York: Harper and Row, 1969).

12 Bhabha, "DissemiNation," 300.

13 *The Latin Epigrams of Thomas More*, ed. Leicester Bradner and Charles Arthur Lyman (Chicago: Univ. of Chicago Press, 1953), 144.

14 In *Imagined Communities*, Benedict Anderson discusses the fixing of national identity in relation to the new "languages-of-power" created by "print-capitalism" (45).

15 For an excellent discussion of sources and the transmission of utopianism from the classical period to the Renaissance, see the Manuels' *Utopian Thought in the Western World*, 33–116. Some critics locate the origins of secular utopianism in the Renaissance. It was in the early modern period, according to Richard Helgerson, that people "began to consider the possibility of perfecting human society—or at least of

defining its ills in terms proper to a particular and contingent set of social institutions and customs." "Inventing Noplace, or the Power of Negative Thinking," in *The Power of Forms in the Renaissance*, ed. Stephen Greenblatt (Norman: Univ. of Oklahoma Press, 1982), 102.

16 Sidney discusses the utopia in his *Defense*, Donne, in a verse letter to Sir Henry Wotton in the 1590s, and Lyly, in a play entitled *The Woman in the Moone*, performed before Elizabeth in 1597, set in "the bounds of fayre Utopia." See *The Complete Works of John Lyly*, ed. R. Warwick Bond (Oxford: Oxford Univ. Press, 1902), 3:239–88.

17 Thomas Lupton, *Siquila, Too Good to Be True* (London, 1580) and *The Second Part and Knitting Up of the Book Entituled, Too Good to Be True* (London, 1581). Jameson discusses genre both as social contract and as institution in *The Political Unconscious: Narrative as a Socially Symbolic Act* (Ithaca: Cornell Univ. Press, 1981), 106.

18 Glenn Negley's bibliography, *Utopian Literature* (Lawrence: Regents Press of Kansas, 1977), fulfills its aim to "provide for scholars a listing of an important and neglected area of Western literature" from the sixteenth century to the present.

19 I am particularly indebted to several studies of nationalism, colonialism, and capitalism. On the subject of nationalism, I've found especially helpful the essays in Bhabha's *Nation and Narration;* though it focuses on a later period, E. J. Hobsbawm's *Nations and Nationalism Since 1780* (Cambridge: Cambridge Univ. Press, 1990); and Anderson's *Imagined Communities*, esp. chap. 3, "The Origins of National Consciousness," 37–46, were also useful.

20 A recent study argues that writing in the age of Elizabeth is acutely nationalist. See Richard Helgerson, *Forms of Nationhood*. Helgerson does not discuss *Utopia* or utopianism, but he has a very interesting chapter on travel narrative and some brief remarks about chorographies and land surveys under Elizabeth, 131–39.

21 Jeffrey Knapp, *An Empire Nowhere* (Berkeley: Univ. of California Press, 1991).

22 See Fernand Braudel, *The Wheels of Commerce: Civilization and Capitalism, 15th–18th Century* (New York: Harper and Row, 1982), 2:448–60. Enthusiasm for investing in these companies intensified in the second half of the century. Braudel notes that there were twenty-four British joint-stock companies in the year 1688; "between 1692 and 1695, 150 joint stock companies were founded, not all of which survived" (451). Other important studies of colonialism and its effects in the period include David Quinn's *Explorers and Colonies:*

America, 1500–1625 (London: Hambledon Press, 1990) and Joyce Appleby's *Economic Thought and Ideology in Seventeenth-Century England* (Princeton: Princeton Univ. Press, 1978).

23 Kenneth R. Andrews, *Trade, Plunder, and Settlement: Maritime Enterprise and the Genesis of the British Empire, 1480–1630* (Cambridge: Cambridge Univ. Press, 1984), 13.

24 James Holstun, *A Rational Millennium: Puritan Utopias of Seventeenth-Century England and America* (New York: Oxford Univ. Press, 1987).

25 Mary Douglas, *How Institutions Think* (Syracuse: Syracuse Univ. Press, 1986), 55.

26 J. C. Davis, for example, distinguishes utopian fictions from "Cockaygne," "arcadia," the "perfect moral commonwealth," and the "millennium." See *Utopia and the Ideal Society*, (Cambridge: Cambridge Univ. Press, 1981), 12–40. Eliav-Feldon distinguishes utopias from "the good government," "idealizations of existing societies," "designs of ideal cities," "glorifications of a primitive Golden Age," and "secret societies (real or imaginary)"; she also distinguishes between "world empires and plans for universal eternal peace" and "theocratic millennial kingdoms (plans or experiments)" in *Realistic Societies*, 1–4.

27 The most helpful book-length study of dialogue as a genre in the Renaissance that I have found is K. J. Wilson's *Incomplete Fictions* (Washington, D.C.: Catholic Univ. of America Press, 1985). Darko Suvin argues that utopian dialogue is deictic rather than Socratic. "At the basis of all utopian debates, in its open or hidden dialogues, is a gesture of pointing, a wide-eyed glance from here to there": *Metamorphoses of Science Fiction*, 37. Two interesting theorizations of travel romance can be found in Michel de Certeau, *Heterologies: Discourse on the Other*, trans. Brian Massumi (Minneapolis: Univ. of Minnesota Press, 1986), 139 ff., and in Michael Nerlich, *The Ideology of Adventure: Studies in Modern Consciousness, 1100–1750* (Minneapolis: Univ. of Minnesota Press, 1987). According to de Certeau, "explorations semanticize the voids of the universe." Nerlich reads the travel romance as a masterplot of mercantile acquisition and aggrandizement.

28 Louis Marin discusses the neutralizing effect of utopian literature in *Utopics*; Darko Suvin discusses the estrangement of utopian fiction in *Metamorphoses of Science Fiction*, 53–55; and Stephen Jay Greenblatt discusses *Utopia* and anamorphic art in *Renaissance Self-Fashioning: From More to Shakespeare* (Chicago: Univ. of Chicago Press, 1980), 23.

29 Erving Goffman, *Asylums: Essays on the Social Situations of Mental Patients and Other Inmates* (New York: Anchor Books, 1961), 4.

30 Pierre Macherey, *A Theory of Literary Production*, trans. Geoffrey Wall (London, 1978), 17.

31 Nietzsche, in *The Twilight of the Idols*, made this remark: "Liberal institutions straightaway cease from being liberal the moment they are soundly established: once this is attained no more grievous and more thorough enemies of freedom exist." Most of Michel Foucault's work can be described as the reassessment of so-called liberal institutions—the clinic, the hospital or asylum, the modern penitentiary. Perhaps the most relevant of Foucault's texts for my project is *Discipline and Punish*, trans. Alan Sheridan (New York: Pantheon Books, 1977), which I found especially illuminating in terms of the development of English public schools and public workhouses.

32 The Italian editor Ramusio, for example, reprinted the travels of Iamboulous alongside accounts of the voyages of Vespucci and Columbus, declaring the journey to have been authentic or at least "part truth, part fable." As the Manuels put it in *Utopian Thought in the Western World*, "the two geographies, the imaginary and the real, were sometimes confused" (23). The Manuels discuss Hellenistic utopian novels on page 83 and Iamboulous's account on 86–87.

33 *Diodorus Siculus*, trans. and ed. C. H. Oldfeather (Cambridge, 1935), 2:69–71.

34 Stephen Jay Greenblatt, *Marvelous Possessions: The Wonder of the New World* (Chicago: Univ. of Chicago Press, 1991), 103.

35 Iamboulous sees this feature in an apparently positive light, but the traditional understanding of the double or "forked tongue" is not complimentary. The Bible warns against the "double-tongued" (I Timothy 3.8), as do the maxims found in Aesop's Fables, translated in the fifteenth century by Caxton ("Therefore men must not trust in hym that hath two faces and two tongues" and "Tongue double brings trouble"). The pejorative image of the split or forked tongue dates back at least to Euripides in the fourth century B.C. ("No man am I of double tongue") and to Plautus in the second century B.C. ("He's got a two-forked tongue like a snake"). The association between the forked serpent's tongue and human duplicity has a similarly ancient history. In *The Aeneid* Virgil describes the flickering and forked tongues of serpents (2:211). Shakespeare in *A Midsummer Night's Dream* uses the image in a misled lover's angry accusation: "With doubler tongue than thine, thou serpent, adder never stung!"

And in Milton's Hell, the fallen angels, suffering God's punishment in which they must periodically take the form of serpents, try to speak, only to return each other's hisses "with forked tongue / to forked tongue" (10:518). In Thomas Fuller's *Gnomologia* (1732), a new conjunction between doublespeak and the diabolic is represented in the phrase "His tongue is cloven as the Devil's Foot." See Burton Stevenson, *The Home Book of Proverbs, Maxims, and Familiar Phrases* (New York: Macmillan, 1948), 2344. Euripides' citation is from *Rhesus* (450 B.C.), 1:395; Plautus' is from *Poenulus* (194 B.C.), 1:1034. By the early seventeenth century, the word *forked* was beginning to be used to suggest linguistic ambiguity as well as deliberate falsehood. Jonson in *Volpone* uses the phrase *forked counsel* to describe ambiguous advice (I:i). Sayings, maxims, and homilies warned that people in general were double tongued, as speech had the capacity for great harm as well as great good. As Sir Walter Raleigh put it in his *Instructions to His Son* (1616), "The tongue is the instrument of the greatest good and the greatest evil that is done in the world." To be double tongued, then, came in the early modern period to imply ambiguity if not treachery through language, to offer not only double meanings but meanings that were qualitatively and morally opposed.

36 A better and more detailed definition is given by Vincent Crapanzano: "Dialogue comes from the Greek *dialogos*. *Dia* is a preposition that means through, between, across, by, of. It is akin to *dyo* and *di-*, two. As a prefix in English *dia* suggests a passing through, as in diathermy, thoroughly or completely as in diagnosis, a going apart as in dialysis, and opposed in moment as in diamagneticism. *Logos* comes from *legein*, to speak. It may also mean thought as well as speech— thought, as Onians (1951, 76 n. 9) points out, that is conceived materially as breath, spirit, pneuma. Hence, etymologically, a dialogue is a speech across, between, through two people. It is a passing through and a going apart. There is both a transformational dimension to dialogue and an oppositional one—an agonistic one. It is a relationship of considerable tension." See Crapanzano, "On Dialogue," in *The Interpretation of Dialogue*, ed. Tullio Maranhao (Chicago: Univ. of Chicago Press, 1990), 276.

37 This distinction may help to explain why the dialogue in utopian fiction is almost without exception disappointingly flat or stilted. The utopia's formal dialogues can hardly be considered "dialogic" in the privileged sense granted that term by Bakhtin, in which discourse

"there are two voices, two meanings, and two expressions." See
M. M. Bakhtin, *The Dialogic Imagination* (Austin: Univ. of Texas
Press, 1981). The flat world of utopian dialogue presents two figures,
both shadows: the shadow of curiosity ("Let me implore you to describe that island to us . . . you can take it for granted that we want to
know everything that we don't know yet") and the shadow of gratifi-
cation ("There's nothing I'd rather do, for these things are fresh in
my mind"). Though two speakers are present, these exchanges are
not necessarily "true dialogue." Jochen Mecke points out: "If, on the
one hand, a true dialogue may take place within a single person, on
the other hand, the existence of several participants in communication does not guarantee its dialogic character. As the example of so-
called discussions in totalitarian systems illustrates, one voice or subject may be disseminated through different individuals having the
same opinions, sharing the same value system and the same language.
Even though all external premises for dialogue are fulfilled, the internal condition, the tension between two or more semantic contex-
tures, is completely missing." See Mecke, "Dialogue in Narration,"
in *The Interpretation of Dialogue*, 202.

38 Eliav-Feldon, *Realistic Utopias*, 1; J. C. Davis, *Utopia and the Ideal Society*, 17.

39 "The book speaks plainly and directly . . . it does not require readers
with critical sophistication, and to dwell for long on the 'literary'
qualities of the book would be, Morris would say, beside the point."
William Morris, *News from Nowhere; or, An Epoch of Rest*, ed. James
Redmond (London: Routledge and Kegan Paul, 1970), xxiv–xxv.

40 The most rigorous studies of utopianism have been historical, rather
than literary. See J. C. Davis, *Utopia and the Ideal Society*; Miriam
Eliav-Feldon, *Realistic Utopias*; and Keith Thomas, "The Utopian
Impulse in Seventeenth-Century England," *Dutch Quarterly Review*
15.3 (1985), 162–88. An encyclopedic study can be found in Frank
and Fritzie Manuel's *Utopian Thought*. Other historical surveys in-
clude Alfred Braunthal, *Salvation and the Perfect Society: The Eternal
Quest* (Amherst: Univ. of Massachusetts Press, 1979), J. O. Hertzler,
The History of Utopian Thought (New York, 1965), Harry Levin, *The
Myth of the Golden Age in the Renaissance* (Bloomington: Indiana
Univ. Press, 1969), Lewis Mumford, *The Story of Utopias* (New York,
1922), and Ernest Lee Tuveson, *Millennium and Utopia: A Study in
the Background of the Idea of Progress* (Gloucester: Peter Smith, 1972).
Surprisingly, few or no studies of early modern fiction mention

utopias. Michael McKeon, for example, touches only briefly on the utopian aspects of travel narrative in his survey of seventeenth-century romance. Given the thoroughness of *The Origins of the English Novel, 1600–1740* (Baltimore: Johns Hopkins Univ. Press, 1987), it seems surprising that he doesn't discuss *New Atlantis, The Blazing-world,* or *The Isle of Pines.* Nor is utopian fiction mentioned by J. Paul Hunter in *Before Novels: The Cultural Contexts of Eighteenth-Century English Fiction* (New York: Norton, 1990).

41 J. C. Davis proposes reading Bacon's *New Atlantis* as a play: "Like More's *Utopia, New Atlantis* may usefully, but somewhat arbitrarily, be seen in form as a drama . . . [this] does enable the work to be broken down into clear phases": *Utopia and the Ideal Society*, 196.

1. Founding the "Best State of the Commonwealth"

1 Malcolm Seaborne, *The English School: Its Architecture and Organization, 1370–1870* (London: Routledge and Kegan Paul, 1971), 12.

2 Joan Simon, *Education and Society in Tudor England* (Cambridge: Cambridge Univ. Press, 1966), 75.

3 "Dean Colet's *Statutes* for the foundation of St Paul's School, 1518," *English Historical Documents, 1485–1558*, ed. David C. Douglas (London: Methuen, 1967), 1039–45.

4 Ibid.

5 Ibid. See Penry Williams, *Life in Tudor England* (New York: Putnam, 1974), 127.

6 Mary Thomas Crane, *Framing Authority: Sayings, Self, and Society in Sixteenth-Century England* (Princeton: Princeton Univ. Press, 1993), 78.

7 Donald Leman Clark, *John Milton at St. Paul's* (New York: Columbia Univ. Press, 1948), 52, 39.

8 Crane, *Framing Authority*, 83.

9 Foster Watson, *The English Grammar Schools to 1660: Their Curriculum and Practice* (London: Frank Cass, 1968), 533–34.

10 Liah Greenfield, *Nationalism: Five Roads to Modernity* (Cambridge, Mass.: Harvard Univ. Press, 1992), 47.

11 A. F. Leach, *The Schools of Medieval England* (London: Methuen, 1915), 250.

12 Simon, *Education and Society*, 73.

13 Leach, *Schools of Medieval England*, 305.

14 Erving Goffman, *Asylums: Essays on the Social Situations of Mental Patients and Other Inmates* (New York: Anchor Books, 1961), 6.

15 *Elizabethan People: State and Society*, Documents of Modern History Series, ed. Joel Hurstfield and Alan G. R. Smith (London: Edward Arnold, 1972), 74–75.

16 Goffman, *Asylums*, 7.

17 *Elizabethan People*, 75.

18 Leach, *Schools of Medieval England*, 306.

19 *Elizabethan People*, 75.

20 Watson, *English Grammar Schools*, 533–34.

21 William Roper, *The Life of Sir Thomas More* (rpt.; Springfield, Ill.: Templegate,), 9.

22 Fredric Seebohm, *The Oxford Reformers: John Colet, Erasmus, and Thomas More* (London: Longman, Green, 1896), 24–25.

23 Roper, *Life*, 38, 11.

24 Marius, *Thomas More*, 224–25, 222.

25 Thomas More, *Utopia*, in *The Complete Works of Thomas More*, 15 vols., ed. Edward Surtz and J. H. Hexter (New Haven: Yale Univ. Press, 1965), 4:127. Subsequent references to *Utopia* will be made from this edition and noted parenthetically in the text by page number.

26 "In the elementary schools, the divison of time became increasingly minute; activities were governed in detail by orders that had to be obeyed immediately: 'At the last stroke of the hour, a pupil will ring the bell, and at the first sound of the bell all the pupils will kneel, with their arms crossed and their eyes lowered.'" Michel Foucault, *Discipline and Punish*, trans. Alan Sheridan (New York: Pantheon Books, 1977), 150.

27 Ibid., 181.

28 Northrop Frye, "Varieties of Literary Utopias," in *Utopia and Utopian Thought*, ed. Frank Manuel (Boston: Houghton Mifflin, 1966), 27.

29 Pierre Macherey, *A Theory of Literary Production* (London: Routledge and Kegan Paul, 1985), 202.

30 Richard Halpern, *The Poetics of Primitive Accumulation: English Renaissance Culture and the Genealogy of Capital* (Ithaca: Cornell Univ. Press, 1991), 168.

31 Macherey, *A Theory of Literary Production*, 17.

32 Pierre Bourdieu, *Outline of a Theory of Practice*, trans. Richard Nice (Cambridge: Cambridge Univ. Press, 1977), 196.

33 Editions vary in the prefatory material they include with the text of *Utopia*. Gary Morson makes an insightful comment in this regard: "I have before me six English translations of *Utopia* (as well as one Russian version), none of which—even apart from their different renderings of the same passage in the original—agrees with any of

the others as to where the work begins and as to what material it contains." Morson, *The Boundaries of Genre: Dostoyevsky's Diary of a Writer and the Traditions of the Literary Utopia* (Austin: Univ. of Texas Press, 1981), 165. See Peter Allen, "Utopia and European Humanism: The Function of the Prefatory Letters and Verses," *Studies in the Renaissance* 10 (1963): 91–107.

34 Thomas Greene, *The Light in Troy* (New Haven: Yale Univ. Press, 1982).

35 *The Correspondence of Sir Thomas More*, ed. Elizabeth Frances Rogers (Princeton: Princeton Univ. Press, 1947), 83–85.

36 More's *Utopia*, trans. Ralph Robinson (1551), *English Reprints* (New York: AMS Press, 1966), 4:18–19.

37 Etíenne Balibar, "The Nation Form," in *Race, Nation, and Class: Ambiguous Identities*, ed. Balibar and Immanuel Wallerstein (London: Verso, 1991), 98.

38 G. R. Elton, *Reform and Reformation England, 1509–1558* (Cambridge, Mass.: Harvard Univ. Press, 1977), 366. J. H. Lupton, *The Utopia of Thomas More* (Oxford: Clarendon Press, n.d.), lxxiii.

39 Claudio Guillen, *Literature as System: Essays toward the Theory of Literary History* (Princeton: Princeton Univ. Press, 1971).

40 John Colet, "A Lytell Proheme to the Booke called *Grammaticus Rudimentia,*" in *The Pauline Muses*, ed. Edward Pine (London: Victor Gollancz, 1947), 11–12.

2. A Land of Experimental Knowledge

1 Rosalie Colie, "Cornelis Drebbel and Salomon de Caus: Two Jacobean Models for Salomon's House," *Huntington Library Quarterly* 18.3 (1955), 257.

2 C. Van der Woude (1645) in William Benchley Rye, *England as Seen by Foreigners in the Days of Elizabeth and James the First* (London: John Russell Smith, 1865), 234.

3 Colie, "Cornelis Drebbel," 254.

4 Van der Woude, *England as Seen by Foreigners*, 234.

5 Brahe, the astronomer best known today as Kepler's teacher, was granted tenancy of a small island off the Danish coast to establish a research colony dedicated to celestial observation. For more than a decade Brahe presided over Uranibourg, the small scientific community on the island of Hveen, living in eccentric fashion with a jester, a servant he eventually married, and a series of student-apprentices

and builders. At Hveen Brahe also ran a laboratory in which he conducted chemical experiments and made medical elixirs he dispensed to visitors without charge. Stjernebourg, the island's observatory, was manned at all times, enabling what was to constitute an entirely new method for the recording of scientific data. One of the most revolutionary features of the colony was Brahe's attention to the recording of information, as well as its accumulation. Uranibourg's library was dominated by a brass globe erected so that each newly recorded star could be etched on its surface. A paper mill was built on the island, and in 1584 Hveen installed a printing press so that the scientists could publish astronomical predictions and "weather prognostications" in the form of calendars. Brahe's colony on Hveen drew aristocratic and royal visitors from all over Europe, including James himself, traveling in Denmark after his marriage to Anne in 1589. Information about Hveen has been culled by scholars from Brahe's diary and from his correspondence. See J. L. E. Dreyer, *Tycho Brahe: A Picture of Scientific Life and Work in the Sixteenth Century* (New York: Dover, 1963).

6 Other English visitors to Hveen included Lord Willoughby d'Eresby and his physician, Thomas Muffet, in 1582, and Daniel Rogers, also in the service of Queen Elizabeth. See Dreyer, *Tycho Brahe*, 137.

7 Peter J. French, *John Dee: The World of an Elizabethan Magus* (London: Routledge and Kegan Paul, 1972), 44.

8 Francis Johnson, *Astronomical Thought in the Renaissance: A Study of English Scientific Writings from 1500 to 1645* (Baltimore: Johns Hopkins Univ. Press, 1937), 138.

9 French, *John Dee*, 180.

10 James Spedding, Robert Ellis, and Douglas Heath, eds., *The Works of Francis Bacon*, 12 vols. (London, 1864), 11:25, 66. All references to the works of Francis Bacon will be made from this edition, marked parenthetically by volume and page number.

11 Bacon's "reduction" of Ireland was to consist of four points—the extinguishing of the relics of war, the recovery of the hearts of the people, the removing of the root and occasions of new troubles, and the establishment of plantations and buildings. Julian Martin has a useful summary of Bacon's positions on Ireland and Spain in *Francis Bacon, the State, and the Reform of Natural Philosophy* (Cambridge: Cambridge Univ. Press, 1992), 132ff.

12 Julian Martin argues that *New Atlantis* "must also be considered in terms of centralised government and a reformed, civil polity. The

story is, in the first instance, about an imperial state": ibid., 135. Charles Whitney, in "Merchants of Light: Science as Colonization in *New Atlantis*," claims *New Atlantis* is "in effect, a political allegory. A socially symbolic meaning, in many specifics unattempted, thus supplements the main argument about science," *Francis Bacon's Legacy of Texts*, ed. William A. Sessions (New York: AMS Press, 1990), 256. Despite its relative paucity of social references, Whitney sees *New Atlantis* as offering "a vision of science linked inseparably to external and even internal colonialism" (257). In "The New Atlantis and the Uses of Utopia," *English Literary History* 57 (Fall 1990): 503–26, Denise Albanese argues that in *New Atlantis* colonialism "becomes both *topos* and trope, a culturally available validation of the novelty proclaimed by [Bacon's] philosophical program" (507).

13 Vincent Todd Harlow, *Ralegh's Last Voyage* (1932; rpt., New York: Da Capo Press, 1971), 344.

14 Paolo Rossi, in the *Dictionary of the History of Ideas: Studies of Selected Pivotal Ideas*, 4 vols., ed. Philip P. Wiener (New York: Scribner, 1968), 1:174.

15 As Albanese puts it, "When all of Bacon's text are to one degree or another 'unperfected'—from the twice-revised and augmented *Essays* to the *Great Instauration* and all the components nested within it—it becomes fair to question the textual and ideological functions of imperfection in the Baconian program": "New Atlantis," 523. Charles Whitney has suggested that Bacon's "modernity" lies in part in what he considers to be a "compulsion not to finish": "Much of the force of Bacon's aphorisms, natural histories, and essays depends on their prospective quality as beginnings or representations of beginnings. But Bacon's philosophical work, and much of his other work as well, seems always to be just getting started. Its revolutionary character is manifested mainly in claims, statements of intent, and in exhortation. One assumes that Bacon would have liked to finish more than he did, but works that inadequately realize their projected plan are in such a majority that they must be viewed as fulfilling some unstated (and perhaps unconscious) pattern—one that reveals the modernity of his project." Whitney, *Francis Bacon and Modernity* (New Haven: Yale Univ. Press, 1986), 189.

16 *Leonardo da Vinci and a Memory of his Childhood* (1910), in *The Complete Psychological Works of Sigmund Freud*, trans. James Strachey (London: Hogarth Press, 1964), 11:57–137.

17 Caroline Merchant, *The Death of Nature: Women, Ecology, and the Scientific Revolution* (San Francisco: Harper and Row, 1983), 183.

18 In *Panopticon; or, The Inspection House* [(1787; reprinted in *Works*, ed. John Bowring, 11 vols., New York: Russell and Russell, 1962)], Jeremy Bentham laid out the principle of "central inspection" (40). This was elaborated on by Michel Foucault in *Discipline and Punish*, trans. Alan Sheridan (New York: Pantheon Books, 1977): "The more constantly the persons to be inspected are under the eyes of the persons who should inspect them, the more perfectly will the purpose of the establishment have been attained." "The essence [of the plan] consists, then, in the *centrality* of the inspector's situation, combined with the well-known and most effectual contrivances for *seeing without being seen*." In Foucault's chapter on "Panopticism" (*Discipline and Punish*, 195–228), he points out that the Panopticon "also does the work of a naturalist" and that "the Panopticon was also a laboratory" (203), and that both inform the disciplinary procedures of modern culture. Foucault mentions Bacon, though not *New Atlantis*, in this discussion: "On the threshold of the classical age, Bacon, lawyer and statesman, tried to develop a methodology of investigation for the empirical sciences. What Great Observer will produce the methodology of examination for the human sciences?" (226).

19 In a "total institution," Erving Goffman argues, "minute segments of a person's line of activity may be subjected to regulations and judgments by staff; the inmate's life is penetrated by constant sanctioning interaction from above, especially during the initial period of stay before the inmate accepts the regulations unthinkingly": *Asylums* (New York: Anchor Books, 1961), 38. The inmate, Goffman notes, "is never fully alone; he is always within sight and often earshot of someone, if only his fellow inmates" (25). Goffman is especially interested in the procedures of initiation through which the individual is "converted" to inmate. "The admission procedure can be characterized as a leaving off and a taking on, with the midpoint marked by physical nakedness. Leaving off of course entails a dispossession of property, important because persons invest self-feelings in their possessions. Perhaps the most significant of these possessions is not physical at all, one's full name; whatever one is thereafter called, loss of one's name can be a great curtailment of the self" (18). In *New Atlantis*, the mariners' names are "left off" in this fashion even as the narrative begins.

20 Whitney points out that the name Solomon powerfully links Bacon's story to Spanish colonization and to fabulous legends of a rich Southern Pacific land, an Australia or Ophir. Richard Hakluyt's compendium of travel accounts includes that of the Spanish captive Lopez Vaz on the Solomon Islands discovered by Mendana in 1568: they are called the "Isles of Salomon" after "those from whence Salomon fetched gold to adorn the Temple of Jerusalem." Many contemporaries of Bacon also knew the widely circulated memorial of a later explorer of the Solomons, Ferdinand Quiros, who wanted to found an egalitarian "New Jerusalem" there—an apt model for Bacon's own South Sea, Christian, Solomonic utopia, trading however not gold but "light": "Merchants of Light," 261. Bacon's use of Solomon as the eponymous founder of his utopia's scientific institute is part of the Hebraism not merely of *New Atlantis* but of his entire oeuvre. See Joan Wyle Hall, "Salomon Saith: Bacon's Use of Solomon in the 1625 Essayes," *Univ. of Dayton Review* 15 (spring 1982): 83–88.

21 James Hilton's *Lost Horizon* (New York: Grosset and Dunlap, 1933) has recently been read as an "archive-state" that "operates not only as a fortress but also as a museum that spreads its capillaries all over the world to recruit the best and the brightest personnel from among a shifting pool of state nomads." See Thomas Richards, "Archive and Utopia," *Representations* 37 (winter 1992): 125. This system of utopian exchange dates back at least as far as Tommasso Campanella's *City of the Sun:* "When I marveled that they knew the histories of these men, they explained to me that they understood the languages of all the nations and that they dispatched ambassadors throughout the world to learn both what was good and bad in each of them. They profit a good deal by doing this." *The City of the Sun*, trans. and ed. Daniel Donno (Berkeley: Univ. of California Press, 1981), 37.

22 The presence of Joabin in *New Atlantis* has elicited surprisingly little commentary. Clearly Joabin is part of the Davidic subtext of *New Atlantis* and is linked as well to its narrative of conversion. Messianic and rabbinical literature was fairly popular among Puritan ministers in the first part of the century, and a belief persisted that Jewish people must be represented in every nation before the millennium, which encouraged some English citizens to militate for their return. In 1621 William Gouge published an anonymous work entitled *The Calling of the Jewes*, anticipating the convergence of Jewish people in a kind of new Jerusalem. Walter Begley has a lively, albeit racist, account in his appendix to volume 1 of Gott's *Nova Solyma*, 349–59,

which Begley attributed (incorrectly) to Milton (2 vols., [London: J. Murray, 1902]). In *Nova Solyma* the hebraism in English utopias of this period reaches its apex, as two Englishmen, Eugenius and Politian, are brought to "Zion" by their friend Joseph and taught by his father, Jacob, of the perfection of that city. See the account in J. C. Davis, *Utopia and the Ideal Society* (Cambridge: Cambridge Univ. Press, 1981), 140–67.

23 "The Uncanny" (1919), in *The Complete Psychological Works of Sigmund Freud*, 17:219–52.

24 Julie Solomon has traced connections between science in *New Atlantis* and "conjury" in Thomas Harriot's ethnography of the Algonquin Indians in *A Brief and True Discovery*. See Solomon, "To Know, to Fly, to Conjure: Situating Baconian Science at the Juncture of Early Modern Modes of Reading," *Renaissance Quarterly* 44 (autumn 1991): 513–55.

25 Claudio Guillen, "On the Uses of Literary Genre," in *Literature as System: Essays toward the Theory of Literary History* (Princeton: Princeton Univ. Press, 1971), 107–34. After *New Atlantis* was published posthumously in 1627, it became a commonplace to pair Bacon's utopia with More's. As early as 1627 Burton's Democritus linked the two "witty fictions" in his own embedded utopia in *The Anatomy of Melancholy*. In the preface to *A Description of the Famous Kingdome of Macaria* (1641), Gabriel Plattes announced his plan to deliver his message "in a Fiction, as a more mannerly way, having for my pattern Sir Thomas Moore, and Sir Francis Bacon once Lord Chancellour of England," and in 1642, Milton had praise for "our two famous countreymen, the one in his *Utopia*, the other in his *new atlantis* . . . [who] chose . . . to display the largeness of their spirits by teaching this our world better and exacter things." Robert Burton's "utopia of mine own" was written before *New Atlantis* but substantially revised in subsequent editions between 1627 and 1638. *The Anatomy of Melancholy*, 3 vols., ed. Rev. Shilleto (London: George Bell, 1896), 1:113. The allusion to More and Bacon appears on page 9 of Plattes's *Description of the Famous Kingdome of Macaria* (London, 1641); Milton's reference appears in his *Apology . . . against Smectymnuus*, in *The Complete Prose Works of John Milton*, 18 vols., ed. Frank Patterson (New York: Columbia Univ. Press, 1931), 3:294.

26 Gary Saul Morson, *The Boundaries of Genre: Dostoyevsky's Diary of a Writer and the Traditions of Literary Utopia* (Austin: Univ. of Texas Press, 1981), 74–75.

27 Bensalem deliberately assumes a filial position, as its name derives from the Hebrew *ben*, meaning "son of."

28 Pierre Macherey, *A Theory of Literary Production*, trans. Geoffrey Wall (London: Routledge and Kegan Paul, 1978), 240–48.

29 Two important studies credit Bacon with modernity, or modernism. The first is Timothy Reiss's *The Discourse of Modernism* (Ithaca: Cornell Univ. Press, 1982). Reiss claims that science fiction and utopias in the seventeenth century gave rise to "the dominance of a new class of discourse, the analytico-referential" (13), to which he largely attributes the birth of "modernism." Even more detailed attention to the subject is paid by Charles Whitney in *Francis Bacon and Modernity*.

30 *New Atlantis* "imitates" Campanella's *City of the Sun* in this passage. Cf. Campanella (123): "They have discovered the art of flying, the only art the world lacks, and they expect to discover a glass in which to see the hidden stars and a device by which to hear the music of the spheres."

31 Keith Thomas, "The Utopian Impulse in Seventeenth-Century England," *Dutch Quarterly Review* 15.3 (1985):176.

32 Solomon, "To Know, to Fly, to Conjure," 552.

33 Cited by Macherey, *A Theory of Literary Production*, 215.

34 Rossi, *Dictionary*, 1:178.

3. Houses of Industry

1 A few examples of usage from the 1640s make the variety of connotations evident. Sir Thomas Browne (*Pseudodoxia Epidemica*, vol. 3, pt. 12, p. 132) remarks, "Some say it liveth in Aethiopia, others in Arabia, some . . . in Utopia" (1646). Charles I objected to "that new Utopia of Religion and Government into which they endeavour to transform this Kingdom" (1642). In *Mercurius Anti-pragmaticus* (no. 6. 4.) the author claims "they are likely to wander forty yeeres . . . ere they arrive in their Utopian Paradise." In *Soveraigne Power of Parliaments and Kingdomes*, William Prynne refers to "a new Utopian absolute Royall prerogative . . . not bottomed on the Lawes of God or the Realm" (1643); in 1646 Cook objects (*Vind. Law* 28), "That's but a Utopian consideration, a possibility which never comes into Act." These allusions are from the *Oxford English Dictionary*, 12 vols. (Oxford: Clarendon Press, 1933), 11:485–86.

2 For Milton's remarks, see *Areopagitica* and *An Apology . . . against*

Smectymnuus, in *The Works of John Milton*, 18 vols., ed. Frank Patterson (New York: Columbia Univ. Press, 1931), 4:318, 3:294. Subsequent references to Milton's prose will be from this edition, cited parenthetically by volume and page number.

3 Christopher Hill discusses the impact of printing and freedom from censorship on English radicalism in *The World Turned Upside Down: Radical Ideas during the English Revolution* (Middlesex: Penguin Books, 1975), 17–18. Frank and Fritzie Manuels' remarks on sects and utopianism in the Civil War appear in *Utopian Thought in the Western World* (Oxford: Basil Blackwell, 1979), 334.

4 Charles Webster, *The Great Instauration: Science, Medicine and Reform, 1626–1660* (New York: Holmes and Meier, 1976), 32.

5 Webster discusses Hartlib's plans for Antilia in *The Great Instauration*, 46–47, 86–87, and 98, and Robert Child and John Winthrop's plans, 46–47. For a detailed discussion of John Eliot's "praying towns," see the chapter in James Holstun's *A Rational Millennium: Puritan Utopias of Seventeenth-Century England and America* (New York: Oxford Univ. Press, 1987), 102–65.

6 Robert Burton, *The Anatomy of Melancholy*, ed. Holbrook Jackson (New York: Vintage Books, 1977), 98.

7 Samuel Hartlib, *Clavis Apocalyptica, or, a Prophetical Key* (1651), epistle to the reader. J. C. Davis's discussion of millenarianism and utopia is a useful survey; see *Utopia and the Ideal Society* (Cambridge: Cambridge Univ. Press, 1981), 314 ff. Holstun, who draws a distinction between "hermeneutical" and "catalytic" millennialism in *A Rational Millennium* (45), explores the subject throughout his study.

8 *Olbia. The New Iland Lately Discovered. With its Religion and Rites of Worship; Laws, Customs, and Government, Characters, and Language; With Education of Their Children in their Sciences, Arts, and Manufactures, with other things remarkable.* By a Christian Pilgrim [John Sadler], driven by Tempest. . . . London, 1660. Sadler discusses his predictions concerning the end of time on 380 ff.

9 Daniel 12.4. See Webster, *Great Instauration*, 18 ff., and Holstun, *A Rational Millennium*, 49–50.

10 Webster's *Great Instauration* treats the subjects of agricultural and educational reform in such careful detail that only a general debt to his study can be acknowledged here. See especially chap. 5, "Dominion over Nature," 324–483. For a feminist perspective on Hartlib and the reformers, see Carolyn Merchant, *The Death of Nature: Women,*

Ecology, and the Scientific Revolution (San Francisco: Harper and Row, 1980), 186–90.

11 Spenser's description in *A View of the Present State of Ireland* (1633), for example, draws a comparison between the starving Irish and New World "cannibals": "Out of everie corner of the woodes and glennes they came crepinge forth upon theire handes, for theire legges could not beare them, they looked Anotomies of death, they spake like ghostes cryinge out of theire graves, they did eate of the dead Carrions, happye were they could fynde them, yea and one another soone after in so much as the verie Carcases they spared not to scrape out of their graves" (ed. W. L. Renwick [London: Eric Partridge / Scholar's Press, 1934), 135.

12 See Richard Dunn's remarks on this subject in *Sugar and Slaves: The Rise of the Planter Class in the English West Indies, 1624–1713* (New York: Norton, 1973), 137–39, 147–48, 154.

13 *Nova Solyma, the Ideal City; or, Jerusalem Regained. An Anonymous Romance written in the Time of Charles I. Now First Drawn from Obscurity and Attributed to the illustrious J.M.*, ed. Rev. Walter Begley (London: J. Murray, 1902). On the subject of Plattes's authorship of *Macaria*, see Charles Webster, "The Authorship and Significance of *Macaria*," in *The Intellectual Revolution of the Seventeenth Century*, ed. Charles Webster (London: Routledge and Kegan Paul, 1974), 369–85.

14 Davis mentions Plattes's identification with More in choosing the name Macaria in *Utopia and the Ideal Society*, 319.

15 Max Weber, *The Protestant Ethic and the Spirit of Capitalism*, trans. Talcott Parsons (Gloucester, Mass: Peter Smith, 1988), 155–83. Weber focuses in his discussion on the Puritan Richard Baxter, who denounces wealth and its pursuit but, as Weber points out, actually denounces relaxation in wealth and its enjoyment, emphasizing the necessity for activity, labor, or the rational work of a "calling" (162). "When the limitation of consumption is combined with this release of acquisitive activity," Weber remarks, "the inevitable practical result is obvious: accumulation of capital through ascetic compulsion to save" (172).

16 Christopher Hill critiques Michael Walzer's argument (from *The Revolution of the Saints*, 1965) in *The World Turned Upside Down*, suggesting that what "produced alarm and anxiety in some was an opportunity for others," allowing, at least in relative terms, for social and economic mobility for some individuals (48).

17 On the inscription in Plattes's manuscript, see Davis, *Utopia and the Ideal Society*, 313 n. 37.

18 *Nova Solyma*, 88. The relationship between utopianism and the New Christianity has not, it seems to me, been sufficiently explored. For a summary of the history of New Christians, especially in Spain, see Ronald Sanders, *Lost Tribes and Promised Lands* (New York: Harper Books, 1992), 65–73.

19 Cf. Bunyan's description of the fair in the town called Vanity: "A fair wherein should be sold all sorts of vanity . . . [where] are all such merchandise sold, as houses, lands, trades, places, honours, preferments, titles, countries, Kingdoms, lusts, pleasures, and delights of all sorts." *The Pilgrim's Progress*, ed. Roger Sharrock (Middlesex: Penguin Books, 1965), 125. Interestingly, Gott makes his Bazaar a Ladies Bazaar, suggesting that it is women who are the market for such "tiring houses."

20 Thomas Hobbes, *Leviathan*, ed. C. B. Macpherson (Middlesex: Penguin Books, 1981), 81.

21 C. G. A. Clay, *Economic Expansion and Social Change: England, 1500–1700*, 2 vols. (Cambridge: Cambridge Univ. Press, 1984), 1:230.

22 Richard Lachman, *From Manor to Market: Structural Change in England, 1536–1640* (Madison: Univ. of Wisconsin Press, 1987), 16.

23 Clay, *Economic Expansion*, 1:219. Andrew Appleby, in *Famine in Tudor and Stuart England* (Palo Alto: Stanford Univ. Press, 1978), 155, discusses the severity of harvests between 1647 and 1649. One of his general claims is that a "different pattern of mortality was emerging as early as 1649."

24 As Weber puts it, "Waste of time is thus the first and in principle the deadliest of sins" for the Puritans (*Protestant Ethic*, 157). In Robert Burton's *Anatomy of Melancholy*, Democritus banishes idleness from his utopia: "Wherefore I will suffer no beggars, rogues, vagabonds, or idle persons at all, that cannot give an account of their lives how they maintain themselves . . . [for why should] an idle drone . . . live at ease, and do nothing?" (104).

25 Foucault, *Discipline and Punish*, 144. Webster discusses the establishment of workhouses in *The Great Instauration*, 361. On restrictive controls of the poor, see Clay, *Economic Expansion*, 1:233.

26 Webster discusses vocational training schemes in *The Great Instauration*, 363 n. 97, and Hartlib's specific plans on 362.

27 Webster, *The Great Instauration*, 214, 212, 363.

28 I am indebted in this summary to the account by George H. Sabine in *The Works of Gerrard Winstanley* (Ithaca: Cornell Univ. Press, 1941), 5–11, and to the introduction in Robert W. Kenny's edition of *The Law of Freedom in a Platform; or, True Magistracy Restored* (1941; rpt. New York: Schocken Books, 1973), 1–8.

29 Sabine, *Works*, 9.

30 Sabine, *Works*, 511.

31 See Perry Miller, *The New England Mind: From Colony to Province* (Cambridge, Mass.: Harvard Univ. Press, 1962), and Sacvan Bercovitch, *The American Jeremiad* (Madison: Univ. of Wisconsin Press, 1978). Holstun has a useful discussion in *A Rational Millennium*, 256–65.

32 Holstun, *A Rational Millennium*, 254.

33 Joyce Oldham Appleby, *Economic Thought and Ideology in Seventeenth-Century England* (Princeton: Princeton Univ. Press, 1978), 73.

34 See the discussion by Holstun in *A Rational Millennium*, 269.

4. "No Subjects to the Commonwealth"

1 The event is described by Charles North in a letter to his father, 13 April 1667, cited by Sophie Tomlinson in "My Brain My Stage: Margaret Cavendish and the Fantasy of Female Performance," in *Women, Texts, and Histories, 1575–1760*, ed. Clare Brant and Diane Purkiss (New York: Routledge, 1992), 159. Tomlinson uses the phrase "outrageous upstaging" on the same page.

2 See Catherine Gallagher, "Embracing the Absolute: The Politics of the Female Subject in Seventeenth-Century England," *Genders* 1 (March 1988): 24–29, and Rachel Trubowitz, "The Reenchantment of Utopia and the Female Monarchical Self: Margaret Cavendish's *Blazing World*," *Tulsa Studies in Women's Literature* 2 (fall 1992): 229–45, for a discussion of this identification.

3 Cavendish, "To the Readers" (London, 1668).

4 Wendy Wall, "Our Bodies / Our Texts?" in *Anxious Power: Reading, Writing and Ambivalence in Narrative by Women*, ed. Carol J. Singely and Susan Elizabeth Sweeney (Albany: SUNY Press, 1993), 52.

5 On "inwardness" and Renaissance theater, see Katherine Eisaman Maus, *Inwardness and Theater in the English Renaissance* (Chicago: Univ. of Chicago Press, 1995). The quote is from Sophie Tomlinson, "My Brain My Stage," 150.

6 Helen McAfee, *Pepys on the Restoration Stage* (1916; rpt. New York: Benjamin Blom, 1964), 39, 59–60.

7 Laura Lunger Knoppers, *Historicizing Milton: Spectacle, Power, and Poetry in Restoration England* (Athens: Univ. of Georgia Press, 1994), 1.

8 Richard Helgerson, *Forms of Nationhood: The Elizabethan Writing of England* (Chicago: Univ. of Chicago Press, 1992), 253, 245.

9 For Pepys's responses to seeing women and children on stage, see McAfee, *Pepys on the Restoration Stage*, 47.

10 Tomlinson, "My Brain My Stage," 137–38. For a discussion of the "martial queen" in Cavendish's plays, see Elaine Hobby, *Virtue of Necessity: English Women's Writing, 1649–88* (London: Virago, 1988), 109. Kate Lilley discusses the empress as "a kind of warrior queen, Elizabeth redivivas" in "Seventeenth-Century Women's Utopian Writing," in *Women, Texts, and Histories,* 119.

11 On the frightening aspects of crowds at Restoration plays, see E. G. Hundert, *The Enlightenment Fable: Bernard Mandeville and the Discovery of Society* (Cambridge: Cambridge Univ. Press, 1994), 150.

12 McAfee, *Pepys on the Restoration Stage*, 53–54.

13 *The Description of a New World, Called The Blazing-world. Written by the Thrice Noble, Illustrious, and Excellent Princesse, the Duchess of Newcastle.* London, Printed by A. Maxwell, in the Year M.DC.LX.VIII, 4. I use the Huntington manuscript of Cavendish's utopia, hereafter cited parenthetically in the text by page number.

14 Margaret Cavendish, *The Life of William Cavendish* (London, 1667).

15 Predictably no questions were raised concerning the fertility of Newcastle, fifty-eight when his wife was twenty-five. Instead, Cavendish was prescribed a number of medicines intended to facilitate conception, including ram's excrement, and urged by friends and family to spend less time hunched over her books. See Kathleen Jones, *A Glorious Fame: The Life of Margaret Cavendish, Duchess of Newcastle, 1623–1673* (London: Bloomsbury, 1988), 63. Cavendish's own views of her childlessness have been interpreted unsympathetically by most critics, who believe her disparagement of motherhood was nothing more than envy. In fact, Cavendish herself never mentions missing children, and rather than seeing her writing as a substitute for offspring, she appears rather to have struggled, as did her contemporary John Milton, for a literary contribution that would be remembered (in his terms) for "three generations and downwards" or (in her terms) for a "glorious fame" won by "noble achievements." Even if she had borne Newcastle children, they would have belonged to him and not to her. As she put it

in one of her *Sociable Letters* (London, 1664), "a Woman hath no such Reason to desire Children for her own sake, for first her name is lost . . . also her Family, for neither Name nor Estate goes to her Family. . . . Also she hazards her Life by bringing them into the World, and hath the greatest share of trouble in bringing them up." Women were not entitled under the law even to guardianship of their own children. When Cavendish's father had died, years earlier, a custodian for the Lucas children was appointed by the courts, although they were still living with their mother. For a discussion of women and the law in the early modern period, see Ian McClean, *The Renaissance Notion of Women: A Study in the Fortunes of Scholasticism and Medical Science in European Intellectual Life* (Cambridge: Cambridge Univ. Press, 1980), 68–81.

16 See discussion in Jones, *A Glorious Fame*, 117.

17 *The Diary of Samuel Pepys*, ed. R. C. Latham and W. Matthews, 11 vols. (Berkeley: Univ. of California Press, 1972), 8:196–97, 8:209, 9:123. Surprisingly, this judgment followed the reading of Cavendish's biography of her husband, the one work that received praise during her lifetime. Pepys had stayed home one evening reading the book to "ease his eyes," as he claimed its print was "fair." For Pepys's discussion of Cavendish as "Romantick," see 8:163; for his discussion of her invitation to the Society, see 8:243.

18 Thomas Sprat, *The History of the Royal Society of London* (1667), 64–65. Despite the all-embracing nature of this statement, Sprat's *History* is overwhelmingly nationalistic. He contends that the Society must succeed because it epitomizes the "present prevailing Genius of the English Nation" (78) and "the present Inquiring Temper of this Age" (372). In a lengthy paean to the English, Sprat ascribes to them the "unaffected sincerity" and "sound simplicity" of the middle qualities, "between the reserv'd subtle southern, and the rough unhewn Northern people. . . . So that even the position of our climate, the air, the influence of the heavens, the composition of the English blood . . . seem to joyn with the labour of the Royal Society, to render our Country, a Land of Experimental Knowledge" (114). In Sprat's view even within England the Society will not provoke differences but resolve them. Sprat ends the third part of his *History* with the assurance that scientific inquiry, rather than leading to civic unrest, will make the country prosperous and busy, augmenting rather than diminishing the newly restored king's authority.

19 Ibid., 158, 175.

20 Jones, *A Glorious Fame*, 163.

21 Pepys, *Diary*, 8:243–44.

22 Luce Irigaray, "Is the Subject of Science Sexed?" trans. Carol Mastrangelo Bove, in *Feminism and Science*, ed. Nancy Tuana (Bloomington: Indiana Univ. Press, 1989), 65.

23 Knoppers, *Historicizing Milton*, 143.

24 Pepys, *Diary*, 7:271–72.

25 Daniel Defoe, interestingly enough, draws a comparison between the rampant spread of the Plague and the Great Fire in his *Journal of the Plague Year* (1722). See the discussion by Donald Scott, *The Psychology of Fire* (New York: Scribner, 1974), 15. An interesting survey of fires in early modern England can be found in G. V. Blackstone, *A History of the British Fire Service* (London: Routledge and Kegan Paul, 1957), 19–31. According to Blackstone, accounts of fires became more detailed during the Elizabethan period. The first illustrations of specific fires appeared during the sixteenth century, along with pamphlets detailing their devastation: *The True Report of the burnyng of the Steple and Churche of Poules in London* in 1561, for example, and *The Great Fire of Beccles* in 1586. Despite improvements in fire engines and in fire prevention, cities continued to be destroyed: Tiverton in 1612 and Marlborough in 1653. It was not until after the Great Fire that the city of London regulated either fire prevention equipment or fire insurance. See the account in Blackstone, esp. 19–31.

26 *The Diary of John Evelyn*, ed. John Bowle (Oxford: Oxford Univ. Press, 1985), 213. All subsequent references to Evelyn's diary will be cited parenthetically from this edition by page number.

27 Knoppers, *Historicizing Milton*, 150.

28 See, for instance, the account in *Londinium Redivivum*, cited by Scott, in *Psychology of Fire*, 17 ff.

29 "It is not indeede imaginable how extraordinary the vigilanc[e] and activity of the King and Duke was, even labouring in person, and being present, to command, order, reward, and encourage Workemen; by which he shewd his affection to his people, and gained theirs": *Diary of John Evelyn*, 5–7 September 1666, 212.

30 Millennialists, who held the year's triple sixes in dread, saw the hand of God in the Fire. Apocalyptic prophecies had been abundant throughout the Civil War and Interregnum. In 1658, for instance, one Daniel Baker had warned that a "consuming fire shall be kindled, which will scorch with burning heat all hypocrites, unstable, double-minded workers of iniquity. Yea, a great fire and smoke shall increase,

howling and great wailing shall be on every hand in her streets."
Cited by Blackstone, *A History*, 34.

31 Apparently Hubert, who was hanged at Tyburn, died reasserting his
guilt amid clamors of denials from eyewitnesses. See Blackstone, *A
History*, 20–21, and Scott, *Psychology of Fire*, 15–19. Hubert was not
the only scapegoat. At various times the list of suspects included
Charles II, but the favorite targets among the English were the
Catholics. See the discussion by Knoppers in *Historicizing Milton*,
158–59.

32 Evelyn, for example, gives this account in his diary: "There was (I
know not how) an Alarme begun, that the French and the Dutch
(with whom we were now in hostility) were not only landed, but en-
tring the citty; there being in truth, greate suspicion some days before, of those two nations joyning, and even now, that they had been
the occasion of firing the Towne; this report did so terrifie, that on a
suddaine there was such an uprore and tumult, that they [the Lon-
doners] ran from their goods, and taking what weapons they could
come at, they could not be stop'd from falling on some of those nations whom they casually met" (214–15).

33 Concern for less susceptible buildings follows a sentiment already articulated by early modern utopists. Miriam Eliav-Feldon notes that
"fire precautions are to be adopted in [most utopian] cities: not only
are all buildings to be made of non-inflammable materials, but they
would also have fire-proof walls to separate the buildings" (Andreae)
and "armouries in which shall be kept engines for quenching the fire"
(Burton). See *Realistic Utopias: The Ideal Imaginary Societies of the
Renaissance, 1516–1630* (Oxford: Clarendon Press, 1982), 37. Cavendish's description of the capital city in the Blazing-world makes an interesting comparison: "The City it self was built of Gold: and their
Architectures were noble, stately, and magnificent, not like our Modern, but like those in Romans time; for our modern Buildings ar like
those Houses which Children use to make Cards, one story above another, fitter for Birds, then Men" (9).

34 Dryden's characterization of the fire suggests associations to an ambitious underclass. The progress of the blaze from the city's poorest
sections to the wealthiest areas north and west seemed almost to
parody an aristocratic fear that the underclass might rise up and
consume the governing elite. Earlier chronicles of fires suggest this
rhetoric was not uncommon. In a 1612 tract on the "Lamentable
Burnyng of Tiverton," the transgressive power of fire had been set

forth in distinctly class-coded terms: "the fury of that Mercilesse Element, that consuming Servant of the world, that subject of man, Fire, I mean, which being kept under, without getting too rigorous a head, proves obedient to all our needful uses, (without which we could not live) but obtaining the upper hand, grows rebellious, and ruinates where it comes, as lately the tyranny thereof was shewed." Cited by Blackstone, *A History*, v.

35 *Annus Mirabilis*, stanza 295 (1176–80), *The Works of John Dryden*, 24 vols., ed. Edward Niles Hooker and H. T. Swedenberg Jr. (Berkeley: Univ. of California Press), 1:103.

36 Before the late 1980s, only a handful of critics had published responses to *The Blazing-world*, and that handful had not been admiring. Henry Ten Eyck Perry disparaged the text at the beginning of this century in his biography of Cavendish, seeing it as a "confused result," "well-nigh impossible to analyze": *The First Duchess of Newcastle* (London: Ginn, 1918), 258. Douglas Grant called *The Blazing-world* "confused ridiculous fantasy," arguing that as "either narrative or speculation it is quite hopeless": *Margaret the First* (London: Rupert-Hart Davis, 1958), 208. Frank Manuel sees Cavendish's romance as a "solipsistic manifestation" bordering on insanity, claiming it has much in common with the delusional ravings of Freud's Dr. Schreber: "Towards a Psychological History of Utopias," *Utopias and Utopian Thought* (Boston: Houghton Mifflin, 1966), 69. More recently, Sara Mendelson has objected that Cavendish "was not a true champion of her sex, but an egoist who happened to be of the female gender." See *The Mental World of Stuart Women* (Brighton, Sussex: Harvester, 1987), 55. Dale Spender, in *Mothers of the Novel: A Hundred Good Women Writers before Jane Austen* (New York: Pandora, 1986), 42, has a brief review of Cavendish in her chapter on "Biographical Beginnings" in which she credits her for "literary innovation," but her remarks are limited to one paragraph. Two important new essays reclaim Cavendish's utopia as a serious piece of political and scientific fantasy. See Catherine Gallagher, "Embracing the Absolute," and Rachel Trubowitz, "The Reenchantment of Utopia."

37 Most studies of utopianism in the period exclude Cavendish: for example, J. C. Davis, *Utopia and the Ideal Society: A Study of English Utopian Writing, 1516–1700* (Cambridge: Cambridge Univ. Press, 1981); Miriam Eliav-Feldon, *Realistic Utopias;* and Keith Thomas, "The Utopian Impulse in Seventeenth-Century England," *Dutch Quarterly Review* 15.3 (1985): 162–88.

38 Gallagher, "Embracing the Absolute," 24–29.

39 Knoppers, *Historicizing Milton*, 2.

40 Gaston Bachelard, *The Psychoanalysis of Fire*, trans. Alan C. M. Ross (Boston: Beacon Press, 1964), 10 ff. Bachelard explicitly associates fire with what he calls the "masculine principle," a principle "of the center, a principle of power, active and sudden as the spark and power of will" (53).

41 "The Acquisition and Control of Fire" (1931), in *The Complete Psychological Works of Sigmund Freud*, trans. James Strachey (London: Hogarth Press, 1964), 22:188–190.

42 From *The Common Reader*, cited by Jones, *A Glorious Fame*, 180. Woolf, in fact, was raised with the figure of Margaret Cavendish as a "bogey," in some ways as threatening and silencing a forebear as Milton, that other seventeenth-century author who earns, in Woolf's recollections, the same epithet. If Milton's "bogey" for Cavendish was his authority—his patriarchy, scholarship, and exclusiveness as an author, as Gilbert and Gubar have so provocatively suggested—Cavendish's "bogey" was her "madness," her inability to combine poetic ambition with a "normal" existence. Like so many writers who happen to be women, Cavendish was later represented as having chosen art over life. For Woolf, as I suspect for many other readers, Cavendish's example was impeachable whereas Milton's was not. No doubt she was a more terrifying bogey for Woolf than Milton could ever have been.

5. Nation, Miscegenation

1 *Patriarcha and Other Political Works of Robert Filmer*, ed. Peter Laslett (New York: Garland, 1984), 58. Epigraph is quoted from page 84.

2 Ronald Sanders in *Lost Tribes and Promised Lands* (New York: Harper Books, 1992), 224.

3 *The Isle of Pines (1668): An Essay in Bibliography*, ed. Worthington Chauncy Ford (Boston: Club of Odd Volumes, 1920). Ford acknowledges Defoe's "widely known" debt to Neville on page 48 of this edition. Harold Weber has a brief essay on Neville's utopia entitled "Charles II, George Pines, and Mr. Dorimant: The Politics of Sexual Power in Restoration England," *Criticism* 32 (spring 1990): 193–219. Weber discusses only the first section of the text, and he focuses rather narrowly on George Pine's relationship as patriarch in relation to Charles II. J. C. Davis, who discusses *The Isle of Pines* in the intro-

duction to his study of utopias in the period, classifies the text as an arcadia and thus omits it from further analysis. See *Utopia and the Ideal Society: A Study of English Utopian Writing, 1516–1700* (Cambridge: Cambridge Univ. Press, 1981). The most elaborate discussion of the text that I have found is David Fausett's *Writing the New World: Imaginary Voyages and Utopias of the Great Southern Land* (Syracuse: Syracuse Univ. Press, 1993), 81–90.

4 For a discussion of Campanella's eugenics, see Frank and Fritzie Manuel, *Utopian Thought in the Western World* (Oxford: Basil Blackwell, 1979), 276, and Miriam Eliav-Feldon, *Realistic Utopias* (Oxford: Clarendon Press, 1982), 45–46. Campanella and Patrizi follow Plato, Eliav-Feldon says, in advocating eugenic breeding. Campanella also recommended that during pregnancy women should observe statues of great heroes to improve the physiognomy of their unborn offspring.

5 *The Political Works of James I*, ed. Charles Howard McIlwain (Cambridge, Mass.: Harvard Univ. Press, 1918), 36.

6 The term *race* was changing in meaning during the seventeenth century. According to the *Oxford English Dictionary*, in the Elizabethan period *race* was mostly used to mean the offspring or posterity of a person, a lineage (such as the race of Abraham or of Adam). By the 1660s, Milton was using the term in new ways: for example, in the first book of *Paradise Lost*, he refers to "that Pigmean Race beyond the Indian Mount" (780); in the tenth book he refers to a "Race of Satan" (385). In the late sixteenth and early seventeenth centuries *race* could also be used to describe natural disposition, as Shakespeare's Angelo intended it in *Measure for Measure:* "Now I give my sensuall race the rein."

7 This point is strongly made by Dryden in *Absalom and Achitophel* (1681), in which Charles II's infidelities are presented as kingly and patriarchal duties. In the opening lines of the poem, the speaker laments the advent of piety and priestcraft and the loss of polygamy, "when man on many multiplied his kind." Here is the description of King David in the opening lines of the poem, representing the promiscuous Charles II: "after Heaven's own heart / His vigorous warmth did variously impart / To wives and slaves; and wide as his command, / Scattered his Maker's image through the land."

8 Ronald Sanders, *Lost Tribes*, 287. Sanders discusses English reactions to the marriage of John Rolfe and Pocahontas at length on 263–96.

For an account of Hugh Davis's sentence, see Robert Sickels, *Race, Marriage, and the Law* (Albuquerque: Univ. of New Mexico Press, 1972), 123.

9 England's attitudes on this subject were by no means representative of all Europe: the Spanish attitude toward intermarriage in the colonies, for example, was very different. See the summary in Stanley and Barbara Stein, *The Colonial Heritage of Latin America* (New York: Oxford Univ. Press, 1970), 57–66.

10 Sanders, *Lost Tribes*, 360.

11 See Abbot Emerson Smith, *Colonists in Bondage: White Servitude and Convict Labor in America, 1607–1776* (Gloucester, Mass: Peter Smith, 1965), 30–35, for a discussion of the proportionate numbers of white servants in the colonies and a discussion of "deficiency acts," laws established to prop up the numbers of whites. In *Sugar and Slaves: The Rise of the Planter Class in the English West Indies, 1624–1713* (New York: Norton, 1973), Richard Dunn uses tables to compare the use of white servants and black slaves on West Indian plantations in the seventeenth century. See, for example, "The Labor Force on Fifteen Barbados Plantations, 1640–1667," 68. On the population of Barbados in 1650, see Sanders, *Lost Tribes*, 341.

12 See Dunn, *Sugar and Slaves*, 240, 256–62. Dunn's discussion of slave uprisings is rather uneven in tone. Although he is occasionally sympathetic with the slaves, in other passages he is uncomfortably judgmental, saying, for example, that in Barbados "slaves were deeply rebellious and unwilling" (73), Caribs in Dominica "were far too savage to catch and tame" (74), and the Negroes "brought over in chains" were "hostile and rebellious" (69).

13 Abdul R. JanMohamed discusses the specular nature of colonialist fiction in his essay "The Economy of Manichean Allegory: The Function of Racial Difference in Colonialist Literature," in *Race, Writing, and Difference*, ed. Henry Louis Gates Jr. (Chicago: Univ. of Chicago Press, 1985), 84. For a discussion of Cromwell's "Western Design," see Arthur Percival Newton, *The Colonising Activities of the English Puritans* (New Haven: Yale Univ. Press, 1914), 314–30.

14 *Plato Redivivus* provides the most interesting comparison with *The Isle of Pines*. In it, an English gentleman converses with a doctor and a noble Venetian, trying to understand England's "turbulent position" (20) and how English government has "decayed" (26).

15 To better understand the nature of the Phils' consecutive insurrections, it is important first to consider the place and disposition of

Pine's island. Unlike his predecessors, Neville is quite deliberate in the geographical location of his fictitious island, claiming in his subtitle that it is a "fourth island" in Terra Australis Incognita. Three times, however, the Isle of Pines is associated with Africa. Both Pine's and Van Sloetten's ships stop in the Cape Verde islands, a crucial slave post in the seventeenth century. Both ships pass Madagascar as well, and Pine's passes the Cape of Good Hope at the southern tip of Africa before it is "lost." By situating his utopia so close to Africa, Neville would seem to be referring to changing patterns in English colonial traffic, which (after the formation of the Royal African Company in 1660) increasingly involved the purchase and trade of slaves. But despite Neville's specificity about the location of the island, confusion arises about its geographical setting. There was (and is) a real Isle of Pines, known to the English both through Peter Martyr's description of Columbus's discovery of it in 1494 and through Francis Drake's skirmish there in 1572 in which he stole two boats and several African slaves from Spanish mariners. This island, which served as a penal colony after a period as a haven for pirates and buccaneers, is situated off the coast of Cuba (then Hispaniola). One source suggests that Drake actually attacked the island in 1596, killing its inhabitants and destroying the colony they had built there. Though there is another Isle of Pines (Isla das Pinos) in French New Caledonia, it was not discovered until the late eighteenth century, and it may actually have been named for Neville's island rather than vice versa. So the Isle of Pines that Neville and his audience would have known was situated in the West Indies and not in the South Pacific. In other words, Neville locates his utopian fiction on an island already associated for the English, however confusedly, with piracy, international combat, and the repossession of African slaves.

16 Homi Bhabha has an essay on the "sudden, fortuitous discovery of the English book" in the "wild and wordless wastes of colonial India, Africa, the Caribbean" which would suggest that the Bible becomes a fundamental instrument of colonial authority for each Pine. See "Signs Taken for Wonders: Questions of Ambivalence and Authority under a Tree outside Delhi, May, 1819," *Critical Inquiry* 12 (autumn 1985): 144–65; rpt. in *Race, Writing, and Difference*, 163–84.

17 René Girard discusses the use of the scapegoat in *La Violence et le Sacré* (Paris: Bernard Grosset, 1972), 63 ff.

18 Henry Weber points out that Neville uses an economic metaphor here ("longed for her share"). See Weber, 206.

19 Cf. Eve's relation to Adam of her dream of "flight and change" in book 5 of *Paradise Lost*.

20 See Patricia Morton, *Disfigured Images: The Historical Assault on Afro-American Women* (New York: Greenwood Press, 1991), 6. Tillinghast is quoted by Morton in the same volume, 69.

21 Sanders, *Lost Tribes*, 348–49.

6. Out of the Mouth of History

1 Richard Dunn discusses the Guiana settlements and their failure in *Sugar and Slaves: The Rise of the Planter Class in the English West Indies, 1624–1713* (New York: Norton, 1973), 17.

2 See Peter Hulme, *Colonial Encounters: Europe and the Native Caribbean, 1492–1797* (London: Routledge, 1986), 159.

3 *The discovery of the large, rich, and beautiful Empire of Guiana, with a relation of the great and golden city of Manoa (which the Spaniards call El Dorado).* Performed in the year 1595 by Sir Walter Ralegh, Knight. In Richard Hakluyt, *Voyages and Discoveries*, ed. Jack Beeching (Middlesex: Penguin Books, 1972), 401.

4 On the anachronistic nature of Raleigh's expedition, see Stephen Jay Greenblatt, *Walter Ralegh* (New Haven: Yale Univ. Press, 1973), 165.

5 V. T. Harlow, *Ralegh's Last Voyage, Being an account drawn out of contemporary letters and relations . . . concerning the voyages of Sir Walter Ralegh, Knight, to Guiana in the year 1617 and the fatal consequences of the same* (London, 1932), 344.

6 See George Guffey, "Aphra Behn's Oroonoko: Occasion and Accomplishment," in *Two English Novelists: Aphra Behn and Anthony Trollope*, by George Guffey and Andrew Wright (Los Angeles: William Andrews Clark Memorial Library, UCLA, 1975), for a discussion of the topicality of Behn's romance.

7 Earlier this century Behn was charged with cribbing her Guiana details from George Warren. See Ernest Bernbaum, "Mrs. Behn's Biography, a Fiction," *PMLA* 28 (1913): 432–53. Bernbaum's charge is sharply refuted by Katherine Rogers in "Fact and Fiction in Aphra Behn's *Oroonoko*," *Studies in the Novel* 20 (spring 1988): 1–15. For further discussion on the subject, see Elaine Campbell, "Aphra Behn's Surinam Interlude," *Kunapipi* 7.2–3 (1985): 25–35; William J. Cameron, *New Light on Aphra Behn: An Investigation into the Facts and Fictions Surrounding Her Journey to Surinam in 1663* (Auckland: Univ. of Auckland Press, 1961); and the discussion by Angeline Goreau in

Reconstructing Aphra: A Social Biography of Aphra Behn (New York: Dial Press, 1980), 41–69.

8 George Warren, *An Impartial Description* (London, 1667), 23.

9 *Oroonoko; or, The History of the Royal Slave*, in *Three Histories By Mrs Aphra Behn* (London, 1688), 149–51, 154.

10 In fact, Behn's narrator introduces Anglo-Carib relations to contrast the Caribs with the real subjects of her story, the Coramantien slaves imported from Africa to work the English plantations. Like Surinam's utopian landscape, the Caribs remain part of her backdrop. But even here the distinction she draws between caressing and enslavement is complicated at the very least. Late in the romance, the narrator and several other English women gather the courage to visit some Indian villages, considered especially dangerous since recent English-Indian feuds. Protected by the noble Oroonoko, the women witness various Carib rituals, visit an Indian house, and meet several "fiendish" war-captains. On their way back they encounter "Indians of strange Aspects; that is, of a larger size," apparently from a different tribe, who are carrying bags of gold dust with them from an upcountry river. Behn's narrator reports that these men were taken back to Parham House to be kept until the governor's return, fretfully suspecting in retrospect that the "advantage" of all that gold has gone, with the rest of Surinam's riches, to the Dutch. This entire expedition, we learn in a matter-of-fact aside, was made possible by none other than "Our Indians Slaves, that row'd us" and served as the women's interpreters. Some of the Caribs, caressed "as Friends" or not, are obviously slaves to the English. It would seem that everyone in Surinam is either a slave or at risk of becoming one—everyone, that is, except the English masters.

11 Hakluyt, *Voyages and Discoveries*, 390.

12 The nature of this "truth" has been a subject of great critical interest. See the discussion, for example, by Robert Chibka in "'Oh! Do Not Fear a Woman's Invention': Truth, Falsehood, and Fiction in Aphra Behn's *Oroonoko*," *Texas Studies in Literature and Language* 30 (winter 1988): 510–37.

13 Margaret Ferguson, "Juggling the Categories of Race, Class, and Gender: Aphra Behn's *Oroonoko*," *Women's Studies* 19 (August 1991): 159–81.

14 As Laura Brown points out, the narrator's account of "Oroonoko's classical European beauty" is a "locus classicus of sentimental identification," serving to erase his face rather than to describe it. "The Ro-

mance of Empire: Oroonoko and the Trade in Slaves," in *The New Eighteenth Century*, ed. Felicity Nussbaum and Laura Brown (New York: Routledge, 1991), 47.

15 See Nancy Vickers, "Diana Described: Scattered Women and Scattered Rhyme," in *Writing and Sexual Difference*, ed. Elizabeth Abel (Chicago: Univ. of Chicago Press, 1982).

16 Laura Brown discusses parallels between Oroonoko and Charles I, who was popularly known as Caesar, in "The Romance of Empire," 57–59. James II also used Caesar as a nickname.

Afterword

1 Cited by Timothy Brennan, "The National Longing for Form," in *Nation and Narration*, ed. Homi K. Bhabha (London: Routledge, 1990), 55.

2 Laura Brown, "The Romance of Empire," in *The New Eighteenth Century*, ed. Felicity Nussbaum and Laura Brown (New York: Routledge, 1991), 59.

3 James Sutherland, *The Restoration Newspaper and Its Development* (Cambridge: Cambridge Univ. Press, 1986), 25.

4 Brennan, "National Longing for Form," 52.

5 Nancy Armstrong and Leonard Tennenhouse, *The Imaginary Puritan: Literature, Intellectual Labor, and the Origins of Personal Life* (Berkeley: Univ. of California Press, 1992), 198.

6 See the discussion of "unisonance" in Homi K. Bhabha, "DissemiNation: Time, Narrative, and the Margins of the Modern Nation," in *Nation and Narration*, esp. 308–20.

7 Ernest Gellner, *Nations and Nationalism* (Ithaca: Cornell Univ. Press, 1983).

8 Bhabha, *Nation and Narration*, 4.

INDEX

Abraxa (*Utopia*), 20, 49, 50

Absolutism, defeat of, 179

Actresses, Restoration, 119–20, 203 (n. 9)

Aesop, 187 (n. 35)

Agriculture: reforms in, 87, 199 (n. 10); as metaphor for education, 89

Air, weighing of, 125, 126

Albanese, Denise, 194 (nn. 12, 15)

Algonquin Indians, 197 (n. 24); "praying towns" for, 86, 199 (n. 5)

Amaurotum (*Utopia*), 20

America, utopian communities in, 85–86

Anamorphic art, 16, 186 (n. 28)

Anatomy of Melancholy, The (Burton), 8, 11, 197 (n. 25); parody of spatial location, 86; idleness in, 201 (n. 24)

Anderson, Benedict, 183 (n. 2), 184 (n. 14)

Andrews, Kenneth R., 12

Anne (consort of James I), 165, 193 (n. 5)

Annus Mirabilis (Dryden), 130, 206 (n. 34)

Anonymity, 5, 180

Antimiscegenation laws, 147

Antiquity Reviv'd, 11

Anti-utopias, 16, 111

Aporia, 19

Appleby, Joyce, 111–12

Arcadia, 186 (n. 26); *The Isle of Pines* as, 209 (n. 3)

Aristocracy, of early modern England, 3, 27

Armstrong, Nancy, 180

Army: in early modern England, 4; New Model, 14, 87

Ashmolean Museum, 14

Authors. *See* Utopists

Bachelard, Gaston, 138, 208 (n. 40)

Bacon, Francis, 5; investment in Virginia Companies, 54, 63; scientific program of, 61, 63, 65, 77–78; *Advancement of Learning*, 62, 64, 66, 67, 68–69; on colonialism, 63, 64–65; *Essays*, 63, 64, 194 (n. 15); *Great Instauration*, 63, 66, 194 (n. 15); reduction of Ireland, 63, 193 (n. 11); *An Advertisement Touching an Holy War*, 64; *De Dignitate et Augmentis Scientiarum*, 64, 65; *History of Henry VII*, 64; retirement from public life, 64; *Sylva Sylvarum, or A Natural History*, 64, 66, 68; discursive structures of, 65–67, 76, 81, 194 (n. 15); aphorisms of, 66, 194 (n. 15); incompleteness in, 66, 194 (n. 15); modernity of, 66, 194 (n. 15), 198 (n. 29); use of essay form, 66, 73; nature in, 67–68; *Novum Organum*, 68; literary genres of, 73; "Of Empire," 73; "Of Studies," 73; imitation of *Utopia*, 74; as father of Royal Society, 81; influence on utopists, 83, 93, 197 (n. 25); philosophical works of, 194 (n. 15); Foucault on, 195 (n. 18). See also *New Atlantis*

Baker, Daniel, 205 (n. 30)

Bakhtin, M. M., 188 (n. 37)

Barbados, slavery in, 147, 210 (n. 12)

Basilikon Doron (James I), 144–45

Baxter, Richard, 200 (n. 15)

Letters, 124–25; visit to Royal Society, 125, 127; and Great Fire of London, 130, 132; *Grounds of Natural Philosophy*, 130; *Sociable Letters*, 130, 203 (n. 15); self-deprecation of, 139; biography of husband, 204 (n. 17); Virginia Woolf on, 140, 208 (n. 42). See also *Description of a new world, call'd The Blazing world, The*

Cavendish, William (duke of Newcastle), 116, 203 (n. 15); biography of, 204 (n. 17)

Caxton, William, 187 (n. 35)

Censorship: freedom from, 85, 199 (n. 3); in *Macaria*, 94

Chapman, George, 162–63

Charity, 101

Charles I (king of England), 175; on utopias, 84, 85, 198 (n. 1); and Oroonoko, 214 (n. 16)

Charles II (king of England): and Cornelis Drebbel, 57; patronage of Royal Society, 81, 127; opening of theaters, 117; love of spectacle, 119; coronation of, 128; and Great Fire of London, 129–30, 205 (n. 29); promiscuity of, 145, 209 (n. 7); death of, 168; as patriarch, 208 (n. 3), 209 (n. 7)

Child, Robert, 199 (n. 5)

Chorographies, 185 (n. 20)

Christianity: teleology of, 10; and utopianism, 201 (n. 18)

Citizenship: in utopian narratives, 21; in *Utopia*, 37

City of the Sun (Campanella), 98, 198 (n. 30); eugenics in, 143, 209 (n. 4); exchange in, 196 (n. 21)

Civic obedience: education for, 25, 26, 27, 31, 36; in *The Isle of Pines*, 151

Civil War: utopian narratives of, 4, 5, 89; self-consciousness in, 11; national identity in, 16; utopists of, 83; reform in, 85; poverty following, 100–101; in *Blazing-world*, 136; utopianism during, 199 (n. 3); millennialists during, 205 (n. 30)

Classical utopianism, 178, 179

Clay, C. G. A., 201 (n. 23)

Cockaygne (genre), 186 (n. 26)

Colet, John: and St. Paul's Cathedral School, 5, 23–26, 28; use of monitors, 30; bust of, 31, 32; friendship with More, 31; *Grammaticus Rudimentia*, 54–55

College of Six Days' Work (*New Atlantis*), 66, 69, 76, 78, 79, 80

Colonialism, 185 (n. 19); in utopian narratives, 8, 16, 22; in *Utopia*, 12, 41; and national identity, 16; and capital venture, 54; Bacon on, 63, 64–65; Roman, 64–65; as scientific experimentation, 78; role of poor in, 90; imaginary worlds in, 121; and intermarriage, 146, 210 (n. 9); and racial differences, 146–49; racial proportion in, 147, 210 (n. 11); Elizabethan, 162–64; seventeenth-century, 169, 185 (n. 22); in *New Atlantis*, 194 (n. 12); Spanish, 196 (n. 20); authority of Bible in, 211 (n. 16). *See also* Plantations, colonial; Slavery, African

Columbus, Christopher, 18, 52, 187 (n. 32); in Guiana, 162; discovery of Isle of Pines, 211 (n. 15)

Comenius, Johann, 89

Commonwealth Defended, A, 90

Commonwealth government: English utopists on, 5; didactic treatises on, 14–15; in *The Law of Freedom in a Platform*, 105, 106,

England (*cont.*)
of power in, 179; status of
women in, 204 (n. 15). *See also*
State, early modern
Erasmus, Desiderius: and St. Paul's
school, 24, 25; and Thomas More,
47, 48, 49
Ergastula literaria (Petty), 102
Estrangement: from society, 9, 184
(n. 10); of utopian fiction, 16, 186
(n. 28); in *Blazing-world*, 132
Eton, prepostors in, 30–31
Eugenics: in *City of the Sun*, 143, 209
(n. 4); in Plato, 209 (n. 4)
Euripides, 187 (n. 35)
Europe, utopian narratives of, 3, 183
(n. 3)
Evelyn, John: on Margaret
Cavendish, 123, 125; on Great Fire
of London, 129, 206 (n. 32); on
Charles II, 130, 131
Everard, William, 102
Experimental communities, 85–86
Experimentation, scientific, 65; in
Bacon, 68; colonialism as, 78; audi-
ence for, 79–80; Bacon's influence
on, 81; and royal authority, 204
(n. 18). See also *New Atlantis;*
Research; Science

Factories, model, 101
Fairfax, Lord, 103
Famines, 100, 101, 114; in Ireland,
200 (n. 11)
Feudalism, deterioration of, 100
Fiction: science, 9, 132, 184 (n. 11),
198 (n. 29); specular, 149, 210
(n. 13); effect on utopian narratives, 178; seventeenth-century,
179, 189 (n. 40)
Filmer, Robert: colonialism in, 16;
on Noah, 141; *Patriarcha*, 145–46

Fire: in early modern England, 128,
205 (n. 25); in prevention of
plague, 129; as spectacle, 137–38;
in *Blazing-world*, 137–39, 140;
masculine principle of, 138, 208 (n.
40); myths of, 138; transgressive
power of, 206 (n. 33). See also *Description of a new world, call'd The
Blazing-world, The;* Great Fire of
London
Ford, Worthington Chauncy, 208
(n. 3)
Foucault, Michel: on institutions, 17,
187 (n. 31); on timetables, 36; on
punishment, 39; on education, 191
(n. 26); on surveillance, 195 (n. 18)
Founding fictions: in *New Atlantis*, 2;
in utopias, 50, 178, 180; *Utopia* as,
54; in *Blazing-world*, 133
Freedom: and institutions, 17, 19;
from censorship, 85, 199 (n. 3); to
work, 107
Freud, Sigmund, 66, 138
Frugality: in *Macaria*, 94; in *Nova
Solyma*, 96–97
Frye, Northrop, 9, 40, 184 (n. 10)
Fuller, Thomas, 188 (n. 35)

Gallagher, Catherine, 120
Gassendi, Pierre, 122
Gellner, Ernest, 5, 180
Genres, conventionalization of, 54
Geography, utopian, 9–10, 15–16,
19–21
Gerbier, Balthazar, 102
Giles, Peter, 48
Girard, René, 151
Gnomologia (Fuller), 188 (n. 35)
God and the King (textbook), 27
Godwin, Francis, 132
Goffman, Erving, 16, 28–29, 195
(n. 19)

Holstun, James: on demographics, 14; on Milton, 111; on millennialism, 199 (n. 7)

Hooke, Robert, 124

Households, in *Utopia*, 37, 38

House of Industry (Carey), 102

Hubert (watchmaker), 129, 140, 206 (n. 31)

Humorous Lovers (duke of Newcastle), 116

Husbandry: in *Macaria*, 89, 95; in seventeenth-century utopias, 89; as metaphor for salvation, 93; in *The Law of Freedom in a Platform*, 106

Huygens, Christiaan, 56–57

Hveen (Denmark): research colony at, 60, 192 (n. 5); visitors to, 193 (n. 6)

Hythlodaeus, Raphael (*Utopia*): on Abraxa, 20; on timetables, 33, 36; on education, 39; on English culture, 40; on colonialism, 41; on the marketplace, 43; as narrator, 47, 49, 51; on marriage, 74; on Macaria, 93–94

Iamboulous (Diodorus Siculus), 17–18, 187 (nn. 32, 35)

Idleness: and poverty, 90–91; Winstanley on, 100, 106, 110–11; reformers on, 101; in *The Isle of Pines*, 150; in *The Anatomy of Melancholy*, 201 (n. 24)

Imagination, in *Blazing-world*, 121, 135–36, 140

"Imagined community," 2, 183 (n. 2)

Imitation, in *Utopia*, 39–40, 47

Imoinda (*Oroonoko*), 170, 171, 175

Impartial Description of Surinam upon the Continent of Guiana, An (Warren), 165–67, 212 (n. 7)

Imperialism: English, 12–13; and science, 61, 63, 64, 83

Indians, American, 90, 197 (n. 24), 199 (n. 5)

Individualism: in utopias, 8; and institutions, 19

Industry: workhouses as model of, 5; in utopian narratives, 21, 89, 91–92, 94, 112; Dutch as model of, 92, 111–12, 113–14; in *Macaria*, 92, 95; in *Nova Solyma*, 96; in *The Law of Freedom in a Platform*, 107

Institutions: of early modern state, 3, 14; in utopias, 5, 15, 16, 21, 180; "total," 16, 28–29, 195 (n. 19); Foucault on, 17, 187 (n. 31); dialogue with individuals, 19; corruption in, 40; in *Utopia*, 51–52; reform of, 54, 87; "entrance," 70; transfer of power to, 179; Nietzsche on, 187 (n. 31)

Insurrection: in utopias, 143; in *The Isle of Pines*, 147, 150, 157–58, 159, 161, 210 (n. 15); in *Oroonoko*, 147, 148, 169, 170–71, 173, 175; of slaves, 147, 210 (n. 12); as spectacle, 177. *See also* Slavery, African

Interregnum: national identity in, 16; utopists of, 83; reform in, 85; disillusionment with, 111; millennialists during, 205 (n. 30)

Inventions, scientific, 57, 60; in *New Atlantis*, 57, 60, 76, 194 (n. 12). *See also* Experimentation, scientific; Laboratories; Science

Ireland: Bacon on, 63, 193 (n. 11); famine in, 200 (n. 11)

Irigaray, Luce, 127

Irony: in More's *Utopia*, 46; in depiction of ideal commonwealth, 179

Islas das Pinos (French New Caledonia), 211 (n. 15)

Isle of Pines, The (Neville), 11; dialogue in, 19; location of, 20, 211 (n. 15); publication of, 141; national identity in, 142–43, 160–61; patriarchy in, 142–43, 208 (n. 3); racial differences in, 143, 144, 155; as source for *Robinson Crusoe*, 143, 208 (n. 3); insurrection in, 147, 150, 157–58, 159, 161, 210 (n. 15); master-slave relations in, 149; narrative structure of, 149; popularity of, 149; Bible in, 150, 211 (n. 16); as Noah legend, 150, 160; possession in, 150; scapegoating in, 150; reproduction in, 150–51, 156; boundaries in, 152, 153; as Paradise, 152–53; sexual relations in, 153, 154–55, 157, 158, 159, 160; social status in, 153; power relations in, 154–55; population in, 156; marriage in, 158; as satire on the Civil War, 160; as arcadia, 209 (n. 3). *See also* Neville, Henry

Isle of Pines (West Indies), 211 (n. 15)

Isolation: in *New Atlantis*, 72–73; in *Blazing-world*, 132

Jamaica, slavery in, 147, 148

James I (king of England): and Cornelis Drebbel, 56–57; and Bacon's scientific program, 61–62; *Basilikon Doron*, 144–45; and Guiana expedition, 164, 165; and Tycho Brahe, 192–93 (n. 5)

James II (king of England), 165, 177; and Great Fire of London, 205 (n. 29)

Jameson, Fredric, 9; on genre, 11; 185 (n. 17)

Jamestown colony, 63

JanMohamed, Abdul, 149, 210 (n. 13)

Jeremiad: Winstanley's use of, 108–9

Jewels: in *Blazing-world*, 134–35, 140

Joabin (*New Atlantis*), 74–75, 196 (n. 22)

Joint-stock companies, 12, 185 (n. 22)

Jonson, Ben, 57, 188 (n. 35)

Kenny, Robert W., 108

Kepler, Johannes, 132

Killigrew, Thomas, 117, 119

King, Susan, 104

Knapp, Jeffrey, 12

Knoppers, Laura, 119, 128; on spectacle, 135

Knowledge: in works of Bacon, 68–69; reproduction of, 73, 74; as commodity, 99; "laborious," 102

Labor: in *New Atlantis*, 80–81; idealization of, 92; in seventeenth-century utopias, 100–102; rehabilitative, 102. *See also* Industry

Laboratories: in *New Atlantis*, 5, 65, 68, 76–79; at Eltham Palace, 57, 60; alchemical, 58; as homology for state, 83; in *Macaria*, 95

Laboring class, seventeenth-century, 16. *See also* Industry

Ladies Bazaar (*Nova Solyma*), 97–98, 201 (n. 19)

"Lamentable Burnyng of Tiverton," 206–7 (n. 34)

Land surveys, Elizabethan, 185 (n. 20)

Land utilization, 42; reform of, 89; for peasants, 101; Diggers' belief in, 103; in *The Law of Freedom in a Platform*, 110

Law: humanist debate on, 46; R. H. on, 115

Law of Freedom in a Platform, The (Winstanley), 11, 20, 105–11; land use in, 89, 110; monarchy in, 90, 109; commonwealth government in, 105, 106, 107, 109; education in, 106; idleness in, 106, 110–11; industry in, 107; patriarchy in, 107; dialogue in, 108, 109–10; regulation of population in, 108; scripture in, 108; as model for utopists, 110; goals of, 111. *See also* Winstanley, Gerrard

LeGuin, Ursula, 9

Leicester, earl of, 61

Leonardo da Vinci, 66

Leviathan (Hobbes), 11, 99–100

Libraries, 60–61

Licensing Act, 179–80

Lilley, Kate, 203 (n. 10)

Lily, William, 24, 26

Lincoln's Inn Theater, 116

Literacy rates, 180

London Corporation for the Poor, 101

London Stock Exchange, 14, 54, 63

Lost Horizon (Hilton), 71, 196 (n. 21)

Lucas, Margaret. *See* Cavendish, Margaret

Lucian, 45, 132

Lupset, Thomas, 48

Lupton, J. H., 53

Lupton, Thomas, 11

Lyly, John, 11, 185 (n. 16)

Macaulay, Thomas Babington, 180

Macherey, Pierre, 16, 76; on shortage, 42

Man, as machine, 99–100

Mandeville, John, 17, 52

Man in the Moone, The (Godwin), 132

Manley, Mary de la Rivière, 179

Mannheim, Karl, 9

Manoa (Guiana), 163, 212 (n. 3)

Manuel, Frank and Fritzie, 187 (n. 32), 189 (n. 40); on sects, 199 (n. 3)

Marcuse, Herbert, 9

Marin, Louis, 9, 16, 184 (n. 10), 186 (n. 28); on *Utopia*, 51

Marketplace: in *Utopia*, 40, 42–45, 54; in *Nova Solyma*, 97–98, 99. *See also* Capitalism

Marriage: in *Utopia*, 74; royal, 145; interracial, 146–47, 209 (n. 8), 210 (n. 9); in *The Isle of Pines*, 158. *See also* Race

Martin, Julian, 193 (nn. 11–12)

Marx, Karl: on *New Atlantis*, 80

Massachusetts Bay Colony, 12, 63

Master-slave relations, 144, 146–48; in *The Isle of Pines*, 149; in Warren, 166–67; in *Oroonoko*, 170–73, 176, 213 (n. 10)

McKeon, Michael, 178–79, 190 (n. 40)

Mecke, Jochen, 189 (n. 37)

Mendelson, Sara, 207 (n. 36)

Mercer's Company (London), 24

Merchant, Caroline, 67

Merchant's Exchange (*Nova Solyma*), 97–98

Merry Wives of Windsor, The (Shakespeare), 163

Millennialism, 87, 186 (n. 26); radical, 108; types of, 199 (n. 7); in Great Fire of London, 205 (n. 30)

Milton, John: on utopias, 8–9, 197 (n. 25); *Areopagitica*, 84–85; *Readie & Easie Way To Establish A Free Commonwealth*, 89, 111–13; attribution of *Nova Solyma* to, 91; on nationalism, 111; on monarchy, 112, 113; "Lycidas," 113; *Paradise Lost*, 188 (n. 35), 209 (n. 6), 212 (n. 19); *Apology . . . against*

Restoration, 141; and racial differences, 142; in *The Isle of Pines*, 142–43, 208 (n. 3); monarchy as, 145

Peacham, Henry, 57

Peasants, poverty of, 101

Penal codes, 46

Pepys, Samuel: on Margaret Cavendish, 116–17, 123–24, 125, 127, 204 (n. 17); on theater audiences, 120; on Great Fire of London, 128; on actresses, 203 (n. 9)

Perry, Henry Ten Eyck, 207 (n. 36)

Peter, Hugh, 102

Peter Martyr, 46

Petty, William, 101, 102

Phils (*The Isle of Pines*), 156, 157, 158, 159, 160, 210 (n. 15)

Pilgrim's Progress (Bunyan), 93, 98, 201 (n. 19)

Plague (1665), 116, 128; use of fire against, 129

Plantations, colonial, 5; Bacon on, 63; interracial marriage on, 146–47; effect on utopian narratives, 148–49; racial proportion on, 210 (n. 11). *See also* Colonialism; Slavery, African

Plato: and More's *Utopia*, 19, 45, 47, 48–49, 51, 75; Atlantis in, 75; *Critias*, 75; *Timaeus*, 75; on slavery, 143; eugenics in, 209 (n. 4)

Platt, John, 103–4

Plattes, Gabriel: starvation of, 5, 95–96; and English commonwealth, 81; on *New Atlantis*, 81; and More's *Utopia*, 86, 91, 200 (n. 14); *A Discovery of Subterraneal Treasure*, 92, 93; *The Profitable Intelligencer*, 92, 93; *A Discovery of Infinite Treasure*, 92–93; *The Trea-*

sure House of Nature Unlocked, 95. See also *Description of the Famous Kingdome of Macaria, A*

Plautus, 187 (n. 35)

Plockhoy, Peter Cornelius, 85

Plutarch, 45

Pocahontas, 209 (n. 8)

Poenulus (Plautus), 188 (n. 35)

Political service, humanist debate on, 46

Political tracts, seventeenth-century, 16

Polygamy, 209 (n. 7)

Poor: colonization of, 90; comparison with savages, 90, 200 (n. 11); utopists on, 90–91, 100; in works of Plattes, 92–93; in *Nova Solyma*, 100; in London, 101; peasants among, 101; restrictive controls on, 101, 201 (n. 25); children of, 102; Winstanley on, 104; in *A Modest Plea*, 113; in seventeenth-century utopias, 115

Poor Laws, 101

Population: in Puritan utopias, 14; in *Utopia*, 41–42, 44; in *The Law of Freedom in a Platform*, 108; slave, 147–48; in *The Isle of Pines*, 156

Possession: in *The Isle of Pines*, 150; in *Oroonoko*, 169

Power: in early modern England, 3, 14; of Restoration theater, 119, 140; in *The Isle of Pines*, 154–55; in *Oroonoko*, 165; transfer to institutions, 179; language of, 184 (n. 14)

Praying towns, 86, 199 (n. 5)

Pride, in *Utopia*, 44, 45

Principal Navigations (Hakluyt), 12, 196 (n. 20)

Printing: impact on radicalism, 85, 199 (n. 3); in *Macaria*, 85; and spread of utopianism, 85; early

Printing (*cont.*)
modern, 183 (n. 7); effect on national identity, 184 (n. 14); Brahe's use of, 193 (n. 5)
Privacy, in *Utopia*, 38
Production: in utopian narratives, 8, 180; authorial, 50; in *New Atlantis*, 80
Productivity, in *Utopia*, 39–40
Prometheus, 138, 139
Promiscuity, royal, 145, 209 (n. 7)
Promotion, in *Utopia*, 39, 45
Property, in total institutions, 195 (n. 19)
Proposals for Raising a College of Industry (Bellers), 102
Protestants, English: martyrdom of, 4; reading of *Utopia*, 53
Prynne, William, 119, 198 (n. 1)
Public education: in early modern England, 3, 4; in utopian narratives, 22; hierarchy in, 24, 28, 36; as "total institution," 28; surveillance in, 29–31; Foucault on, 187 (n. 31). *See also* Grammar schools, Tudor
Puritanism: utopian communities in, 85; reform literature of, 87, 89; and capitalism, 99; and workhouses, 101

Quiroga, Vasco de, 52
Quiros, Ferdinand, 196 (n. 20)

R. H. (utopist), 11, 83, 114–15
Race: and patriarchy, 142; and national identity, 142–46, 160; and slavery, 143; and hierarchy, 144; and colonialism, 146–49; in *The Isle of Pines*, 155; and sexuality, 155–57; categorization of, 161; seventeenth-century interpreta-

tion of, 209 (n. 6). *See also* Marriage: interracial
Radicalism, English, 84, 199 (n. 3)
Raleigh, Sir Walter, 64; first Guiana voyage, 162–64, 212 (n. 4); *Discovery of the large, rich, and beautiful Empire of Guiana*, 163, 165, 169, 212 (n. 3); death of, 165; second Guiana voyage, 164–65; *Instructions to His Son*, 188 (n. 35)
Raleigh, Wat, 165–66
Ramusio, Giovanni Battista, 187 (n. 32)
Rastell, William, 52
Redmond, James, 21
Reform: ambiguities in, 9; state as organ for, 17; in utopian narratives, 19, 108; of national institutions, 54, 87; as machine, 79; agricultural, 87, 199 (n. 10); economic, 87, 91–92, 112; educational, 87, 199 (n. 10)
Reformation, English, 4
"A Reformation of Schools" (Comenius), 89
Reformers, seventeenth-century, 102, 103
Reform literature, Puritan, 87, 89
Reiss, Timothy, 198 (n. 29)
Relief bills, for the poor, 101
Reproduction: of knowledge, 73, 74; in nature, 78–79; in *The Isle of Pines*, 150–51, 156
Republic (Plato), 19, 47, 48–49, 51, 75; slavery in, 143
Research: maritime voyages as, 67; in *New Atlantis*, 69. *See also* Experimentation, scientific; Science
Restoration: national identity in, 14, 16; utopias following, 114–15; opening of theaters in, 117–19; patriarchy during, 141; end of, 177. *See also* Theater, Restoration

Slavery, African (*cont.*)
  utopias, 143; in Virginia, 146;
  transmission through mother,
  146–47; in West Indies, 147–48; in
  seventeenth-century utopias, 149;
  and national identity, 160; in Suri-
  nam, 170; in *Oroonoko*, 170–73
Slave trade, 166–67
Society of Antiquaries, 4
Socratic dialogue, 15
Solomon, Julie, 80, 197 (n. 24)
Solomon Islands, 196 (n. 20)
Southerne, Thomas, 174
*Soveraigne Power of Parliaments and
  Kingdomes* (Prynne), 198 (n. 1)
Spain: as model of empire, 64, 65;
  New Christians in, 201 (n. 18);
  attitude toward intermarriage,
  210 (n. 9)
Spatial location: in utopian narra-
  tives, 9–10, 19–21, 86; Burton's
  parody of, 86
Spectacle: in Restoration theater, 5,
  117, 119–20; Great Fire of London
  as, 129, 130, 137; in *Blazing-world*,
  135; in utopias, 161; insurrection
  as, 177
Spenser, Edmund: *Faerie Queene*, 14;
  *A View of the Present State of Ire-
  land*, 200 (n. 11)
Sprat, Thomas, 81, 82, 124, 127; on
  nationalism, 204 (n. 18)
St. Anthony's School (London), 31
St. George's Hill (Surrey), 102–4,
  105
St. Paul's Cathedral School, 5, 23;
  curriculum of, 24, 25, 28; goals of,
  24–26; monitors at, 30–31; hierarchy within, 36
Stanbridge, John, 26
State, "archive," 196 (n. 21)
State, early modern: institutions of,
  3, 14; values of, 5, 21, 27; produc-

tion of citizens in, 8, 21, 31; as
  organ for reform, 17; obligation
  to, 25, 26, 27, 31, 36; education in,
  27, 31; as research institution, 83;
  status of women in, 204 (n. 15)
State, modern: characteristics of,
  180; homogeneity in, 180
Stjernebourg (observatory), 193
  (n. 5)
Storehouses, common, 105–6
Strangers' House (*New Atlantis*), 69,
  70, 78
Strype, John, 26
Submarines, 56–57
Sulpicius (textbook), 28
Surinam: in Warren, 165–67; as mi-
  crocosm of England, 167, 177; in
  Oroonoko, 167–68; slavery in, 170;
  loss to Dutch, 177. *See also* Guiana
Surveillance: in public education,
  29–31; in *Utopia*, 37; in *New At-
  lantis*, 69–71, 72–73; in *Oroonoko*,
  177; importance in state, 180;
  Foucault on, 195 (n. 18)
Suvin, Darko, 9, 16; on estrange-
  ment, 184 (n. 10), 186 (n. 28); on
  dialogue, 186 (n. 27)
Swift, Jonathan, 179
Sybil (Disraeli), 101
Symonds, William, 146
Systema Agriculturae (Wolidge), 88

Tadlowe, George, 53
Teleology, Christian, 10
Tennenhouse, Leonard, 180
Texts, representational nature of,
  22
Theater, Restoration, 119–20; spectacle in, 5, 117; inwardness of, 117,
  202 (n. 5); inclusiveness of, 119;
  power of, 119, 140; women in,
  119–20; audience of, 120, 203
  (n. 11)

Tillinghast, Joseph, 155
Timetables, in *Utopia*, 33, 36
Time travel, 9
Tiverton, burning of, 205 (n. 25), 206 (n. 33)
Tomlinson, Sophie, 119, 202 (n. 1)
Totalitarianism, 189 (n. 37)
Trading companies, 12, 164
Travelers, utopian: dialogue with hosts, 19, 46
Travel narratives, 185 (n. 20); sixteenth-century, 12; in utopias, 15, 180; in seventeenth-century utopias, 90; Winstanley's rejection of, 108; as genre, 186 (n. 27)
Trefry (*Oroonoko*), 170, 171, 172, 173, 176
True Levellers. *See* Diggers
True Report of the burnyng of the Steple and Churche of Poules, The, 205 (n. 25)
Tymme, Thomas, 60

Unisonance, 180, 214 (n. 6)
Uranibourg (Hveen), 60, 192 (n. 5); library of, 193 (n. 5)
Utopia (More): imitations of, 3, 51, 74, 197 (n. 25); national consciousness in, 3, 10, 11, 52; Robinson's translation of, 3, 10, 52–53; education in, 5, 33, 38, 39–40; "Debate of Counsel" in, 10; golden age in, 10; publication of, 10; models for, 11, 45–46, 48; popularity of, 11; colonialism in, 12, 41; geography of, 19–20; influence of grammar schools on, 31, 54; timetables in, 33, 36; gold in, 36, 44–45, 53; waste in, 36; visibility in, 36–37, 44; confession in, 37, 38; monitors in, 37, 45; social status in, 38–39, 45; promotion in, 39, 45; imitation

in, 39–40, 47; productivity in, 39–40; marketplace in, 40, 42–45, 54; regulation of want in, 40–45, 51; regulation of population in, 41–42, 44; avarice in, 43, 44; boundaries of, 44; control of value in, 44, 45; discipline in, 44; pride in, 44, 45; as new genre, 46; traveler's accounts in, 46, 52; use of irony, 46; wisdom-dialogue in, 46; prefatory letters of, 47–48, 50, 191 (n. 33); as handbook, 50; misinterpretation of, 50; listening in, 50–51; institutions in, 51–52; political nature of, 53; Protestant audience of, 53; concealment in, 54; as founding fiction, 54; marriage in, 74; and *New Atlantis*, 74–75; Plattes on, 86; Macaria in, 93–94; as news, 180; Milton on, 197 (n. 25). *See also* More, Thomas
Utopianism, 84; printing's spread of, 85; classical, 178, 179; Renaissance, 183 (n. 3); Frye on, 183 (n. 7); transmission from classical period, 184 (n. 15); historical studies of, 189 (n. 40); during Civil War, 199 (n. 3); and New Christianity, 201 (n. 18)
Utopian narratives: narrators of, 2–3; Continental, 3, 183 (n. 3); strategies of, 3, 21, 22; colonialism in, 8, 16, 22; human ability in, 8; individualism in, 8; political function of, 8, 53; readers of, 8, 178; criticism on, 9, 16; self-criticism in, 9; spacial location in, 9–10, 19–21, 86; beginning of, 10; after *Utopia*, 11–12; Puritan, 14, 85; as genre, 14–15, 186 (n. 26); dialogue in, 15, 17–19, 188 (n. 37); as "speaking picture," 15, 179, 180; neutralizing effect of, 16, 186

Utopian narratives (*cont.*)
(n. 28); two voices of, 17–19; reform in, 19; self-representation
in, 21; textual representation in,
22; as founding fictions, 50, 178,
180; misinterpretation of, 50;
form of, 90; as guides to reform,
108; spectacle in, 161; inaccessibility in, 177; effect of newspapers
on, 178; as protonovel, 178–79; as
allegory of authorship, 179;
eighteenth-century, 179; hybrid
nature of, 179; as news, 180
—Seventeenth-century, 11;
Bacon's influence on, 83; freedom
from censorship, 85, 199 (n. 3); dialogue in, 87, 90; economic reform
in, 87, 91–92; institution of labor
in, 100–102; poor in, 115; effect of
colonial plantations on, 148–49;
fictional qualities of, 179, 180
Utopias: election in, 2, 5, 8; "found"
nature of, 2; cultural formation in,
5; institutions of, 5, 15, 16, 21,
180; production in, 8, 180; Milton
on, 8–9, 84–85; geography of,
9–10, 15–16, 19–21; in John Lyly,
11, 185 (n. 16); population in, 14,
41–42; as ideal commonwealth, 15,
179; masculinist aspect of, 15; as
ideal places, 15–16, 20–21; dis-
function within, 16; systems of,
16; of classical era, 17–19; industry
in, 21, 89, 91–92, 94, 112; values
in, 21, 180; boundaries of, 21–22;
Charles I on, 84, 85; in seventeenth-century discourse, 84–85;
eugenics in, 143; inaccessibility of,
177; preeminence of state in, 180;
hebraism of, 197 (n. 22); fire precautions in, 206 (n. 33)
Utopists, 4–5; use of spatial relocation, 9–10; following More, 50,

179; of Civil War, 83, 89; influence
of Bacon on, 83; use of realism,
86–87; on the poor, 90–91, 100;
post-Restoration, 114–15

Values: of early modern state, 5, 21,
27; in utopias, 21, 180
Vaz, Lopez, 196 (n. 20)
Verne, Jules, 80
Vespucci, Amerigo, 45, 46, 187
(n. 32); on native women, 156
Vickers, Nancy, 171
Vigilance, culture of, 30–31, 36
Virgil, 187 (n. 35)
Virginia Companies, 12, 164;
Bacon's investment in, 54, 63
Visibility, in *Utopia*, 36–37, 44
Volpone (Jonson), 188 (n. 35)

Walsingham, Sir Francis, 61
Walzer, Michael, 200 (n. 16)
Warren, George, 165–67, 177, 212
(n. 7)
Waste: in *Utopia*, 36; Weber on, 201
(n. 24)
Watson, Foster, 27
*Way Propounded to make the poor . . .
happy, A* (Plockhoy), 85
Weber, Harold, 208 (n. 3)
Weber, Henry, 211 (n. 18)
Weber, Max, 93; on consumption,
200 (n. 15); on waste, 201
(n. 24)
Webster, Charles, 85, 199
(nn. 4, 10); on workhouses, 201
(n. 25)
"Western Design" (of Cromwell),
16, 148
West Indies: English in, 12, 13, 63;
racial mix in, 147, 210 (n. 11); slave
revolts in, 148
Westminster School: statutes of,
29; monitors in, 30

Whitney, Charles, 194 (nn. 12, 15),
196 (n. 20); on modernism, 198
(n. 29)

Wilkins, John, 132

Williams, Penry, 26

Williams, Raymond, 9, 184 (n. 10)

Willoughby d'Eresby, Lord, 193
(n. 6)

Winstanley, Gerrard, 5; on idleness,
100, 106, 110–11; on labor, 102,
109; at Digger Colony, 102–4;
early life of, 104; "An Humble Request," 104; *The Saint's Paradise*,
104; *The New Law of Righteousness*,
105. See also *The Law of Freedom
in a Platform*

Winthrop, John, 86, 199 (n. 5)

Witch trials, 67

Wolidge, John, 88

Women: as authors, 117; in Restoration theater, 119–20, 203 (n. 9);
authority of, 120, 136; role models
for, 122; in *Blazing-world*, 127, 140;
African, 155–56; status in early
modern England, 204 (n. 15)

Woolf, Virginia: on Margaret
Cavendish, 140, 208 (n. 42)

Workforce, 16; prisoners in, 80;
reform of, 83. *See also*
Labor

Workhouses, 4, 201 (n. 25); as
model for industry, 5; models in
New Atlantis, 81; establishment
of, 100, 101; Puritan views on,
101; "literary," 102; Parliament's
funding of, 102; in *A Modest
Plea*, 113; Foucault on, 187 (n. 31)

Works and Days (Hesiod), 10